"Dr. Rix has exposed reparative therapy in ~~pares the features of the ex-gay movement~~ hyper-religiosity. The similarities are so nu difference between the two."

　　— THOMAS ERWIN GERTZ, ED.D.
　　　Dean of Students, Institute for Advanc
　　　San Francisco, California

"Jallen Rix, a young man who has suffered through ex-gay therapy, tells how he found new hope and healing for his wounded, gay soul. Please, if you are struggling to know the truth about homosexuality for yourself or for one you love, read *Ex-Gay No Way*. It could save your life or the life of a gay or lesbian person who needs to know that homosexuality is not a sickness to be healed or a sin to be forgiven but another of God's mysterious gifts to be accepted, celebrated and lived with integrity."

　　— MEL WHITE, Author, *Stranger at the Gate: To be Gay* and *Christian in*
　　　America and *Religion Gone Bad: Hidden Dangers from the Christian Right*

"Ex-Gay therapy is both ineffective and traumatizing and often leaves wounds which may feel impossible to heal. Until now, there were few books that offered hope for people who have endured this torture and brainwashing. In *Ex-Gay No Way* Jallen Rix shares his inspiring story and delivers a groundbreaking book that serves as beacon of hope. Finally the path that leads out of self-loathing and depression has been illuminated. Survivors of so-called 'conversion therapy' have been tossed a life preserver in this uplifting and life-changing book. It is a must read for survivors and all those who wish to support them."

　　— DARREN MAIN, author of *Hearts & Minds: Talking to Christians about*
　　　Homosexuality

"The Ex-Gay Movement is stripped naked, and through an abundance of snapshots we get to see its vulnerability and cover-ups. These perspectives are mounted together with Jallen's moving story telling and in-depth research. The naming of religious abuse, the dispelling of sex-phobic myths, the raw emotion of personal experience make this a great resource for pastors and counselors; yet possibly the greatest accomplishment of this book is that it brings the reader to a conclusion – a motive and means for recovery without feeling forced to accept or abandon."

　　— PAUL WHITING, International advocate, author and pastor

SURVIVAL AND RECOVERY FROM RELIGIOUS ABUSE

Jallen Rix, Ed.D.

FINDHORN PRESS

© Jallen Rix, Ed.D. 2010

The right of Jallen Rix, Ed.D. to be identified as the author
of this work has been asserted by him in accordance with the
Copyright, Designs and Patents Act 1998.

Published in 2010 by Findhorn Press, Scotland

ISBN 978-1-84409-187-4

Edited by Jean Semrau
Cover design by RixArtz
Cover Photo: Brian Ashby
Interior design by Damian Keenan

Printed and bound in the USA

1 2 3 4 5 6 7 8 9 17 16 15 14 13 12 11 10

Published by
Findhorn Press
117-121 High Street,
Forres IV36 1AB,
Scotland, UK

t +44 (0)1309 690582
f +44 (0)131 777 2711
e info@findhornpress.com
www.findhornpress.com

Contents

Introduction
A Peaceful Place in the Past 7

1 Refreshing My Memory with Some Not-So-Refreshing Memories
My Religious and Ex-gay Story 17

2 More Ex-gay Experiences
Stories of Other Ex-gay Survivors 47

3 Religious Abuse & the Ex-gay Movement —
Twins Hatched from the Same Egg
A Comparison 63

4 Drinking the Kool-Aid
All about Denial 83

5 My Voice in the Crowd
Becoming My Authentic Self 93

6 What Ex-gays Cannot Do
The Challenge of Unconditional Love 109

7 Taking My Spirituality Personally in Every Way
My Spiritual Journey 117

Contents

8 Our Obsessively Negative View of Sexuality
The Source of Much of the Problem 139

9 Sexuality and Spirituality —
Twins Hatched from the Same Egg
Solutions to the Problem 153

10 Embracing Adulthood
More Steps in My Recovery Process 187

11 All I've Learned Comes Home
Keeping Love the Focus with My Family 199

Conclusion
An Invitation
My Hope for the Future 221

Acknowledgments 235

Appendix
Steps to Telling Your Story 237

Bibliography 239

Endnotes 243

A Peaceful Place in the Past

To: Those left with the question, "Why did he do it?"
I must confess that there were things in my life that I could not gain
control of. No matter how much I prayed and tried to avoid the temp-
tation, I continually failed. It is this constant failure that has made
me make a decision to terminate my life here on earth. If I remain, it
could possibly allow the devil the opportunity to lead me away from
the Lord. I love my life, but my love for the Lord is so much greater,
the choice is simple. It is the continuing lack of strength and/or lack
of obedience and/or lack of will power to cast aside certain sins — to
continually go before God and ask forgiveness and make promises I
know I can't keep is more than I can take. I feel it is making a mockery
of God and all He stands for in my life. I regret if I bring sorrow to
those that are left behind. If you get your heart in tune with the word
of God you will be as happy about my "transfer" as I am. I also hope
that this answers sufficiently the question, why. May God have mercy
on my soul. A brother and a friend.

— *Jack McIntyre*

THIS IS A PORTION OF THE LETTER a friend showed me years ago when I wondered out loud if anyone had killed themselves as a result of going to an ex-gay ministry. I had attended an ex-gay support group for a few months, but it never evoked so much turmoil that I contemplated suicide. However, the environment certainly affected my life for years to come. I so wanted to believe what they declared: "You can change from gay to straight!" I read it in their materials. They affirmed it face-to-face. It was preached from the pulpit. It was argued on talk shows.

Enthusiastic prayers for healing were proclaimed by sincere people. And I believed it with all my heart. But over time, once the flash was gone and people were forced to get on with life, we who called ourselves "ex-gay" were still attracted to the same gender. After enduring the rigors of conversion .therapy, I came out feeling far worse than when I first entered. No matter how hard I tried, no matter what I did, no matter how loyal and obedient I was to who I believed Christ to be, I did not become straight. It seemed I had failed myself, everyone I loved, and most of all, God. Without question, it was one of the most devastating times in my life. I could not have sunk any lower in what seemed to be bottomless despair. It was during these moments that some ex-gays attempt suicide, and with this letter, I knew for a fact that at least one succeeded. Unfortunately, over the years I've known others.

A lot of ex-gay survivors lost everything they held dear when they left the various ex-gay ministries and still were homosexual. Jobs were lost. Reputations were destroyed. Families split. Individuals were excommunicated. When they failed at being straight, they didn't even have pieces of their lives to put back together. Literally alone, they had to start over completely. Hearing more and more similar experiences started me wondering why the ex-gay movement had so much influence on these peoples' lives, not to mention my own. Thus began my journey toward understanding a much larger and more pervasive phenomenon, of which ex-gays were only a part: religious abuse.

During this period I was keenly aware of the absence of information, resources and support for ex-gay survivors. Sure, there was public debate (especially during election years) about "change" groups, conversion therapies and whether gays and lesbians could actually become straight. There was a handful of books about coming out, but there were even fewer about coming out in a religious environment. And there was nothing — zip, nada, zero — on how to deal with what had happened to those of us who wanted to recover from the damaging effects of the ex-gay experience. It was as if there was no measuring stick to determine how very badly wounded we were. Looking back, it seemed that even when I learned to hold my head high and walk proud as a gay man, I couldn't see how my ex-gay experience continued to cause me to limp painfully. This partially resulted from not seeing the larger picture.

Yet, as I stepped further out of the closet, I began to write about lessons learned from trial and error, as an ex-gay survivor. Occasionally I would be asked to speak about my ex-gay experience, or lead a workshop about it. Because my website addressed the subject, the media would occasionally contact me to get my side of the story. The most exciting occasion was when ABC's 20/20 News Magazine flew me to New York to be on a segment about ex-gay ministries. My story ended up being the only dissenting voice in the piece. This kind of attention would help people with similar backgrounds find me. They had no one to confide in about what had happened to them. They often felt caught between Christian gay-haters or gay Christian-haters. Even today, as more and more people come forward and tell of their ex-gay years, there is little information on the aftermath and recovery process.

So I wrote the first incarnation of this book. The first effort was a workbook which was copied onto regular-sized paper, folded in half and stapled into pamphlets. Nonetheless, it did help to fill the void, and the purpose has always been the same — to help people recover from the damaging effects of the ex-gay experience.

However, I realized over the years that I had to address the larger problem of a somewhat newly-identified (within the past several decades) phenomenon called religious abuse. The more I understood the nature of religious abuse, the better I was able to recover from the ex-gay experiences. It was as though I finally figured out the right questions to ask, which uncovered answers that deeply resolved life-long conflicts.

Clarifications

The structure of this book generally aligns into two parts: First, determining the scope and seriousness of this phenomenon, including the ex-gay movement, religious abuse, my personal experience, and others' stories; and second, the processes I used and paths I took to recover from it. This is not a volume of scientifically-tested research. Although I reference plenty of supportive data, I mainly write from my own experiences and relate what has helped me over the years.

I have wrestled with how much theology to put in this book. I do not have any conscious religious agenda. Where I am today in my spiritual journey is a liberal far cry from where I was during my ex-gay period, and that is, oddly enough, putting it conservatively. That said, there are several important steps that got me to where I am today that are clearly Western Christian ideas. Because they have been key to my recovery process I have included them. Furthermore, because the ex-gay phenomenon was completely fabricated by contemporary Christianity, I can't but address its shortcomings head on. Often, I will be using their own theological "yardsticks" to measure the incompatibility of reparative therapy with Christianity.

Ah. That's the first time I've mentioned reparative therapy and it, along with a lot of other terms, needs some initial clarification. There are a number of general titles for the ex-gay movement: reparative therapy, conversion therapy, restoration therapy, ex-gay ministries (this does not even begin to cover the names of specific organizations under this category). As this book was going to print, the American

Psychological Association released one of the most comprehensive studies on the movement to date.[1] In it, they use the term Sexual Orientation Conversion Efforts (SOCE), which I hope over time will become the standard term. Although there may be subtle differences in the definitions, at this point please consider that they all loosely mean the same thing: the movement that believes homosexuality is a sin and unhealthy and therefore should be and can be cured.

Religious abuse, the way I use it, also needs clarification. Other labels for it include religious addiction, religious compulsivity, religious obsessiveness, and religious dependence. For now, allow me to use these interchangeably. I promise that the details and various nuances will soon be explored. Eventually, even the ex-gay movement in many ways will become synonymous with religious abuse.

I have decided to approach this writing not only from my personal experiences, but also from my professional perspective, as a sexologist. It is important not to hem and haw about sexuality and how integral it is to the subject. Indeed, the whole point of contention is with whom gays and lesbians have sex and whom they love romantically. Even most ex-gay groups will admit they may not be able to make people straight. At best, they can only help them attempt celibacy. With an emphasis on behavior, they believe that you're as good as straight just as long as there is no gay sex involved. Whatever you think about the ex-gay movement, if sex did not exist, neither would this conflict. Of course, there are subjects other than sex that come into play. But nearly all the theological debates, prayer services, pseudo-psychological studies, self-destructive behaviors, and failed attempts at celibacy, are fueled by a severe erotophobia (a fear of or disdain for sex). This is why I decided to pursue my doctorate in sexology.

It's true. One of the biggest reasons I made sexology the focus of my post-graduate work was the ex-gay movement. I spent the first quarter century of my life intently focused on the study of the Bible, Christianity, and spirituality. Somewhere in the coming out process I realized I had better get the sexual side of the story if I was going to speak with any balanced authority on the ex-gay subject.

What is sexology, you ask? It is not psychology, though there are aspects of sexuality and the psyche that overlap. As one of the most outspoken sexologists of our time, the Rev. Ted McIlvenna, defined it, "Sexology is the study of what people do sexually and how they feel about it."[2] Although this definition is about as straightforward as it can get, for this society at the beginning of the twenty-first century to seriously seek to understand sex may seem strange, frivolous, scandalous and even perverted. This makes the research and education about sex anything but simple. Yet, there could not be a more important aspect of humanity than sexuality. After all, it is the activity that has propagated the world. And when you consider that the vast majority of sexual activity is not about procreation, we have a significant chunk of adult behavior influenced by sex for pleasure's sake, not to mention how much of our society alternately idealizes, exploits and stigmatizes it. This makes sex important in my eyes. And when people begin to treat it as such and really educate themselves about it, we will see the resolution of a lot of society's problems. From sexually-transmitted diseases and infections to sexual satisfaction in a relationship, from online chat rooms to sexual abuse, from what should be taught to our children to what happens in the Oval Office, the neglect of sexual wisdom is the source of many of our cultural challenges that we must begin to seriously address, the ex-gay movement included.

On the related topic of gender, this book is not without its weaknesses. Due to the fact the ex-gay movement is primarily populated by men, this volume has a disproportionate lack of female presence. I "scraped the barrel" to find quotes from women to tell their stories. Ultimately, as a man, I will be writing from my male (and gay) perspective.

Recovery from…?

I am aware that the term "recovery" is often used in association with 12-step programs, but there will be no such association here (though these programs do indeed help people recover from various challenges). There are even ex-gay groups that view their own work as a recovery process. Be that as it may, knowing we are all different suggests that our recovery processes will be just as diverse. Although I'm hoping that by reading this book people can take some steps in their recovery away from the damaging effects of the ex-gay and religiously abusive environments, this book is certainly not the only step. So I use the word "recovery" in its broadest sense to mean the process by which we attempt to compensate for the setbacks the ex-gay organizations have caused that keep us from embracing life in all its abundance.

In the early nineties, I helped staff a booth for a gay-positive Christian organization at the San Francisco LGBT (Lesbian, Gay, Bisexual, Transgendered) Pride Festival, and I had made a huge banner that said, "Gay/Lesbian and Christian? There is a connection!" During the day, a lot of people would ask us questions, take brochures, and occasionally debate the merging of Christianity and homosexuality. For the most part, these were civil conversations. However, I remember distinctly a guy walking through the crowd who, when he saw our banner, abruptly changed course to intersect directly with our booth. "Jesus doesn't love gays and lesbians," he screamed with fire in his eyes, not two inches from my friend's face. "Fuck him. Christians hate us, so I hate you!" And he would not stop his diatribe. My friend (in charge of the booth and more experienced with folks like this) made a bee-line over to security, who got the man calmed down and moved him along.

Despite being rattled by the unabashed show of hatred, we didn't let his anger get to us. Why? Because we understood. We all had felt the pain and sting of rejection that this man clearly felt. Each one of us in that booth could cite legitimate reasons to spit words of rage because of our painful experiences in the conservative church and, specifically, in ex-gay Christian ministries.

When I consider what elements helped me recover from the damaging effects of my ex-gay experience, I have tried to consider my goals. What does recovery look like? Am I ever fully recovered? At the very least, recovery is subjective if not elusive. I can tell you, I do not want to be like that screaming man — someone who seemed so unable to let go of his pain that he was consumed by it when the subject passed before his eyes.

Initially, I can say one goal that is easily identified and already achieved is that I am no longer in an ex-gay environment. It is in my past. I made it out, and that's saying something all by itself. The ex-gay environment I was a part of can no longer cause me direct pain. Just like getting a cut: I can remember what it felt like, and that memory can be vivid. I can know I don't want to feel it again, but the actual experience — the sharp edge being pressed into my skin — is behind me. This is not to minimize or invalidate the horrible abuse that occurred, and the potent effect it still has on me and many others. In fact, this is where I think the majority of ex-gay survivors find themselves: what is to be done with this experience, these memories, and these often overwhelmingly painful feelings?

Some years back, I met with a survivor fresh out of a live-in ex-gay ministry. He chose to meet for tea in the Castro of San Francisco (known the world over as a haven for LGBT folk), never having been there before; he wanted to walk the streets comfortably without fear or shame. As we walked, he immediately laid a ground rule for our conversation: "No talking about ex-gays!" We could talk about anything else, but not that. We walked about a half block, and he began talking about his ex-gay experience. Eventually I chimed in with my thoughts, and he realized what we were talking about, saying, "I said we weren't going to talk about that." We would walk another block or two, and he would be right back talking about it again and again and again. Despite the desire to leave it behind him, despite his attempts to avoid his feelings and to get on with life, his need to process what had happened just burst, nearly uncontrollably, out of him. I think this is a telling example of where many ex-gay survivors find themselves — wanting to put the whole thing behind them yet unable to do so. Just when I think all has fallen silent, once again, it begs for attention, and sometimes at the most inopportune situations.

There are others who are much better at shutting out their past. Some ex-gay survivors have stepped out of the church and have never spoken or thought of it again. Who am I to judge a recovery strategy that seems to have worked well for them? For myself, however, I have found great healing and strength from acknowledging my religious history — for better or for worse — much like I might acknowledge my ethnic heritage. I've met many former Christians who reject their religious background by negating it. They declare, "I don't believe in Christianity," as if they never had any connection with it or it does not bear any relevance on their lives now. But if asked, "Were you raised a Christian?" They will respond with a litany of their religious upbringing and its bearing upon them. It's as if they think that no longer believing in Christianity somehow stops it from being a part of their historical makeup. I think this does a disservice to self-acceptance. It's almost as if they are saying, "I don't accept this part of who I am, this part called my past."

If I asked a person if she were Russian, would it make sense for her to say, "Oh, I don't believe in Russians." Huh? Of course not. My religious upbringing had a part of making me into the person I am today. In fact, it may have more influence on who I am today than my ethnic heritage does. It is part of what makes me unique. No, I no longer believe like the Southern Baptists I grew up with, but I once did. To pretend it did not happen in hopes that the memories will hurt less is a way of not accepting who I am. To wish it did not happen is a waste of energy — a lost cause — because no one can change the past. Accepting our past is like accepting our skin color and our sexuality. A quote from Lily Tomlin that I often meditate on is, "Forgiveness is giving up all hope for a better past." Wishing our ex-gay experience had not happened, ignoring it with the hope of forgetting it, avoiding the painful memories when they come up, could be another way of resisting forgiveness for myself or others for what has occurred.

It seems most ex-gay survivors aren't suppressing the fact of what happened simply for the sake of it. They're actually wanting to avoid the deep pain and hurt these memories still bring up. Granted, when someone is faced with uncomfortable, scary, difficult, and painful circumstances, it is natural and often wise to run in the opposite direction to get as far away from the unpleasantness as possible. However, there's a difference between maneuvering around negative influences that are outside myself and resisting what I am emotionally experiencing inside me. When it comes to my own feelings, I have learned that the quickest route to the other side of pain is directly through it. This approach is what M. Scott Peck speaks of in his landmark book, *The Road Less Traveled*, in which he stresses that we must end avoidance and face our fears if we are to be truly healthy.

Besides, all that suppressing and avoiding of feelings sounds all too familiar.

Indeed, it's one of those ingrained patterns that I learned so well in the ex-gay environment. Sure, I justified it by giving it another name, like, "focusing on godly thoughts," or "memorizing Scripture," or "keeping busy in ministry." Yet I was doing everything I could to avoid and suppress what I deeply knew was there — my true sexual feelings.

What was true then is true now — avoiding and suppressing does not dissipate the heart's natural and innocent yearnings. On the contrary, it just stock-piles emotional energy. Some people analogize that painful memories are like hidden tumors that could someday grow and poison one's entire being. Sooner or later that emotional energy will find its way out, be it in heart trouble, ulcers, nervous break-downs, or a triggered explosion — as in the case of the screaming man. I know this. I experienced it first hand as an ex-gay survivor. It's time to try another approach. Why not practice some preventative medicine and deal with the "cancer" while I am healthy and strong, rather than be forced to deal with it while I'm sick and my life hangs by a thread because of it?

Yet, I warn you. Anyone reading my story whose background is similar may very well have their "buttons" pushed, and pushed hard. It may not take a rocket scientist to figure this out, but it might take a professional therapist to help process some of these "hot spots" while reading this book. Sexuality and spirituality are not often happy-pappy topics in our society, especially for those who have experienced ex-gay and religious abuse first hand. Some have been so upset they became suicidal. This is seriously no laughing matter. Reach out for support, and hopefully professional support. It is not my intention to create further trauma. I want this "read" to be one of healing.

Self-Directed Recovery

One thing is for sure, ex-gay survivors have had it up to their eyeballs with "cures" and "solutions" to their "problems." Later, you will see this is one of the prominent features of religious abuse — living in a constant state of believing you need to be "fixed." As a result, just the possibility of perusing another's perspective on how to "be a better and happier person" can more easily conjure thoughts of burning a book than reading one. Yet here you are with this book in hand. Therefore, let me affirm for you your own experience. No one else can better decide the ways in which you need to heal than you can. In 2008 a group of ex-gay survivors gathered with LGBT-affirming healthcare providers in Denver to begin determining what might be the best course of supporting those recovering from the damaging effects of reparative/conversion therapies. The number-one element, heard loud and clear,

was that a survivor must be the driving force behind his/her own recovery process. That said, I've met plenty of survivors highly motivated to create a sense of closure to all they have experienced, yet not really knowing how to do it. That is what this book is for. Still, it is in your truly capable hands as to how you will proceed. Even though I am sharing my experience, it is what worked for me alone. Please consider what works for you and let the rest go.

In addition, I constantly considered, in the course of this work, who specifically was my audience and, quite honestly, I couldn't be very specific. What I mean is, although I am writing primarily to benefit people recovering from ex-gay and religious abuse, this particular population can be in a wide variety of places when it comes to dealing with their past. I'm sure some readers are just coming out of an ex-gay environment, and I hope this book will be "just the ticket" for them to get on with living. I know there will be some gay Christians who will find parts of my recovery process too liberal, even borderline blasphemous in terms of traditional Christian ethics. I hope there are some readers with whom just the mention of the name "Jesus" causes their blood to boil with frustration in regards to what happened to them in that name. I figure some straight people will read this book even though the whole gay thing (much less the ex-gay thing) is foreign to them. The truth is that religious abuse hits very close to home for many people.

The Benefits

All in all, I hope you go with me on this journey and stick with it to the end. This book is the result of the time I took to focus on what had happened, and how I got beyond the largest obstacles that kept me from enjoying my life in the present. I hope that you, the reader, use this book as a magnifying glass to create a similar focus for yourself. Mostly, I hope you can let go of suppressing your emotions and avoiding memories as they come up in the course of reading this book, because there are significant benefits to be gained from experiencing them.

There is much to be learned from our ex-gay history and, if avoided, may cause you to repeat the same mistakes. Furthermore, if you try to block out those ex-gay years, there are good and cherished memories during the same time that you may block out, as well. If you take the "I don't want to talk about it" stance, then others will not benefit from your experience and they may fall into the same manipulative traps that you did. In fact, it could be hypothesized that the reason ex-gay groups continue to have a kind of legitimacy in our society is that the vast majority of the people who have been damaged by these groups are too hurt to speak up about it. This has got to change!

Over time, with care and attention, you can defuse the pain around these memories. Harmful patterns and behaviors were often developed while in the ex-gay and religiously abusive world. You can compensate for them — even retread them with healthy patterns — to such a degree that you can freely make responsible and enjoyable choices regarding sex, pleasure, and intimacy.

By reviewing my survival and recovery, I hope to provide others with tools to assess their own experiences and thus help them find a peaceful place for their past to reside. This is not to say that anyone would ever approve of what has happened to you. Rather, it is accepting that what has happened is in the past. You can be unafraid to fully remember the good and the bad without being consumed by it. If a forgotten memory triggers strong emotions, you can be familiar enough with the feelings to manage and express them in a healthy manner. You will learn to access the strength and flexibility to change behavior and circumstances to prevent finding yourself in similar abusive experiences. This book can help you not just survive life; it can lead you to ways of enjoying all the abundant blessings and freedoms that come your way. Maybe you will even find yourself in such a space that you can have a positive impact on others who are in or recovering from ex-gay suppression and religious abuse.

Refreshing My Memory with Some Not-So-Refreshing Memories

My Religious and Ex-gay Story

I'LL BE THE FIRST TO ADMIT that my six- to eight-month stint of going to a once-a-week ex-gay drop-in group was not like the long, drawn-out ordeals of many others who lived in residential ex-gay environments for years (which we will address in detail in the next chapter). Yet, my ex-gay days ended up being the catalyst that eventually illuminated the religious abuse that had gone on all my life. I must emphasize that in terms of my experience, neither my family nor our church was actively trying to do me wrong or abuse me — not at all, and therefore I have no desire to hold them in contempt. As you will see later, the system of power abuse and conformity that is often present in vast regions of religious cultures so subtly permeates our society that, for the most part, it seems perfectly appropriate. At the very least, my family and our church raised me the same way they were raised and they did it well.

Because the ex-gay movement as a whole is rooted in our society's religious abuse, I have to start further back than my ex-gay experience. To give a full and accurate picture, I have to start at my beginning. I offer this story of my upbringing as an example for all that follows in this book.

The Moon over My Shoulder

My childhood was wonderful. My parents were honest, hardworking, devout Christians who were fully committed to raising my brother, sister and me. We were a stereotypical middle-class, tract-house family, and my parents did a great job giving us a happy first couple of decades together, including Barbecues, trips to Disneyland, and a tree house in the backyard willow under which a vegetable garden grew.

I grew up close to my mother's side of the family. She had several brothers and sisters who each married and had several kids. We would spend camping trips and holidays together — Christmas, Thanksgiving, and even Easter. All the cousins

in my generation were probably a little closer than in most families. Somehow, we had been spread out in age so that each of us graduated one at a time — year after year — for about a twenty-year run. We were like a posse that, if entering a mall en masse, could cause an uproar. When the reunions were over and our family would go its separate ways, I would be the one to cry as we said goodbye. I did not want those fun times to end.

My very earliest recollections are happy ones — the gentle and dignified face of a woman who took care of me in the church nursery; playing with our pet turtle, Pepae, in the hot, Sacramento sun; and the moon following me around. It's true. My limited understanding of the world convinced me that everywhere I went the moon seemed to be over my shoulder. It was an easy assumption for a young mind. I'd be outside at night, I'd look up and there it would be, following me.

Then there came the afternoon, I guess around twilight, when I was sitting in the back seat of the family car and I caught sight of the moon coming up just over a set of mountains. The mountains seemed to be following me just like the moon, since they appeared in line with our car while other parts of the landscape — the highway signs, the road, and other cars — seemed to be zooming by. I then made the connection that the moon wasn't following me anymore than the mountains were. So far away were these objects that they only appeared to remain still. That filled me with such insignificance that I felt dizzy.

As if that was not sobering enough for my young mind, I then glanced at a car driving parallel to ours. In the back seat was a little girl about my age looking back at me. Another realization tore at the center of my reality. Here was a little girl who neither knew me, nor had any desire to know me. She causally looked away to go on and have her own life completely separate from mine, and it really didn't matter if she ever saw me again. My brain was expanding so quickly it felt like my skull would crack. Of course, it was my first inkling that my little bubble of life was not always an accurate reflection of the wide and wonderful world.

"I'll Show You Mine, If You Show Me Yours"

It might have been on the very same car ride that my family drove through Golden Gate Park. I must have been between two and seven years of age. Still in the backseat, I recall noticing a Greek-style statue of a female nude. Although it is my earliest memory of seeing the beauty of an unobstructed female form, my reaction was — ho-hum, there she was. Then I saw him — a particular sculpture of a male nude captured my attention (I still know where it is today). Bronzed, flexed and posed with one leg up, he mightily pulled the handle of a large wine press. My breath

fogged up the window — that was a man! And there was no conception of shame or sin in me.

I remember making comic books with a neighbor boy. Somehow the innocently neutral question came up, "Which is more fun, drawing supergirls, or superguys?" I recall him saying that he liked drawing women with their long hair and big tits, like Wonder Woman and the Invisible Girl. Without missing a beat, I responded, "I like drawing supermen, with all their muscles, like Captain America and Batman!" We went right on drawing our comics without so much as an afterthought about our preferences.

Somewhere around the age of four or five, I had a series of steamy, torrid sexual encounters with the neighbor girl, Jackie, who was about the same age. Actually, these three or four experiences were nothing more than, "I'll show you mine if you show me yours." Really, that was it. About all we could muster was a drop of the drawers. Simply showing off the parts that we were told to keep hidden (as well as noticing the differences) was about as titillating as we could figure out. The last time we did it, Jackie's younger cousin was there. We three snuck behind the aluminum tool shed in her backyard and proceeded to dare each other to show our butt cheeks. When it was the cousin's turn, the pressure was too great, and he darted out from behind the shed and proceeded to tell Jackie's mom. Damn! He was a tattler — a big tattler with a very little tale.

When Jackie and I entered her house, her mother was picking up the phone receiver, and she curtly told me to "Go home." Oh, dear. Was she going to call my parents? When I walked into the house my brother had his attention on the television, and my Dad was hanging up the phone. His eyes met mine and I knew. I walked to my bedroom and he followed. He took his belt off and spanked me till I cried. I think there was some relief that my brother hadn't seemed to notice, since his face was still planted on the TV. I think my mom and sister were out of the house. To this day, not one word has ever been spoken about the incident.

How Could I Say No?

My family was solely Southern Baptist, though we all lived in California (yes, Southern Baptists live there, too). I joke sometimes that I was born on a Saturday and in church on Sunday. Of course this is an exaggeration, but it might as well be true. I grew up in a close-knit group of churchgoers that beautifully colored my childhood. My whole world revolved around this community of a few hundred churchgoers. I was fed so much of the Southern Baptist diet, so much of the teachings of Jesus, and so much church, at such a young age, that it was not second nature to me; it was first nature. Long before my own identity was defined — before I had a clear sense of self — I was taught that I should put "Jesus first, others second, and myself last." On the surface, this sounds like an inspiring way to live. Those adults who make a conscious choice to live this way truly have my respect. But I was never really given a choice in the matter. I was handed a template by which to live, before I found my own voice, before the uniqueness of my personality was developed and solidified. Sure, my own personality naturally emerged some, but I always tried to subjugate it to make Jesus, the church, and others predominant.

I remember asking Jesus into my heart as my "personal Lord and Savior" around the wise ol' age of seven or eight. I think I had awareness of what that entailed. I remember being questioned by my parents if I really understood what I was doing. I can remember saying the right answers because, "Well... it is the right thing to do... right?" I did not want to be out of the club. I wanted to be accepted by God, my church, and my family. Summer camps, Sunday school lessons, sermons, revivals — all of these were occasions (literally thousands of them) where people I looked up to were drilling into my heart and mind the need, the imperative, the requirement for complete faithfulness to God. I would have been crazy to choose anything else. I don't think I really knew of anything else to legitimately choose.

Going to summer camp, or to be more precise, Christian summer camp — a place in the California Sierra Mountains — gave me many great childhood memories. Campfires, making friendships, hiking in nature, taking fun workshops, making puppets, and feeling closer to God were just a few of the activities I enjoyed doing. The summer of my sixth-grade year I even went with the intention to find a girl friend — and I found Dorothy. We held hands in the food line. People talked about us. I think I liked most the status and attention it gave me. We sucked face a few times although it gave me a protruding stiffy in my baggy shorts. Sheesh, was I embarrassed. Despite that, I mostly felt normal, acceptable, and even envied.

Every evening, after dinner and before campfire, there was a worship service that included inspiring music, funny skits, prayer, and a speaker specializing in talking to young people. At the end of every service there would be an altar call, where the audience was encouraged to take another step closer to God by coming to the front of the room to receive prayer. I've chosen words that describe this ritual in the best light possible, and indeed, this was exactly how some of these services progressed. Other services were not so benign.

Where Catholics might use guilt to persuade their followers, Baptists use "The fear o' God." Ministers who spoke took advantage of all kinds of tactics to hold our attention and produce an emotional response. Stories of people who resisted the opportunity to accept Jesus into their lives and then were horribly killed in a car crash. "What if, on the way home from this very camp, one of you suffers the same fate? Are you right with the Lord?" Other fear-based angles (I've heard them so many times over) were the detailed descriptions of hell — pain, death, demons, Satan, burning for eternity, gross rotting flesh… (need I go on?). Another is the detailed, graphic telling of the torture and death of Jesus that was so vivid that it would put any Mel Gibson film to shame. Then, of course, it would be brought home that the reason Jesus endured all of this mutilation was to save my undeserving soul. "Wow! I must really be a horrible sinner since Jesus had to die for me." Another angle was the ever-effective interpretation of the last book in the Bible, Revelation, which somehow predicted the end of the world where all the Christians would rise into the sky to be with God and then God would destroy the world, like Sodom and Gomorrah: "Will I be left behind?"

These sermons at camp or at a revival setting at least a couple of times a year would often increase nightly in tension until on the last night the altar call was so persuasive that everyone would be down in front begging for God's mercy. No one was "required" to walk down that aisle and "forced" to give their heart to God, but what would you do at such a young age? I didn't want to risk dying on the way home. I was going to run to the front and get prayer at every opportunity for whatever reason, to make sure that no evil befell me. Then factor in the enormous peer pressure. All the adults wanted the kids to "be right with God" (whatever that means). All my friends were down in front, and look, Johnny, the "rebel kid" (whom everyone's been praying for), just walked down to the front with tears in his eyes. If he could come to Jesus, why wasn't I doing it? What other options did I have except to walk down that aisle whenever possible? And that is what is most important to point out: what choice did I really have?

Body: Bad. Spirit: Good.

Touch in our family occurred, but it seemed, for the most part, obligatory — a hug before I went to bed, or a peck on the cheek from "Aunt Helen" at Thanksgiving dinner. I don't remember much of it being really enjoyed. Sure, I was held and touched a lot while I was very young, but it became a distant memory, as though I was supposed to grow out of it as the unspoken cloud of sexuality loomed on the horizon. There really seemed to be a fear that I shouldn't enjoy touch too much, since it led to this horrible thing called "sex," and "it" was more horrible than any other sin. I don't think that was ever said to me word-for-word, but I got the message somehow. Being suspicious of touch often meant being suspicious of the body. Our Southern Baptist Church was hardly comfortable with either. Our services were sedate, to say the least. Oh, they tried to sing uplifting songs of joy, but how could we when even clapping hands during a chorus or applauding after a solo was often looked down on as being too raucous?

I had a number of different experiences similar to the "I'll show you mine..." experience as I was growing up, but they truly felt more like experimentation than sexual passion. I was trying to figure out what all these amazingly good feelings in my body were. What was it all about, and why was it so scary and "hush, hush"? My upbringing in the church and my home life didn't do much to promote a healthy sense of sexuality. They were simply passing on what they had been taught, which, unfortunately, was fraught with confusing problems from the get-go. So you can imagine my perplexity when I began to realize that it was okay for married adults to have sex. In fact, I figured out in my fifth-grade sex education class (I was fortunate to live in California where it was taught in the 1970's) that this monstrous act was actually what brought me to life.

It got even more confusing. It seemed that the only way for this vile act to be acceptable — perhaps enjoyable (huh?) — was within the confines of a God-approved marriage. A married person having sex outside of that commitment was grounds for divorce. Therefore, sex and commitment were pretty much synonymous. So how was it that what seemed the most horrible sin of all was the very glue that kept couples together? How was it that sex before marriage was punishably wrong and then became instantly glorious once a couple got licensed from the church? How was it that the same act of loving expression was so devil-plagued and evil one day, yet a wonderful gift of God the next? I didn't know of anything else in God's creation that could flip-flop so radically.

When I searched for the texts in the Bible to back these contradictory judgments about sex, I came up empty-handed. I read about holy God-fearing men having multiple wives. I saw female prostitutes contributing to the cause of Judaism and Christ. I read that Jesus said that once a couple is committed there are no grounds for divorce. But none of these scriptures went into to any detail about sex. Not finding a strong correlation between Baptist "sex ethics" and the Bible, I started wondering what else regarding sexuality had I taken for granted. Was this just another moon that I assumed would always be over my shoulder? The more I attempted to understand what I was taught, the more these ideas didn't add up. It seemed the more I learned about the realities of sexuality, the more intrigued I became with all the negative hoopla surrounding it.

For the most part, I kept this perplexing curiosity carefully to myself. I had to be cautious about asking too many questions for fear of people thinking me a pervert. I had no idea that most people my age were wondering similar thoughts. I had to take what was being fed to me, and then figure out what it meant on my own. I certainly was not going to ask my mentors and church leadership questions when all I heard on a regular basis was, "Just say no. Sex is bad!" As an adult, while getting my doctorate in sexology, I learned that one of the most important questions a sexologist can ask is not, "Why?" but "Why not?" Even at such a young age, before I was sexually active, I was mumbling under my breath, in so many ways, "Why not?"

Around puberty I began to recognize that the attraction to the male physique had a name, and it was not a nice one. Soon after this realization, I quickly relegated homosexuality to a back corner of my mind. I naively figured that it would be something I would grow out of. Unfortunately, this set up a dichotomy, and although I did not fully understand it at the time, I began to nurture an outer facade and presented myself as everyone's favorite Christian boy. It wasn't difficult since a significant amount of who I was on the outside was genuinely me, but I also had to hide my more vulnerable aspects. I naturally nurtured my sexuality and anything else that truly felt like me; I just kept it safely hidden for fear of rejection. As a result, I became a finely-skilled liar. Mind you, I was not trying to manipulate people maliciously. It's just how I developed over the years. I was simply hiding, and at the same time desperately craving approval. So I learned to smooth over any "unsightly bumps" with fictitious nuances and exaggerations clever enough to make a grandmother well up with tears of inspiration.

No experience of "the flesh" confounded me more than dancing. (Why do Baptists never have sex standing up? Because it might lead to dancing.) Indeed, it seemed that Southern Baptists from my upbringing truly did rank dancing right up there with sex. In Junior High School when the boys' P.E. class merged with the girls' for a few weeks of basic ballroom dancing, I had the humiliating experience of giving my coach a note from my parents to exclude me from the class for religious purposes. I was placed in a remedial P.E. class with all the physically and mentally challenged kids. When the ballroom dancing ended no one ever bothered to put me back into the regular Phys. Ed. Class. On some level, I was glad, since it would have been all the more embarrassing to return to all those boys' teases. Furthermore, remedial P.E. was a breeze, and I felt strangely comfortable with all the "freaks" and outcasts.

A new youth pastor was hired while I was in Junior High, and he tried to push the dancing envelope. In a number of youth musicals, he actually had us move and stand in different positions from song to song. We even changed positions during the songs — in front of everyone! Dare I suggest calling it (gulp) choreography?

Truthfully it was the simplest of moves — girls on one side, guys on the other, then guys in the front, girls in the back — much like in a marching band. In one rehearsal, he suggesting the guys move downstage at a certain point in a song — about four or five steps. We practiced the steps and he abruptly stopped the music and told us to do it again and "This time don't sway so much to the rhythm." His eyes were on me. There was silence. Then it felt like everyone was staring at me. What had just happened? Did I sway too much? Did I swish too much? I just took five steps forward. How did I even have time to get a beat on? Evidently I had done something. Now I had to do it again and I didn't even know what I did wrong. Should I walk really stiffly? Could it be that in a performance a dim-sighted elderly person might misconstrue the robotic adjustments as chaotic undulations of nubile youths and thus the entire church would split apart and everyone would fall into the tormenting flames of hell? Never!

Yet I liked the exhilaration of standing before people, singing and moving to the rhythm. It felt open and expressive. As a senior in high school, I joined show choir, a singing group that did show tunes — dancing steps included. I think I just didn't mention it to my parents. When they did find out, I downplayed the dancing taboo by suggesting that it was, in fact, choreography. Not dancing. This was an instance when I could see dad and mom not too happy about it, but they let me do it nevertheless.

As my gay desires became clearer to me (not that my swish ever did), I went into a greater degree of denial. I stopped asking, "Why not?" I just wanted to fit in. It seemed that avoiding rejection by putting up an outward facade was gradually reaching obsessive proportions. There were aspects of the church that seemed to encourage it. Gender rolls were clear and strict. The guys in my house were never to wear necklaces — too feminine. My sister (and all the women) only wore dresses in church. I think she was well into high school before she was allowed to wear slacks to a Sunday evening (more casual) service and it was a big deal. I can't recall if mom has ever worn pants in church. It was her way of showing respect.

"Choosing" Jesus?

When my whole world revolved around this church community, there was no way I was going to purposefully disappoint them and risk the sting of their judgment and rejection. This kind of peer pressure for me was far beyond the typical high school problems, such as smoking or drinking or wearing the right clothes. It was a kind of sanctioned, subtle peer pressure. So it was sort of okay as long as it kept me and everyone following Jesus, and I sure was not going to be the odd man out. Is it any wonder that so many of us developed a dichotomous life, putting on conforming appearances, and hiding our true selves far from anyone's gaze?

The most ironic dynamic to being indoctrinated at such a young age is that it made my "relationship with God" not intentional or purposeful, but instead automatic, unconscious and unchosen. I could respond (and still can) with the right theological perspective without thinking. It was my own authentic thoughts that I had to really dig for. Jesus was more a cultural norm than a vibrant, on-going relationship — the very opposite perspective to what I believe my Christian role models were trying to instill in me. Their zealous desires to save me from the fires of hell actually negated the real opportunity for me to freely choose to get to know Jesus. When I was asked to do anything for the cause of Christ, what other response could I have given but, "You bet"? Was that an authentic walk with God chosen freely with my mind, body and soul? Not to me. How could I freely make a choice when I was really only given one option? I certainly do not blame my parents for being protective, and sometimes overprotective, trying to keep me from heartache and suffering. That's what parents should do for their children. But for Christian ministries to limit humanity's ability to choose our paths freely is actually taking away our ability to choose anything — including God. Being given only one choice is no choice at all.

Even being given two choices may not really be a choice either (at least not in my experience). I remember having whole conversations, listening to complete sermons, and even hearing songs written on the subject, "Why can't the sinner — bound for hell — see how great our God is?" I was indoctrinated with the utter horror of evil and hell, and in contrast the total glory, riches and rewards of heaven. What choice is there in that? With that black-and-white scenario, there really is no choice in the matter and, what's worse, no decision-making skill is being taught, either. When I was given really only one choice, it was a no-brainer. Did that help me out in the world when the vast amount of my decisions had several, if not dozens of options to choose from? Nope. I was lost. No wonder I would resist decision-making. I had little to no skill at it, and I was petrified for fear of making the wrong choice (more about this in later chapters).

My Authentic Expression

From a young age my siblings and I were required to learn to play an instrument (we all chose the piano) until we graduated from high school. Having this musical skill created a way for me to help at church and I loved the sense of purpose and attention it gave me. On the one hand, learning music developed skills I am appreciating even to this day, and I have my parents' insistence and perseverance to humbly thank for it. There were plenty of times it was not easy on them to negotiate with three different children to sit and practice the piano. On the other hand, it sometimes felt that Mom and Dad were doing this as a way to pat themselves on the back — especially when they would trot us out to perform for houseguests. I rebelled against this, having no choice in the matter.

It can be argued that I was spoilt and just wanted my way, in the way I wanted it. As the baby of the family, I probably had it the easiest because Mom and Dad had two kids before me to practice on. As I grew, there were a few ways in which they withdrew and let me decide things on my own, but not so with piano practice, and I fixated on this particular lack of freedom. If they were going to make me practice until I graduated, if this was going to be the thing that I had no choice in, I was going to fight tooth and nail against it.

Despite my genuine love for and apparent talent in music, I fought them on a number of fronts. I was supposed to be practicing up to three hours a day, preparing for my high school senior recital. Therefore, whenever I had the chance to practice alone in the house, I'd sit at the piano for five or ten minutes, but lie and tell them I had practiced for 30 or 45 minutes. I "practiced" like this, as well as lied, every chance I got. This set up an odd pattern that plagued me for years, well into adult life. If there was something I really loved to do, like music, I would avoid it whenever possible.

Still, I loved music. I knew it would be my major in college, so another way I rebelled and made it my own was that I started writing my own music. I might have to spend time practicing pieces that other composers wrote, but I could also spend hours writing my own stuff.

The final way I rebelled against the lack of choice in learning music was in angry face-to-face confrontation. I knew in my heart that I would never give up music. I wanted to be a Christian rock star and sing for Jesus. Even if my parents were to stop requiring my intense practice, I would still do it. That was not the point. I didn't have the freedom to choose. They were going to stick to their guns and I was going to make them feel as bad as possible for it. There were times I know I must have seemed possessed with anger. Looking back, I can see that all the spoon-feeding of religion, all the double standard of "freely choosing God," all the hiding of my true sexuality while putting on appearances — all of this helpless, pent-up energy (more than I could understand at the time) got focused and released on my parents over this one issue. No wonder I was so vehement. No wonder they were so shocked — beside themselves, really — and often deeply hurt by my words and frustration.

The Contemporary Christian Music Movement

I completed my senior recital and graduated from high school. True to their word, and probably relieved, my parents no longer required me to take lessons or practice. Yet music was my life. Evangelism (spreading the good news of Jesus' love) found new life on a national, even global scale as the Contemporary Christian Music genre became a legitimate business, and I wanted to be part of it. I was fortunate that I got to see CCM from its start. Its roots were in the 70's Jesus People movement, with bands such as Children of the Day, Second Chapter of Acts, and Maranatha Praise Music. This new "Christian rock" was a way for fundamentalists to be in the world but not of the world: use the musical styles but slap an evangelistic message on top so that the music becomes a tool to win "the lost" from the clutches of hell.

So important was the right message in CCM that music without words was the exception. (Was it Christian at all without lyrics?) Singers would only rarely improvise their words or sings phrases like, "La, la, la, hey, hey, hey, ooooh, shoo-bee doo!" In fact, after hearing a particularly popular Christian song, a friend asked me for the translation, thinking it was some Bible verse in Greek or Hebrew. I replied with a smirk, "Oo, la loo la loo lay." For once, someone was singing just for the joy of singing.

Not only was the message to be Christian, but also CCM, as a business, would develop their musicians into Rock 'n Role Models, if you will, for generations of young Christians. These musicians, simply because of their music (not necessarily their theology or personal lives) were placed on pedestals, and their lives exemplified. They did everything to put their best foot forward. Many of them would go overboard to constantly give God the glory (whatever that meant). The classic scenario was an artist's response to compliments. Often they would reply, "Oh, no, that's wasn't me. That was God singing through me." And the classic joke was, "Really, I could have sworn I saw your lips moving!"

Their influence could not be underestimated, and neither could their music. Literally, die-hard fans would know the reasons songs were written, and they would quote the God-centric lyrics like scripture. In turn, the artists would incorporate all the scripture they could into their songs. That way, fans would learn the Bible at the same time they learned the songs. How convenient! Of course, this made many song lyrics as boring and out of touch as the King James translation of the Bible, including all the thee's, thy's and thou shalt not's. Concerts would overtly push a Christian agenda with all the persuasion of a revival evangelist. But just like any pop-teen idol, it was only a matter of time before these artistic and talented human beings fell from grace. They were human after all. But, oh, the disappointment of thousands of teens when their bigger-than-life role models had feet of clay — just like us.

Every so often there would be a wave of "secular music" that would get caught in the crosshairs of fundamentalists. Christian extremists would denounce "Satan's music" and encourage kids to burn these LPs, cassettes and CDs. It was the era of Backward Masking, when people would claim to find hidden messages from Satan recorded backwards on certain record albums. It was proclaimed as fact that, "These messages supposedly would cause kids to get on drugs, rebel against parents and even kill themselves." It was all hogwash, of course, except that the accused bands would make a lot of cash from the free advertising. Yet, even today, the same old scare tactics crop up in extreme sects. Because of my music training, most of the hype around the "evils of secular music" had little effect — other than to irritate me. I knew both what music could do and its limitations. But I still wanted to write my music and perform in ministry.

Off to College

Just like any youth going off to college, I assumed that the conflicts with my parents would now subside. Much to my dismay, my problems followed me. Now I had difficulty trusting authority — any authority. I was deeply afraid they were only going to limit my freedom, fearful that their motivation was simply to "trot me out for houseguests." Sometimes I wanted to argue with teachers and mentors, and I didn't really know why. It was no longer my actual parents; it was now the parental voice inside me, sounding just as determined as ever, if not becoming distorted, trying to keep me on the straight and narrow path. Although my parents had long since sent their youngest son out into the world, I could not silence the voices in my head. Not surprisingly, a rebel voice emerged in me that could match my parents' strength and volume word for word. Throughout college, I felt continually helpless and exhausted from the never-ending arguments that raged in my head between these voices. It was hard to know if my decisions and behaviors were being dictated by what my parents might have wanted, or if I was just reacting and ricocheting off their words — the rebel doing the opposite of whatever they said.

Music was still the topic in which my confusion was most prominent. I felt that my music career was not my own but something my parents had fabricated for me. Add into the mix my overriding desire to fulfill "God's will" for my life, and no wonder my own sense of identity never got a word in edgewise. From my journal:

I can't tell if I have had a natural talent for music or if after 11 years of lessons I've just acquired it. There were times I hated being "chained" to the piano until I was 18 years old, but now I'm relatively happy to have this talent. Despite all that, what really makes me frustrated is not knowing whether God wants me to do it. I'm not even sure God has that specific of a plan for my life. But if God does not want me to do it, I have to admit, I'm pretty miffed at my folks for all the hell they put me through to learn the piano.

What if it's just a little medal for the folks to wear and say, "Oh. Yes. Our son plays so pretty — and we made him what he is today." I won't be anyone's medal, that's for sure. I wonder if that's why I like music my parents hate? Crap! I can't even trust my love for music. Is it just a rebellion against the kind of music they like? As if my parents would say, "Oh, yes, our son is a rock star!" Ha! Give me a flyin' break! A rock star to them is the incarnation of Satan himself, and I love it! Wow! I'm so riled up! Does God want me to do music as a career? I suppose I can go on the premise that if I can do it, regardless of where it came from, I therefore should do it. Sounds damn good to me — case closed!

Worship in the Body

Although this journal entry was pivotal for my career choice, there were other aspects of Christian music that were causing me more and more angst. Because I attended a Christian college, and because my degree was in music, I spent a lot of time learning to better understand worship. It was to be a genuine, purposeful show of respect from my heart to God's, without any expectations on God to return a favor or "come through for me." It was thanking God, not getting from God. Yet, when I found myself on Sunday morning in a traditional Baptist worship service, I had trouble singing the hymns and worship songs. If I did not agree with what was being sung, if I did not authentically believe from my heart what I was singing, what was I doing it for, especially if I was to be saying these things to God? Often, I didn't even understand much of it. My Bible told me it was just yammering, mindless lip-service.[1]

I knew there were people who genuinely believed what they were singing. I knew that on some level I had to cut this congregation some slack since group singing is sometimes more about the feeling of unity in community than about the words. I knew I had high standards since I was studying music. But I would look around in the church service and I rarely saw anyone who seemed to be singing those words from their souls. Did they really mean all the words that were flowing from their lips? Of course, getting just one congregation to stop and take notice of all the words they say out of simple habit could send the whole way of doing church into chaos. But at least in doing so, there might be some sincerity. I was feeling more and more tension between how I felt on the inside, as opposed to these seemingly meaningless traditions on the outside.

I had been in countless services where the music leader was hollering over the music (albeit encouragingly), "Sing it like ya mean it. Come on, folks, raise your voice to God!" I yearned to hear a church leader say at the beginning of a service, "Today, folks, we want your worship experience to come from the heart, so any of the words in the songs that don't ring true for you, please, don't sing them." And with a little church surfing, that's exactly what I found. It was the newest, most popular, Pentecostal-style denomination, The Vineyard Christian Fellowship. Its focus was to reach the baby-boomers and younger generations, and it was working. I had gone to a few services and I was getting into the swing of its intensified worship. The music was contemporary in style led by a full rock band. The lyrics were in the popular vernacular.

The theme of worship was constantly focused on individual interaction with God through listening to the Spirit. Whatever I sensed in the moment would bring God the most honor and respect, was indeed the most important thing for me to do. This allowed me a sincerity that I had not felt in my past church experiences or in the presence of God. In these extended worship services, I gradually became more sensitive to listening to what was going on spiritually, and I gathered more and more courage to follow through with the Spirit's leading. If I felt it would be best to kneel with my hands over my heart, I was not only free to do that, I was encouraged and supported by others to follow through as the Spirit led. If I was moved to dance, I could go for it! Of course, this was all done with an awareness not to disturb the people around me or interrupt their worship.

It was in one of these early worship experiences that I had a spiritual insight that changed me. I was standing, arms up, humming the melody of what was being sung so that I didn't have to be distracted by the lyrics and I could simply be attuned to the spiritual realm around me. As I listened, I realized that every single part of me was working as one in gratitude to God. My voice, my thoughts, my beliefs, and my body — everything was aligned and completely participating in this celebration of gratitude, and it felt great. It felt whole, and there was no doubt that I distinctly felt God's blessing and acceptance on me within that congregation. It was an "Aha!" moment. I sensed God saying, "Now you're getting it!"

This kind of worship had a positive effect on my body. Since I was already well on my way to becoming a man, the natural, beautiful, wonderful experiences I was having in my body through my five senses flew in the face of conservative body-negative dogma. For the first time, I excelled in gym class — in weightlifting, of all things. I could do more bar-dips and pull-ups than anyone, mainly because I was so lean. I would go rock climbing and conquer walls I never thought I could surmount. How could something so evil, so "fleshy" be so dependably helpful to my well being and feel so good?

Opportunities for dancing would occur. My college roommate bought tickets to go see the English Beat, a high energy ska and reggae band. The music was fast, fun and no one was sitting down. Everyone was up in the front of the theater dancing jubilantly. It was our first time at a real rock concert. At first, we didn't know what to do. We were standing and moving to the beat, but I know I must have looked stiff as a board. My friend was more relaxed and he even went down in the front to dance a couple of times. I didn't feel so much out of place as I felt I had been missing something benignly joyful. Here were people just having a good time. What really struck me was that these people looked no different than my charismatic worshipping congregation. Both groups were enthusiastic. How could I judge what they found to be real? What did that tell me about the body and how good it was? The rhythm, the message, my body all seemed to sum up sincere desire and intense joy, which I no longer had any reason to keep subdued. Deep inside a scared and beaten up part of me — my sexuality — slowly edged its way toward wholeness and it gradually learned to trust my body as a guide.

Not Going Away

In my sophomore year of college I found that sexuality was occupying more of my thoughts. Despite the well-developed hopes and dreams of one day having a wife, children, and the approval of my family, my sexuality yearned for the deepest possible connection with a man. Still, living in the dorms on campus, I dated a girl named Lynn. I also struck up a solid friendship with her best friend, a cute blonde boy named David. On a particular occasion, one where just he and I were praying together, we somehow came out to each other. It sounded something like, "You have a secret sin that needs prayer? I have a secret sin that needs prayer!" Our eye contact locked with the force of a deadbolt, and the pause said everything. Though we prayed for each other to be strong, we ended up making out and eventually more. Here are a few journal entries from that time:

I had ice cream with Lynn, said goodnight at her dorm and went to talk to David about honesty, friendship and "The Problem." We are the same! Oh, God, how am I going to get out of this one? I'm dying inside to fulfill my desires, but it's wrong. Wrong! Help me keep from sin.

I took a walk with David and we wanted to do it. We started making out in the dark of the garden, which was risky, but then we kind of distracted ourselves by going to dinner. Afterwards, back in my room, we went all the way. Later we decided we could not do this anymore. It was, however, okay to be affectionate. Help me, God!

I went to see David in his dorm room and we did homework together. Then he gave me a back rub, and then a facial, but it was too much. His roommate was out of town and I spent the night. Not good! Woke up feeling guilty, mostly sad, depressed and regretful. I left sort of quickly, but then at lunch we talked about it. This can never happen again! I feel too bad. Never! Forgive me, Lord.

This was not the first time for me to have sex with a man. There were a few encounters before this, but they were random enough that I could file them away behind my denial. "How did I get here?" I wondered. "I'm dating a girl and fooling around with her best friend who's a guy!" This was mainly why the amount of time I spent thinking about my sexuality was escalating (raging hormones notwithstanding) and I decided to confide in the Dean of Students to get some help. It took me almost an hour to finally say the word, "homo- homo- homosexual." Luckily, the Dean, a wise and gentle man, showed no sign of condemnation. Through him I happily agreed to meet with one of the school's psychotherapists.

This was the first time I ever had reason to see a counselor and I was excited about the opportunity to work out some of my personal issues. When he got to know my background, we addressed my lying. In fact, on one occasion he called me a borderline compulsive liar which really sobered me up. He made it clear — and I believed him — that if we were going to get anywhere I had to tell the truth at least in our sessions. He promised me that I could say or do nothing that would make him stop seeing me as his client and he remained true to his word. He became my "Tuesday morning friend."

He also was wise enough to know I did not need someone feeding me religious information, Biblical texts, or even psycho-babble. I had plenty of that from my upbringing. What I really needed was to learn to make decisions for myself. However, I did not make it easy for him. I recall a number of times walking into his office, flopping down on the couch and half-joking as I said, "Fix me!" Finally, during one session he spelled it out, "Even if there was a way to 'fix' you, I would probably do everything I could to keep that from you because you need to learn things on your own for a change."

Once that sank in, it fueled my desire to understand homosexuality the best I could, and that way, I assumed, I would overcome it. I never missed a session. In the meantime, I broke it off with both the girl and the guy, which was not easy. I tried to find books on the subject, but there was not much in the mid-eighties on homosexuality — especially from a Christian perspective. Soon I heard about the ex-gay movement. More specifically, I heard about a group in Los Angeles affiliated with my church who were "recovering homosexuals." This sounded perfect. Not only would these people know what I was going through, but it was far enough away that the chance of meeting up with familiar faces was pretty slim. I was able to keep it far removed from school and therefore keep it all a secret. So I drove for two hours down to LA to experience a real ex-gay ministry. I seem to remember that my therapist had doubts whether ministries like this worked, but he was very careful to allow me to explore and make my own decisions.

My Ex-gay Experience

Off to LA I went to attend a group called Desert Streams. There must have been 10 to 15 people when I walked in for the first time and a couple of men welcomed me with eager handshakes. I saw mostly men, a woman or two, and they did not seem straight. I was so nervous I was shaking. I relaxed a bit when they began to worship just like in my church. However, they seemed to be more earnest — standing, raising their arms into the air as they sang. I thought, "Wow. These folks are hard core." I also thought, "Well, God, whatever it takes." At one point I got choked up by the whole scene. These were people who had the same sexual feelings I had. I could tell they really were sincere and that had to count for something. Could it be that I had found what I had been looking for? It certainly looked that way — at least initially.

After about 30 minutes of singing, a guy who appeared to be in charge gave a kind of sermon — a pep-talk, really. Although he did not seem straight, he proclaimed that we were "new creatures in Christ, washed clean, putting off the old and putting on the new, and without Christ we are nothing." He also contrasted our Christian status with those homosexuals "out there" who had not found Jesus yet. He would smirk and offer sarcastic commentary on "those homosexuals," like, "Of course, they can have all the short-lived relationships they want. It's their choice. I can't judge them." Looking back, I now can see that, plainly, he was judging. Just because he said, "I can't judge them" here and there didn't automatically mean he was judgment free, even though he seemed to think so.

Just when I thought we were done, I realized that everyone was going to sub-divide into small groups. I got nervous again. I wanted to cut and run for the door, but they had already accounted for me and cheerfully directed me into a small group of five guys, with one man leading the group. This prayer group was similar to groups in my church, as well. We went around the group and shared our concerns, specifically in terms of our "skewed straight identity," and prayed for each other. One man was married and "just needed to deal with his thoughts." Another man had "fallen" in the past week, which was an unusually arousing realization — this cute guy had actually had sex in the past week. I remember that the group leader, an older, somewhat emotionless gentleman, requested continued prayer for his friend who had disappeared from the group in recent weeks. The words coming out of his mouth sounded distraught, yet his face actually looked as if he was uninterested in what he was saying. I was able to piece together that this leader was a kind of mentor to the missing man. He ended the prayer request by saying something about his fear of his friend falling back into the "lifestyle," and then he said something about how easy it was to get AIDS. This sent a visual chill around our little circle, and it somehow motivated an anxious resolve of devotion in us — at least in me.

The biggest difference between the prayer groups I grew up with and this Vineyard-style group was that each person was put on the "hot seat." This sounds at first scary but it was quite the opposite. Each person when they shared would sit in the middle and we would lay our hands on them — on their shoulders, their forearm or knees — and pray directly to their concerns. Although this might seem odd for a bunch of guys who are attracted to the same gender, it really emphasized to me their "hands-on" approach to participate in each person's healing — just as Christ had done. These people were downright serious about being healed by God and I was ready to find out how to do it. When it came my turn, I didn't have to say anything (thank goodness!) since it was my first time attending. Nonetheless, I sat in the middle while gentle hands touched me and sincere voices articulated my concerns. A wave of acceptance washed over me. At last, I was with a group of people who could understand what I had been going through and could help me with it — or so it felt in that moment.

Over the next six to eight months I made the four-hour round trip to LA every week, up until the summer months. I read everything they gave me. I got more involved with the Vineyard. I became a regular at one of their Bible Studies just off campus, and I had a small prayer/support group with two "ex-lesbians" (whew, that was safe) on campus. I began to exercise spiritual gifts — speaking in tongues, laying hands on people wanting healing, and speaking words of discernment. I submitted myself to any and all the prayer I could receive. It was the height of the 1980's and healing the inner child was all the rage. So the ministry had their own religious twist on pop-psychology trends. We dug in my history for clues about what may have "triggered" my homosexuality. In the process, along with my continued therapy, I learned a lot about myself and dealt with and created closure for some key unresolved past experiences. This part of the experience was helpful to me.

Like any community, as I got to know them, I began to see the dirt on the sole of their "best foot forward." I started to notice the differences between their beliefs and their behavior. What I knew of communities in general told me that no group was perfect, so I was willing to overlook a certain amount. After a while, though, the more I learned, the more disappointed I became.

The group believed, as I later found out most ex-gay groups believed, that homosexuality originates at an early age when a child has an improper relationship with a parent. Maybe the parent is overbearing, passive, or missing. Maybe the child has been molested. I was told that these inappropriate relationships to parents and adults in the past could be counteracted with proper relationships in the present. This relationship would then enable the jump to heterosexuality, or at the very least, allow gays and lesbians to live happily celibate. It sounded perfectly logical, but this is where I observed that the reality hardly conformed to their theory.

For one thing, their methods of countering the missing parental relationship did not seem to bring about heterosexuality. An eager new male recruit would be paired with an older man who, theoretically, replaced the younger man's dysfunctional father-image, filling the void and bringing "healing" for the younger man. I believe some great connections and healing came out of those relationships, but no one ever said they felt heterosexual as a result. I look back now and remember one bonding which was so strong and the "friendship" so close (they were even living together) that in almost every way the two men maintained a gay relationship except for sexual activity — supposedly. I remember another situation when the role model was a straight man, and the recruit dealt with an agonizing crush on the man who could never return the love the recruit desired. This did not seem to bring healing.

There were other ways this theory did not pan out. I knew members whose personal histories simply did not fit the ministry's model for the development of homosexuality. Like me, they had never been molested and they came from healthy, two-parent families. This confounded the leadership. They prayed extensively over us to find the hidden "flaw" that made us gay. I remember a look in one such man's eyes that I now recognize as hopelessness. How would he ever be able to change if he didn't even fit the profile? So they would keep digging.

What really brought the ministry's whole theory into doubt for me came actually from the very source of their theories. Psychologists originally explored the missing parent/mentoring approach in the 1960's,[2] but over time, the results were found to be biased and ineffective. Even some of the psychologists that designed these studies admitted to this. Further research clearly showed these theories were not true (I'll go into detail about this in the next couple of chapters).[3] Yet the ex-gay leadership had no problem presenting the theories as gospel truth. They simply picked out the sentences and paragraphs that supported their views. Under the auspices of religion, they manipulated information to their own purposes — and they did this often. Even after I knew the details of the study, I too disregarded its results and its ramifications about my sexuality. After all, I told myself as they would tell me, the study was "secular" psychology and I had God. I ignored the unpleasant parts of what I was learning because God could do anything, right? God was the eternal trump card. I had to believe God would change me because it was drilled into me that my sexuality was sinful and unacceptable to God.

Those who worked hard enough rose in the ranks as examples of "the healed." One or two were lightly paid as leaders. It was sobering when I realized what kind of bind that put the paid ex-gays in. Could they really be honest about themselves? How could I trust what they say is true when their job depended on it?

Yet, their personalities, sincerity and speaking abilities were so captivating and strong that if we disagreed with them, it felt as if I would be disagreeing with God. Some leaders seemed to earnestly believe that their authority actually was God's authority within the sphere of the group. It felt to me that to question their ministry meant to be unfaithful to God. I felt, and sometimes I was made to feel, that our innocent questions and desires about sexuality were signs of doubt and disloyalty. Faithfulness meant that it did not matter what we thought inside, so long as we conformed to what the leadership believed God wanted.

The more time went by and the longer I attempted to make ex-gay techniques my own, the less they seemed to really work. The focus on "who we were in Christ" began to sound familiar. A great amount of energy was devoted to imagining how I would really be straight one day. The diligence to be "that person for Christ" would often be equated with modifying our appearance, "taking on a masculine nature," even if I still was attracted to the same gender on the inside. Faithfulness to God was in direct proportion to whether members had abstained from sex and masturbation the previous week. We tried to stay busy with church activities (and I with

school) to distract us from looking at our sexuality, which was a kind of success —
a mastery over lust by distraction.

I began to grasp why this all felt familiar. Although I had come to the ex-gay
ministry to find that special spiritual "something" that would miraculously change
my sexuality, their strategy (although hard to pin down) seemed to basically be the
same tactics I had learned growing up in church. All those years of indoctrination
of "All options except God are evil" set me up to accept the ex-gay propaganda as
"the only godly option" — hook, line, and sinker. Although I was always told I was
free to choose, I felt at the mercy of those I looked up to, because I wasn't really
finding the answers I needed from the scripture. I felt flawed and powerless to do
anything about it, except maybe to continue to ignore it. I constantly lived with a
sense of "damned if I do, and damned if I don't," although I could barely recognize
it at the time. These approaches did not make me straight, and they did not seem
to be working for other participants, either.

Still, this was the only thing I knew that might change me. I was not going to
be a failure. I was not going to let God down. I overlooked more and more nonsense to be the person I thought God wanted me to be. I began to notice a cycli-
cal pattern to my behavior. I would go to the LA meeting, share my past week's
"temptations," and get prayer for strength and healing. Then I would drive home
feeling motivated: "Yes, I'm perfect and clean in God's eyes. I'm God's child and
I want to please him in everything I do." I'd get up the next morning and read my
Bible. On the way to class, though, I'd see a cute guy in shorts and I would get
angry at myself for allowing my eyes to wander down his hairy legs. I'd ask God's
forgiveness, quote a scripture, and refocus again. Sometimes I could focus for a
day or two, kind of like keeping a lid firmly on a boiling pot, but eventually that
seemed to burn my hands and make the "fall" all the more disappointing. I would
think I would be gaining ground, but I would get horny, masturbate, and feel like
a tremendous failure. Instead of questioning the routine, I assumed that I must not
be trying hard enough, and I'd start the whole "workaholic" treadmill over again,
and again, and again.

At some point, significant red flags flew for me regarding the ex-gay ministry,
and it really scared me. The more I wanted to believe that many of their "healing
techniques" were sort of based on theological principles, the more I realized that
there were subtle cultic and brainwashing elements to them. I knew better than
to be sucked into something like this. I knew this much: if I was following God's
truth, it could withstand the test of any contradicting view. God was no wimp. If
I had the truth, and God stood with us, why was I so intensely afraid to just get
through the day? What was all the drama about? And most of all, where were all

the straight people who once were gay? Even though I was attending their church, weekly Bible study and a prayer group in my college town, the direct exposure to the ex-gay ministry was only a few hours a week, when I drove down to LA. Gratefully, this allowed me to keep some distance, and I'd like to think it gave me some perspective from really becoming an ex-gay convert.

I often use my composing and writing to work out the deepest of emotional challenges, and my ex-gay experience was no different. Reflecting on my days attending the group, I wrote these lyrics:

You traveled alone 'til we walked up to you.
Good friends and acceptance are what you could use.
Like moist breezes found in the desert you never knew that we accept you.
We drench you with kindness; we tell you you're a friend.
But when your humanness raises its head
Our kindness just dries up. You choke on your breath and the wind.
If you knew we'd look down, you would not have shared.
We stare at your flaws like a sickness that's rare.
As if to smell fumes means to never breathe the air.
Compassion is never a half-hearted thing.
Not everyone can completely agree.
Our words are just air if we cannot stand firm in a breeze.
But we want to change you, to heal and to mend,
As if with a net we will influence the wind.
And now if you change it's as if you will lose and we win.
You now feel a distance. You now feel condemned.
You cannot contribute to flawless men.
The rule that we live by is: "Love the sinner. Hate the sin."
Now we seem at loss when you tell us we're mean.
Unhelpful, cold shoulders are all you'll receive.
You will not stand in a wind that is too cold to breathe.
Rejection stings.
Like bubbles that drift on a desolate breeze,
Our circle of friends have flung out of your reach.
Just what makes us so different from you that would force us to leave?[4]

Exorcism

Nonetheless, I really wanted to be straight, and I still believed that God would change my sexuality, and if the ex-gays didn't know how, what was I going to do? The stress and pressure only seemed to increase when one of the women in my little prayer group had heard about a healer that specialized in "this sort of thing," and my friend arranged for us to go see her. I was hopeful that maybe a special healing like this could help shift things in the right direction, but it began to feel almost subversive, as if we were seeking out a soothsayer. We drove to some church we had never been to before in the middle of the day, and each one of us went in to see this woman one at a time. I was last.

When I walked in, she and her male assistant had me sit in the hot seat while they prayed over me. They asked a few questions, much as a psychic might ask questions: "Do you have siblings? Do you come from a divorced family?" They anointed my forehead with oil. They spoke in tongues over me. There was a lot of praying about roots, "Lord, get to the root of this boy's desire. Lord, pull the improper root of lust clean out of his life." I tried to imagine my problem being a root to a big tree, and I imagined it being pulled out, but somehow the root seemed elusive it felt like I was grabbing for it and nothing was there. I acknowledged this and it somehow spurred them on. They raised their voices. They pressed their fingertips into my skin and vibrated them. Sometimes they would suggest that maybe I was not allowing the Holy Spirit complete freedom to wash me clean, as if I was not doing enough. I squinted. I squeezed. I swayed back in forth in my chair. I stayed as open to whatever God wanted as I possibly could. I wanted to be open in ways I could not yet imagine. Eventually, I felt a certain amount of peace (or exhaustion) while the woman leading the prayer wound down.

I believed. I prayed with her. I pleaded for the Spirit to fill the space where once was the root with God's love and strength. I felt as clean as I imagined clean could be. I was not aware of it, but of the three of us I had taken the longest time. I guess I had deeper roots. I imagined myself completely free to choose heterosexuality, but I was afraid to put it to the test. How would I put it to the test? Was I supposed to get an erection from thinking about women? Was that not a sin all by itself?

Well, the "cleanliness" and the imagined "freedom" lasted until we had dinner at a fast-food spot where a really cute guy was at the register. My sexuality had not flipped, nor did I feel that I chose to be aroused. I just was. My lesbian friends seemed to feel differently, or at least they said, "I really feel like I've been changed." They would kind of chuckle under their breath and say it again. (Recently I've been in touch with one of them and found that she is a happy lesbian woman). I chimed in too, so as not to rouse suspicion, but I was lying through my teeth, as always. I could do it so well.

My Calculated Rebellion

Summer break was just days away. Although friends might not have noticed from the outside, inside I was tied up in knots of frustrated confusion. I suppose this could have been the time when I tried even harder, but I just needed a break. I was so exhausted and so disappointed. I had submerged myself in the ex-gay experience every way I possibly could, and I felt no straighter. If it was going to be this much work for so little reward, I had to be sure of what I was doing. That meant I had to view every perspective. I had spent all my life suppressing my sexuality, especially in the past few months, and it seemed that during these very same months I had been more obsessed with it than ever. I felt confident that I knew what this side of the fence was about. What I hadn't explored was the other side. If I was going to seek God's truth about this in every way, I owed it to myself to know for sure that I was choosing correctly, and the only way to be completely sure was to find out what all the hubbub was about. What was so horribly sinful and desperately lonely about being a homosexual?

When summer began, I prayed a very unique prayer — at least for me at the time. I said, "God, I have to find out for myself what it means to be gay. No more taking ex-gays' word for it. So this is going to be my summer of calculated rebellion. I love you. I will be back, but just give me some space for three months to check things out." As much as I could, I set God on a shelf and turned my back in order to see how the "other half" lived. I stayed on campus with a job in the admissions office, but on off hours I was nowhere to be found. I did not take the long drives down to the ex-gay ministry anymore. The Bible study and prayer group went on vacation with classes. Church definitely took a back seat to other activities.

When I said, "calculated rebellion," it really felt like that. There are several key experiences that summer that I remember like a progressive set of Polaroids in my mind's eye. Like the first day I ever went to a nude beach. I see myself in a regular bookstore downtown. I see before me a brightly-clad catalog entitled, "The Definitive Guide to Nude Beaches in America." I see myself opening it to Santa Barbara. I see the name of a beach I recognize and then I see myself sitting on a public bus that goes directly to that beach. It's effortless, but my heart is pounding out of my chest, and I wonder what could be so wrong about being naked on a beach?

Before I know it, I am standing, shoes in hand, on a public beach. Now all I have to do is walk south a few hundred feet. As I do, I begin to notice less and less clothing on people, until — there, that person just a few feet away from me is completely without a stitch of clothing. I have to sit down. I keep stumbling from my legs trembling so much in the loose sand. I am noticed. There are a couple of (completely naked) guys a short distance away keeping an eye on me. Oh, could it be it's because I'm on a nude beach sporting a shirt and long pants? I remove my shirt and only now does it occur to me that I have come to a beach without a swimsuit. I really can't get in the water with my underwear on. How will I go back to the dorms with wet underwear? So this experience is going to be all or nothing. I will either go in the water without clothes, or I will sit here clothed. It helps that I have unconsciously cornered myself.

I try to calm down — half excited, half petrified. I recline with my shirt between my back and the sand, but I keep sitting up to take in the view. Everything is beautiful — the location, the people, even the "less attractive" people with their courage to be naked are beautiful. It's already late in the day and some are leaving. If I'm going to get in the water, I'll have to do it soon or it will get too cold. Hell, I don't even have a towel to dry off with. So with a big breath, I take off my pants — I'm down to my underwear. The two guys take notice. I think they like what they see, and I don't know whether I like it or not, but it's definitely stimulating. Time passes and I watch the number of people dwindle. Am I going to do this or not?

Soon, even the two guys are starting to pack up, though they are still watching. My head is spinning, and just as they are about to walk away, I stand, drop my tighty-whities and head for the water, which now seems miles away. I notice the watchers have big grins on their faces, but it's not like they're laughing at me. It's like they are genuinely happy for me. When my feet touch the water I am alone before a horizon of deep blue sea. The sun is low and still hot. I wade in up to my thighs and then dive into the waves. It's cold but I have never before felt the ocean wash over me without some kind of clothing on. A thought is revealed to me, "This is what it feels like to be truly washed clean," and it surprises me, just as much as I am transfixed by God's presence. On the sand, in the sun, across the sky, around the salty ocean and against my skin, God is here, and I feel it in every inch of my body. The Spirit is undeniable.

I went back to that beach every chance I got. And yes, a few times I went home with the guys I met there — their homes, not my dorm room. That was out of the question.

Another experience stands out to me that summer and it begins on that very same beach. This time, I have everything I need to last the day — a beach towel, sun block, some food and water, but no bathing suit. On a walk along the beach (completely naked — oh, what a feeling of freedom) a gentleman introduces himself to me. I'm going to call him "Mark." He is a couple of inches taller than I am, beautifully shaped with a light blanket of hair down the center of his chest and no tan line. When he talks, a shining smile beams out from under his sun-bleached blond hair. I learn he is a dance instructor, which explains his body. He has to be a few years older than I am, and although it seems foreign, I admire his streak of fearless femininity. He learns I'm new around here and I'm happy that he respectfully keeps his distance from the subject of my school when he finds out where I attend. We talk for a long time.

As the day goes by, we meet in the water a time or two. We wrestle and play in the waves. I meet his roommate who is tall, lanky, and has an Australian accent. As the day ends, they offer to give me a ride home, but I secretly hope he will invite me back to their house. At that moment, Mark invites me back to their house, saying, "We're going to barbecue some steaks for dinner, would you like to join us?" Would I? I'm going to have what's sure to be a sexual adventure and I'll avoid dorm food as well. When we get to the parking lot, I am struck dumb by their mode of transportation. Mark drives and his roommate is in the passenger seat. I recline, with my arms outstretched across a seat back of white leather upholstery in a giant, candy-apple red, antique Cadillac convertible — with the top down. I own that back seat as that monstrosity drives down the freeway beside a sun-setting beach, and I really don't care who sees me.

We stop at the supermarket and they ask me if I want beer or wine. When I demonstrate little knowledge of either, their grin shows amusement, but they make no fun of me with words. At their house, while dinner is prepared, I discern that Mark's roommate is only that, although at one time they were closer. Mark becomes more affectionate with me, and as uncomfortable as I am with touch, I want all he has to give. When the steaks are ready, the roommate sets his plate down in front of the TV, but Mark suggests the two of us eat in his large master bedroom, just off the patio. I'm going with the flow, and I am again amazed when I enter his bedroom. At the center of a king-size futon is a low-to-the-ground, Asian-style table for two with a spread so elaborate, I am at a loss as to when he had the time to set it up. We sit next to each other over dinner. We flirt and kiss and talk some more. By some of the things he compliments me on, I can tell where he wants to take this. He wants to have anal intercourse with me, and I make it known that although I have never done it before, I want the experience, but only with someone who would be willing to go at a very gentle pace. He can tell I'm serious about the slow approach, and I can tell he is up for the challenge.

Dinner ends, the table is removed and the clothes come off again. I enjoy the soft texture of his chest, his armpits and his abdomen. He explores every inch of my scrawny body and bubble butt. At times, as our excitement builds he has the tendency to become more aggressive, like an animal. I'm intrigued and flattered, but at the point of my concern he slows down — becoming gentler, like a pussy cat — wanting more, holding back. He sticks to his word, and I give him what we both want. Condoms are used — no questions asked. It is not altogether pain-free, but I account for some of it as acquired taste. I can tell he prefers me on my back with our faces nose to nose, but when I get comfortable sitting down on him, it does not take long. I find the spot where I feel him most deeply and hardly any stroking is necessary. I am lost to my eruption mainly by his presence in me. I believe he's right behind me but it's all a little fuzzy at that moment. Soon we are a sweaty-sticky mess, panting, coming down, lying on top of each other every which way.

Here is the crazy part (and the reason I'm going into such detail). During this whole experience and even as we relax to complete peace, at the end of the bed, in the left side of the room is God's presence. I know that sounds silly, and even un-comfortable, but I wasn't looking for it. Yet, I am aware of it the whole time. Mind you, it's not like God's a cheerleader on the sidelines, but I don't sense a wagging finger of shame, either. At one point I even chuckle to think, "Could we please have a little privacy here? Sheesh!" While Mark sleeps and I am cuddling in his strong arms, my eyes are wide open and I ponder what all this means. When I eventually fall asleep, with my cheek on this beautiful man's furry chest, the room is permeated with the Spirit of unconditional love.

I saw Mark a few more times that summer and on the last day of vacation I got out of his bed, returned to campus and never looked back. I accomplished what I set out to do, and I returned, just as I had promised. I did see Mark a year or two later, but it was just in passing. I think we both knew what we were doing for each other, and it was fine for that summer.

All my sex that summer felt, for the most part, positive to me. Call it what you will, but God's presence throughout was a major contradiction in the theology I was given by the ex-gay ministry. I had assumed my calculated rebellion would leave me destitute, morally bankrupt, possibly lying in some alley like an anemic drug addict. From what I was told in the conservative church, I was going to be doing constant battle with Satan for my soul, and the risk of leaving God on the shelf was going to expose me to all kinds of demons. Furthermore, all my life I had been told that the world "out there" beyond our safe little church-approved bubble was unfulfilling, dangerous and on a one-way car-crash to Hell. Yet, in just three months time, I felt that I had glimpsed a number of people's lives that were happy, fulfilled, by no means perfect, but some of them were a lot more loving, peaceful and accepting than many a Christian life I knew. It was a place where, yes, I had to responsibly fend for myself, but God's creations and blessings were everywhere. I simply had never taken the time to experience them. The moon was certainly not following me around, and that was okay.

That summer, something else began to make unexpected spiritual sense. Thanks to my Christian education, I was beginning to see a pattern to God's way of doing things. I could point to any number of historical periods where the status quo, the powers in control, the religious governments and even church leadership would say (and I'm paraphrasing, but not much), "Those evil people out there, those corrupters from Hell, God could not possibly exist in their midst." Yet, wouldn't you know, that's precisely where God dwelt the most. The genuine love of God can grow where we least expect. What better example do we have than Jesus and the Pharisees? These authorities of ancient religion (the Pharisees) would exclaim in horror, "How could Jesus ever spread his message of love to those heathen gentiles (beyond their control, by the way)?" Yet for centuries the whole of Christianity has been made up primarily of gentiles. If this was the way God was going to be made evident in our times, then being gay was right in the fabulous thick of it — right where I should be.

God Speaks

But it was not that easy; it never is. I was a leader on campus, a model student in the music department, working toward a career of performing music and ministry in churches full time. How was any of my sexuality going to fit into this picture of Christian leadership? I'm sorry to say that I put my "summer of love" behind me. School, Bible study and my prayer group became my entire focus. Fortunately, the ex-gay ministry was no longer part of the equation, but I put my sexuality on the back-burner — again. I continued to go to therapy. It had been the most consistent arena for better understanding myself, and I wanted to continue it. I had enjoyed exploring my sexuality, but I still felt that it was in conflict with the rest of my life, school, music, and especially my spiritual journey. These things just seemed more important. Quite frankly, with all of this going on and the friendships through church that I continued to nurture, I could stay busy enough to not think about sex — much.

After living for a year with my unchanged yet relatively docile sexuality, I began to feel a certain amount of peace and clarity. I had explored the challenges of the ex-gay world, and now, I had experienced the other side, too. Still, I had this sense that I really needed to go right to the source for understanding. After all I had learned, I wanted to directly hear the thoughts of God, as best I could figure them out. I decided that the way to accomplish this was to retreat from all the input that was constantly coming at me. I had to get away from the shame, the pleasures, the temptations, the voices of authority — I had to get away and take the time to let everything settle and, in that quiet, hear the still small voice of God. This sounded like a great idea. This was exactly what I should do. Unfortunately, this had occurred to me right at the beginning of my senior year which meant that the soonest I could pull away would not be for another eight months or so. The prospect of waiting so long made me feel frustrated, depressed and at times despondent. My sadness grew. I would be in the middle of something — class, work, or leading worship — and catch myself miles away, thinking, "Why is all of this activity going on when what I really want to do is just hear the voice of God?"

It was at some kind of church planning meeting that I was caught off guard by what I can best describe as God's voice — not booming, but simply clear, present, and re-assuring. "The retreat idea is a great one. I really appreciate your committed desire to know me, but guess what? I'm prepared to tell you what I think about your sexuality right here and now." I blinked as if coming out of a trance, though I was completely unaware of what was going on around me. "Okay, I'll bite," I thought, half skeptical of this simple conversation. "Tell me what you think of my sexuality." As loving as a whisper, I felt as much as I heard, "Please don't worry about it. That is not what it's for." Even before it sank in, I knew in that moment that I would no longer allow my sexuality to keep me from God, or keep me from my goals. Then it sank in, but I was also back in the meeting. The room had fallen silent, all eyes were on me, and my eyes were welling up. Someone asked if I was okay, and my voice cracked when I said, "Yeah, I'm fine." I attempted to stay in the meeting, but I was all too aware of this enormous release that was flooding my existence. It was as if I had exhaled for the first time. I don't know how I got through the rest of the meeting, but when I finally made it to the safety of my darkened room, I let out what I had been holding in for so long and sobbed with a smile on my face. I felt as though the fighting was over, and it amazed me how only then I saw that I had been fighting with myself. I was so tired of fighting. The fear of rejection felt like a poison flowing freely in every one of my veins. I had hated myself in so many ways. I had inflicted so many bruises. "That can end. I am with you. You are safe."

Although I continued to attend the church, I knew inside that God was not the one who had a problem with my sexuality. Mostly, I had the problem with my sexuality. The religious system I grew up in had the problem with my sexuality. This awareness brought about one of the biggest and most important questions in my life: what was I going to do about it?

CHAPTER 2

More Ex-gay Experiences

Stories of Other Ex-gay Survivors

THE ANSWER TO THE QUESTION, "What am I going to do about it?" is what makes up the rest of this book. Of course, having the benefit of looking back over the last 20-plus years helps me understand circumstances, patterns and the overall picture. Therefore, from here on out, I won't be progressing in a strictly chronological manner. It will be clearer to identify different aspects of my recovery when each chapter addresses a specific topic.

Instant Ministry!

Just after college graduation, I took a summer internship at the same charismatic church I had been attending the previous couple of years. I would organize the worship band, practices and other music-related tasks. I also had regular meetings with the senior pastor and, in one such meeting, I told him about my "struggle" with homosexuality. I told him I had attended an ex-gay ministry for a while. Before I could go into any detail of what I believed worked or didn't work, he eagerly delegated to me the responsibility of counseling a couple of church members who were gay. They had each come to him for one-on-one counseling. He didn't know what to do with them and he just assumed that I somehow would know. Looking back, I don't know why I agreed to it, but I did. I think I sincerely wanted to help them.

There I was, in one of the private offices at the church, a couple of times a week listening to two different guys agonize over their sexual desires and the church's negative stance about it. Both of them were having sex in truly risky settings and usually without protection. I quickly realized that the only things I could ethically do for them was to be a good listener, try to help them lower the risk factors, and just accept them. Back at the meetings with the pastor, he would check in with me about the two guys, but he did not ask anything specific. I figured he was respecting confidentiality, but he was probably just uncomfortable about it.

Somewhere in the middle of summer I had a fender-bender. No one was hurt, but I was certainly shaken. For some reason I didn't call friends from church or school. Instead, I called a guy I had met two years prior during my "calculated rebellion." I think I may have wanted some nurturing touch after the accident and I knew I wasn't going to get it from college buddies. I spent the night with him. Later on, I made the mistake of mentioning it to a couple of fellow band members who had been like surrogate parents to me. Within a few days, it had gotten to the pastor. My internship as well as any other connection with that church was over. I remember sitting in his office feeling terribly uncomfortable as he grilled me about what I had been "counseling" the two guys. So much for confidentiality. It was when I wouldn't give him any details that he, in frustration, dismissed me along with a few statements of how I was being used by Satan to divide his church.

I recount this story because it is a typical example of how a number of ex-gay ministries got their start. A church pastor has congregants coming to him about their conflicted sexual feelings and he doesn't know what to do. When he finds someone in the church or denomination that seems to have a "handle" on the subject, or at very least is comfortable talking about it — hallelujah! — a new ministry is born. Not surprisingly, ex-gay leadership has a pretty high turnover rate. With all that pressure, they just can't pretend for very long. I know former leaders who are, to this day, ashamed because they not only feel that they failed at being straight, they also feel that they led a lot of people into seemingly inescapable failure, as well.

It's important to point out that the ex-gay movement was not instigated by a bunch of psychological researchers or therapists basing their treatments on facts. It was mainly spearheaded (and still is) by uneducated (in sexuality) ministers and self-loathing homosexuals. Here was the foundation for this type of abusive religion, and it happens all the time. Distraught churchgoers turn to their pastor with problems far beyond the scope of the leader's education. Instead of passing the members onto a trained professional, like a psychotherapist or sex therapist, the pastor assumes he (usually a man) has the answers to everything, and potentially ends up doing a lot of damage. More details about this will be fleshed out in the next chapter.

Before I more directly explore the connections between religious abuse and the ex-gay movement, it is important to expose just how severe an ex-gay experience can get by citing some stories and quotes of others who have been there. Furthermore, my own experience does not encompass the far-reaching repercussions the ex-gay movement has on our culture, religion and sexuality. Therefore, I am devoting this chapter to a fuller picture of the movement's history and "therapeutic process." To be sure, this is neither a detailed analysis of their "therapies" nor a month-to-month log of their activities.[1] I simply want to hit some of the general highlights, so that we can be on the same page when moving deeper into my recovery process.

"The ex-gay movement began in the latter part of the 20th century in an organized way, but in the late 19th century some doctors tried to cure homosexuality through castration, cauterization, radiation, hormone treatment, shock treatment, aversion therapy, psycho-therapy, prostitution therapy, marriage therapy, lobotomy and other means. What they usually ended up with were castrated, cauterized, radiated, hormoned, shocked, averted, psycho, prostituted, married, lobotomized people. What they never achieved, or rarely achieved were happy healthy heterosexuals."
— *Dr. Sylvia Rhue, Director of Religious Affairs*
National Black Justice Coalition [2]

There have been a number of ex-gay ministries that have popped up over the years, led by parents of LGBT people and former wives of gay men. Even a few straight ministers have felt "called" to start an ex-gay ministry. Such is the case with one of the first known ex-gay ministries, Love In Action. In the early seventies, John Evans, a gay Christian, met with a straight pastor to begin what John thought was simply a Bible study and fellowship time for a few friends who happened to be gay and lesbian. The minister quickly commandeered the group and insisted that they all forsake their homosexual feelings (not to mention long-term relationships) to follow Christ. This led to the eventual suicide of one of the members (the letter that began this book). This "well-meaning" minister also used six members' written testimonies (John's being one of them) in the book, *The Third Sex*. The popularity of the book fueled Love In Action's membership, even after all six members came out of the closet professing that they did not change (more about Love In Action later).[3]

Still, in the mid-seventies (after the gay and lesbian community began actively working for civil rights) and into the eighties (especially as the AIDS epidemic began), dozens of little ministries cropped up like weeds: Be Whole Ministries, The Christian Coalition for Reconciliation, Desert Streams, Eagle Ministries, Emmanuel Ministries, Exodus, Homosexuals Anonymous, Imago Dei, Living In Freedom Eternally (L.I.F.E.), Living Waters, New Christian Ministries, Promise Ministries, and Regeneration Ministries, to name a few. In the 1993 groundbreaking documentary, *One Nation under God*, the late Gary Cooper, one of the original founders of Exodus and an ex-gay survivor, stated that, in the beginning, "Our mailing list went from, maybe, a hundred pieces a month to twenty-five thousand pieces a month, and it made a jump like that in a three-month period."[4] To be sure, as various groups gained recognition, they were striking a definite chord in a lot of people. Just as society was fearful and ignorant of that which was sexually different — homosexuality — the church seemed to be driven by that same fear, making gays and lesbians feel unwelcome. Ex-gay groups were the answers to everyone's prayers — or so they hoped.

The huge surge in interest was a sign to Gary Cooper and Michael Bussee — two of the founders of Exodus — that God was raising them up as ex-gays to minister to all the hurting homosexuals. Unfortunately, by the time Gary and Michael came out to each other, fell in love, came out to their friends and family, and finally left the ministry, Exodus was well on its way to becoming the umbrella organization for all of the smaller ex-gay organizations. Exodus International now calls itself "The largest information and referral ministry in the world addressing homosexual issues." [5] Their website states that they have over 230 local ministries in the U.S. and Canada, as well as affiliates around the world.

God Alone Will Heal You

As most of these little ministries were starting up, they were, if you'll pardon the pun, pretty straightforward: "God can do anything. Simply ask him for healing and he will make you straight." Some of them shunned any use of outside assistance. Even as late as 1993, Joanne Highley from L.I.F.E. Ministries was quoted as saying, "We have had no psychological training. We try not to use psychological techniques. We try to go from the Word of God and what He reveals to us." [6]

Tanya Erzan, after doing extensive research on the ex-gay movement and, in particular, New Hope Ministries, found that, "The problem of Exodus in the seventies was that many ex-gay leaders had been Christians only for several months, and having a testimony was the only qualification for ministry work." [7] Even though over the years a few ex-gay leaders have gotten degrees in various subjects — Marriage and Family Counseling, theology, psychotherapy — the vast majority of those 230 local ministries functions with leaders untrained in therapy or teaching.

As more and more leaders "fell back into the lifestyle," turnover in leadership became almost routine. However, their message began to change:

> *Over the history of the ex-gay movement it has become a little more sophisticated. At first it was just, 'Pray and you'll change.' Then they said, 'Well, it's a long struggle and you'll change.' Then they said, 'Well, maybe with some therapy also, and prayer then you'll change.' So they keep modifying their promises.*
>
> — *Dr. Ralph Blair, psychotherapist and*
> *founder of Evangelicals Concerned.* [8]

Psycho-Babble — From Silly to Serious

Ex-gay ministries incorporated pop psychology and New Age thinking when it suited them. Homosexuals Anonymous (HA) incorporated the traditional 12-Step Program and applied it to homosexuality. Did this work to curb gay sexuality? Not for HA's founder, Colin Cook, who was finally asked to leave the organization after repeated occasions of using phone sex and mutual nude massage as a method of "healing." Did this bring into question the legitimacy of the organization? Of course not. They simply replaced him. Did this ever get him to confront his own sexuality? It seems not. As late as 2007 he was on the air with a radio show in Denver, still promoting the ability to heal homosexuals.[9] In this case, some of their attempts at sounding legitimate seemed laughable, if they hadn't been so detrimental to those who trusted the leaders.

Although most of the techniques used in the contemporary ex-gay world sound quite psychological in style, they are all built upon a premise that is not based in psychology. Underlying all of their work is the religiously-motivated belief that homosexuality is a sin, unhealthy and life-threatening. To be fair, the originators of ex-gay theory did draw from psychoanalytic models, like that of Irving Bieber and Dr. Gerald Davison, with even a little Freud mixed in. These ideas were supposing that a "detached-indifferent father and/or close-binding intimate mother" would produce an "unhealthy" homosexual. But these studies and others were developed in the 1950's and 1960's, when the psychological community also assumed that homosexuality was unhealthy even before doing the research. Even Dr. Davison (Professor of Psychology, USC) has now admitted that his work at that time was biased:

> This [research] was sort of held up as proof of mental illness among homosexuals that they had this close-binding-intimate mother. But if you step back a moment, you have to ask yourself the question, what's wrong with having a mother like that or any other factor in your background unless the outcome that you are trying to explain is judged beforehand to be abnormal. In other words, if you found that factor among heterosexuals, would you conclude that close-binding-intimate mothers are pathogenic? Well you wouldn't. The reason is you would have not decided ahead of time that heterosexuality is abnormal.[10]

In the early 1970's, psychological research began to show that homosexuality was not an illness. In fact, there was evidence that gay male mental health could not even be differentiated from straight male mental health, as in Dr. Evelyn Hooker's ground breaking study on Male Homosexuality.[11] So strong was the proof that the American Psychiatric Association removed homosexuality from the DSM (Diagnostic and Statistical Manual of Mental Disorders), no longer viewing it as a mental illness. However, according to Shidlo, Schroeder and Drescher, "Despite these changes, and perhaps even because of them, a marginal subset of mental health practitioners continues to diagnose and treat individuals with a homosexual orientation as if they are mentally ill."[12]

Further, the ex-gay movement continued to use the outdated psychological material as proof of their theories. One of the early spokespersons for continuing these outdated psychological theories was Elizabeth Moberly. At an Exodus International. Conference in 1990, she is quoted as saying, "When a boy had a good relationship with his father, he never became homosexual."[13] Erzen points out, however, that "Moberly never actually treated ex-gay patients, so her theories were purely speculative, and yet ex-gay-supportive psychiatrists and psychologists at NARTH and elsewhere continue to base their counseling practices on her book."[14] (More on NARTH in the next chapter.) Although Moberly carried the title of Director of Psychosexual Education and Therapy for the Bible Centered Ministries International, any evidence of her psychological credentials has yet to be found. She has disappeared from the ex-gay arena, and Wikipedia says that she is now a cancer researcher in Britain.

Another popular author on the subject of "healing the homosexual" was Leanne Payne, with her books, *The Broken Image: Restoring Wholeness to the Homosexual*, and *Crisis in Masculinity*. She merged the healing power of prayer with "cutting-edge" (questionable) psychological phenomena such as repressed memories and crisis in sexual identity. She popularized the term "inner healing" which is a "form" of prayer therapy used by many ex-gay practitioners. "It involves a prayerful guided imagery experience during which the Holy Spirit is invited to reveal unresolved hurt and woundedness in the life of the ex-gay subject."[15] As with Moberly, no education in psychology or theology was found for Payne.

Dr. Joseph Nicolosi has carried the "change torch" into the new millennium. In fact, he is credited with coining the phrase "reparative therapy," which has become a generic term for any process that purports to facilitate a shift from homosexual orientation to heterosexual orientation.[16] Like almost everyone else in the field, he can't seem to come up with a sound or clear treatment to show real change. Wayne Besen, in his book *Anything But Straight*, followed the ex-gay and reparative therapy phenomena. He found Nicolosi "shifty" when it came to something as simple as getting a clear time frame for people to move through his treatment and become straight. "He [Nicolosi] said that the average amount of time it takes to convert is 6.7 years. At other times, he told the *New Times Los Angeles* that 'We're working two years here,' and, in his book, that 'change' is a 'long-term process,' and one that is 'most probably lifelong.'"[17] He, too, seems to have no problem using the disproved psychological theories; in 2005, at the Love Won Out conference in Seattle, he was quoted as saying, "Every gay man does not value his father," and "Every gay man has a bad relationship with his older brother."[18] Ah, generalizations. As though all gay men are identical.

Reparative therapy and ex-gay theory continue to gain the attention of the psychological community. Evidence, methods and practices have been requested to better understand how the gay-to-straight transition is achieved. Yet there seems to be no therapeutic commonality agreed upon across the various ex-gay groups. Very little actual research or quantifiable proof has been produced or allowed. The vast majority of their "proof" draws from descriptive accounts of people who say it works, and we just have to take their word for it.

As more information has been unearthed about what goes on in ex-gay programs, the more their methods has been brought into question. In fact, the movement was so psychologically unsound that it caused the following organizations to put out warnings about it:

The American Academy of Pediatrics
The American Counseling Association
The American Association of School Administrators
The American Federation of Teachers
The American Psychological Association
The American School Counselor Association
The American School Health Association
The Interfaith Alliance Foundation
The National Association of School Psychologists
The National Association of Secondary School Principals
The National Association of Social Workers
The National Education Association
The School Social Work Association of America

All of the above organizations have published statements warning the public that there is no research to prove that reparative therapy and ex-gay practices work.[19] Furthermore, they warn that participation in such organizations could have damaging repercussions.

Evangelicals Concerned — "The Evil Doppelgänger"

One of the first organizations that provided me a safe place to start understanding my sexuality on a deeper level was Evangelicals Concerned (E.C.). This is a non-profit group that specifically supports LGBT Christians' first steps on the road to unconditionally accepting themselves. They purposefully remain non-denominational so that anyone in the evangelical world can feel relatively safe attending one of their socials, Bible studies, or annual conferences. In my years of working with them, I saw many a person attending an event absolutely petrified and the first thing out of their mouths would be, "I could lose everything if anyone back home knew I was here." Therefore, E.C.'s work is extremely important, and it was very helpful and supportive in my integration process.

I remember attending my very first E.C. Bible study in West Hollywood just after college. I entered an apartment and found a dozen men seated in a circle around the room. A guy knocked on the door and let himself in. A person or two said, "Hi, Jay," evidently knowing the blond-headed man. Jay proceeded across the room, and he returned the greetings by giving one man a kiss — right on the lips — and no one batted an eye. Holy affection! I knew I had found the real deal. Over the years as I got stronger in my faith and sexuality, I served on the Board of Directors and coordinated retreats, Bible studies and conferences. To this day, E.C. maintains a vigilant spot on the forefront of helping those coming out of fundamentalist Christianity. By the way, blond-headed Jay became the person who fulfilled my lifelong desire for a best friend.

It was during my time of leadership in a local E.C. group in San Francisco that I got to know an even more intense version of the ex-gay world. Just across the bay in Marin County was the aforementioned ministry, Love In Action (which eventually changed its name to New Hope Ministries). They developed into a residential, or live-in, program where men would put their lives basically on hold, often moving across the country to live in the Love In Action house with other ex-gays and submerge themselves in a 24/7 program of changing their gay sexuality into heterosexuality. Here are the words of Love In Action ex-gay survivor:

Living in an isolated area of the country, I relied heavily on the integrity of my group's literature to help me decide whether or not to join their ministry. I read their promises of "freedom" and "change" with great hope and decided to move to California to join them. Once there I endured months of painful struggle to deny my sexual orientation with no favorable results, and even more disappointing was the fact that no one, no matter how long they had been there, could look me in the eye and say they had really changed. Only then did I realize that the Ex-gay promises were false. Their literature creates an illusion of freedom that does not exist, and they know it.

— *Sean Greystone.*[20]

Somehow, it got around the residency that if a person had to leave, and had no place to go, Evangelicals Concerned would help. For a while, E.C. San Francisco became the "evil doppelgänger" of Love In Action. Through a few guys who showed up on our doorstep, I heard first-hand how severe these live-in groups could get. Their "change" tactics were extreme to cult-like proportions.

The Love In Action leadership was given near-absolute authority over the members — more so than in the drop-in groups. "...Secular music (other than classical) is not permitted in the house. In addition, the men can only watch videos that are G or PG... They cannot use the Internet because of the availability of pornography, chat rooms, and other places to meet men."[21] At the newer, more sophisticated residential ministry, Love In Action Memphis, "There are no doors on the rooms, the men must wear short hair and modest dress, and there are military-style cleanliness checks of the men and living quarters."[22] I was told the members were restricted from seeing certain people. The ministry provided temp-like jobs so members were monitored at all times. One person contacted us to make plans to leave the house and the only time he could talk with us was on his 30-minute lunch break in which we met him at a fast-food restaurant down the street from where he worked. It felt like a James Bond movie.

There were also confrontations. When live-in members were found out to be breaking one of the many rules, like having sex, the leadership would corner them and aggressively argue with them and pray over them until the person would totally submit, or break down, or both. If the participant did not do exactly what the leadership demanded, he could be kicked out on the spot, or maybe he had to leave within 24 hours, regardless of whether he had anywhere to go. An ousted participant might not even be able to return to his family because they were expecting him to return straight. Leadership would speak horribly of them after the fact. It was as if they made the "rebellious participant" an example of how Satan could destroy a life. The other participants were warned not to communicate with those poor deceived, lost souls. This is where E.C. could help these outcasts, and I'm proud to say I provided a place for a couple of men to stay as they got on their feet.

Unfortunately, the residential-style program has become a standard tool of the ex-gay experience. If a person is really a committed ex-gay, it is a serious option to live — possibly for years — in this kind of environment. In the words of one ex-gay survivor:

> *At the Love In Action program the staff led participants in a game of sorts known as the Five Phases and the Twelve Steps.*
> *Participants preoccupied themselves with moving up (and down) these artificial gradations much like the Chutes & Ladders game I played as a child.*
>
> • *In Phase One the staff forced participants to look at themselves in order to acknowledge they had a problem, in fact that they were a problem— sinful, addicted, and broken.*
>
> • *In Phase Two the focus turned to God, the ultimate perfection and means of escape.*
> • *Phase Three pointed the spotlight onto the family where we created new mythologies about our childhood and family dynamics to fit in with the program theories about dysfunctional families.*
>
> • *In Phase Four we deconstructed former friendships rebranding them as unhealthy, emotionally dependent, and sick with the charge to develop new, healthy relationships with heterosexual mentors from the church.*
>
> • *Finally, we moved to the Fifth Phase where we began to transition into the world outside the program.*
>
> *While slowly working through the phases, the staff also pushed us through an intensive 12-Step program always emphasizing that our desires for people of the same sex had to be always wrong. We needed to account for every sexual encounter and reframe them to fit in with the addiction model the staff gave us. Through our weekly "Moral Inventories" we wrote about and discussed our former sexual experiences reworking them into a clinical narrative designed to reinforce the construct provided by the staff. Instead having sex with someone to express our love or even our horniness, we had to recast our motives*

so that they instead sprung from our own emotional, psychological or spiritual illnesses.

— Peterson Toscano, Ex-gay Survivor
and Performance Activist.[23]

Frank Worthen, the driving force behind Love In Action and New Hope Ministries, takes credit for creating the method of confession as therapy and advertising:

He helped establish the testimony as the basis for a system of public accountability and confession in which he expected ex-gay men and women to testify about their struggles with pornography, masturbation, and an "undisciplined thought life." At New Hope, testimony is a form of therapy. Participants... speak publicly about the most secret and disturbing aspects of their lives as part of their healing... Nothing is too private or painful to share, and it is those with the most unsettling tales who become the most sought-after speakers.[24]

Here's how that kind of "therapy" plays out at the Memphis Love In Action campus:

All the participant had to line up and march in silence into a crowded auditorium of friends and family. We didn't speak to them until we were called on. At that time, we individually shared our "Most Serious Sin" in front of our family and about 100 strangers. One by one, we stood up as if we were preparing for execution and shared private details of our lives. To this day, that event haunts me as I can still see the looks on the faces of everyone. I had to share things than no grown man should ever have to tell his mother.

— Jacob Wilson, Ex-gay Survivor.[25]

After being pushed and coerced to cough up every detail before friends, families, and strangers, no wonder ex-gay survivors sometimes go silent after they have left these religiously abusive environments.

A Political Pawn

Throughout the 1980's and 1990's, political organizations with an overt conservative religious agenda were on the rise, like the Traditional Values Coalition, Family Research Council, and Concerned Women for America, along with mega ministries, such as James Dobson's Focus on the Family and the Jerry Falwell Ministries. These influential groups viewed the ex-gay movement as proof that homosexuals could change and, therefore, the LGBT Community did not need protection under the law. "By creating ex-gay 'superstars' to parade before the media and political decision makers, they hope to stir up just enough doubt and concern to sway the 'malleable middle' toward the 'repressive right.'"[26] Reparative therapy was often cited by politicians lobbying against any legislation that would affirm the human rights of homosexuals. Consequently, this fueled the motivation and finances of the ex-gay movement. Truly, their reach is now global.

The Reasons Why

People whose life experience does not relate to this extreme kind of religion often ask me, "Why in the world would anyone want to be a part of an ex-gay group?" It's a good question and it doesn't have one answer. Of course, there are the religious motivations telling LGBT people that they are sinful. Also, ex-gays can be motivated for fear of losing all credibility, love and status in family and ministry — virtually a person's entire life could be lost if s/he is not heterosexual. Some seek heterosexuality because they believe the only way to have romantic and familial relationships is by marrying someone of the opposite sex. Some turn to ex-gay ministries to deal with unresolved sexual abuse or undesirable behavior. Some join to feel less isolated — at last they are with a group they can relate to. Some have received so much misinformation and negative stereotypes about the LGBT community, not to mention bad sexuality education in general, that they want nothing to do with "those sorts of immoral people." Similarly, some believe they must be heterosexual to avoid getting AIDS, and other STI's (sexually-transmitted infections). "Men and women in heterosexual marriages who are homosexual are especially prone to the allure of reparative therapy... The promise of healing by submitting to counseling can seem tempting because it allows for what is really good in the marriage to continue."[27]

Of course, any number of reasons can be simultaneous motivations, but I believe there is a commonality to all of the reasons people turn to reparative therapy — an overriding sense that their sexuality is not acceptable as it is. They are driven to conform to a set of norms — outside of themselves — to gain the sense of acceptability they so desperately want. The question that is not often asked is whether a deep sense of acceptance can be achieved by conforming to a set of externally-imposed parameters (we'll address that in more detail later).

The kind of ex-gay that seems to do very well in the program is a newly converted Christian. Everything since becoming a Christian has been bright, hopeful, and fulfilling. Often, everything before becoming a Christian was dark, sleazy, addictive and abusive. It's easy to group sexuality with past troubles. The more a participant progresses, the darker that former life becomes. There are so many new things to learn and do as a baby Christian that there's no time to think about the past, for the most part. It seems so cut and dry. I realize this might sound like I'm stacking the deck against the ex-gay movement. In reality, these are the dynamics of one of the most well-known ex-gays, John Paulk. He was the "poster-child" for reparative therapy around the millennium — that is, until he was caught hanging out in a gay bar on a business trip. [28]

More Harm than Good

Still, the psychological basis of ex-gay ministries is outdated and unsound. Their methods and treatments to achieve straightness are vague at best, and unproven. Their evidence is selective, and their "success stories" are questionably transitory. Take, for example, this reflection by Darlene Bogle, who was once a leader in Exodus International:

> In 1988, Exodus LA (the Exodus conference in Los Angeles) had a picture taken with about 200 attendees. The title across the photo was: Can Homosexuals Change? We did. Now, as I look at this poster, more than half of the people in the photo are no longer in ex-gay ministry or involved in the Church. Their orientation wasn't really changed, and neither was mine. We wanted to change behavior that we were told would separate us from a loving God. We were never told that we had an option, that God would still love us as Gay and Lesbian people. [29]

Another ex-gay survivor, Randy Baxter, who rose in the ranks of leadership, had this to say about the lack of success he experienced:

> After three years as a counselee and over a year in ministry leadership, I'd observed and prayed with hundreds of sincere sisters and brothers in Christ who, like me, had diligently read the Bible, led exemplary lives

of faith and submitted themselves to God in every way possible for years — all without any change in sexual preference. The only lasting effects were increased frustration, undiminished desire and increasing self-hatred. A few I knew even attempted suicide, feeling they had failed God.

Sure, a few ex-gays publicly proclaimed themselves heterosexual and found opposite-gender partners, locking themselves into pretending to be straight. Some of these admitted to being bisexual in orientation, while others confessed privately that despite their heterosexual marriages, if they allowed themselves too much temptation, their homosexual thoughts would come flooding back. Change only referred to one's conviction to not act out homosexually, not an inner change of sexual orientation.[30]

Simply because ex-gay ministries and reparative therapists say they have a client's best interest in view when they try to reduce the amount of "unwanted homosexual feelings," that does not automatically mean these organizations are being helpful. On the contrary, there are a number of their own "treatments" that indicate that they do not have their participant's best interest in mind.

How could ex-gay leadership assert such a claim and, at the same time, censor so much information about sexuality, not to mention about homosexuality, from their curriculum and from the participants who place their trust in them? Do they explain to a participant that there are a growing number of Christian denominations that accept gays without changing their sexuality? Do they list all the psychological organizations that do not agree with reparative therapy's premise or methods? Do they list all the different options to let the client decide what course of action to take? Would you go to a doctor if you knew she was going to disregard a number of treatments that could possibly heal you? Would you consider a person a professional in his field if he were indignantly unwilling to incorporate all the facets of his area of specialty?

If they have their participant's well-being as priority, why then is the leadership not happy for a client when he decides that what is best for him is to accept his sexuality as it is — that he is finished examining and has found peace without the struggle of changing. If a woman came to reparative therapists to learn to accept and enjoy her lesbian sexuality, would they treat and support her without bias? They would not.

Christopher H. Rosik, a reparative therapist himself, had the opportunity to lend legitimacy to the cause by having a paper published in the *Journal of Marital and Family Therapy*,[31] yet his words belie his attempts to support the client's best interest as preeminent: "MFTs who engage in reorientation therapy must respect a client's decision to leave treatment and pursue gay-affirmative therapy." At least he is encouraging respect, but as Dr. Robert-Jay Green, in a rebuttal to Rosik's paper in the same journal, pointed out,[32] why would a client have to seek treatment elsewhere unless the therapist's agenda to follow a certain treatment was more important than what the client determines is his or her well-being?

Another paper in the *Journal of Marital and Family Therapy* exposes the agenda of the reparative therapists by simply asking, "Can individuals who are reportedly converted to a heterosexual identity and not satisfied [then] be reoriented back to a homosexual identity?"[33] I've never known a reparative therapist to do that. Besides, even Rosik's words of respect seem to be quite hollow in the light of how participants are treated when they decide to quit, or worse, when they are kicked out of a program. Do they refer clients on to other therapists for further support when the clients accept their sexuality? Do they pat them on the back and say, "I'm so glad you have resolved your conflict?"

> *All of these people who had become my family within this ministry disowned me. I was no longer welcome, I was not "one of them" and I was shunned. I left the ministry, stranded and feeling very abandoned.*
> — *Allyson (Hays) Snicker, Ex-gay Survivor[34]*

As described in the paragraphs below, even the treatment of participants and their families who are faithful to the program seems to indicate that ex-gay leaders are oblivious of the harm they are doing to individuals and families.

> *Adhering to the belief that our families failed us, the Love In Action program leaders served as surrogate parents who attempted to undo the alleged damage inflicted by our real parents. During the Family and Friends Weekend, they not only confronted each participant with their unfounded development theories, they also pushed parents to admit that their child's faulty development stemmed from a dysfunctional family structure. The program buttressed the belief that everyone lives in a flawed sinful state, and by being flawed and sinful parents, they ended up harming their offspring. Sin begets sin. The staff endeavored to lead the families in a corporate confession which included fathers of program participants confessing to the ways they ceded leadership to their wives. The Family and Friends Weekend thus operated under the notion that only by returning to the God-sanctioned patriarchy could the flawed*

*son or daughter experience success in divorcing themselves from homo-
sexuality.*

*I only learned later that my parents experienced deep personal
distress as a result of their initial Family and Friends Weekend. My
sister told me that for the first two weeks after they returned, "there
was something wrong with Mom and Dad." They seemed depressed
and spoke little. It also affected their appetite and energy level. She
said it was like a light had gone out in them. She felt so concerned that
she called the Love In Action office and demanded, "What did you do
to my parents?" Love In Action never followed up.*

*Years later, when I told one of the Love In Action leaders, who had
been part of that weekend, about my parents' distress and how it
resulted in years of self-doubts and emotional upheaval, he responded
with program jargon and put the blame back on my parents by sta-
ting, "Healthy people ask for what they need." He suggested that since
my parents were not healthy to begin with, they didn't know how to
seek the help they needed. By constantly turning the blame around and
pointing to what they see as the flawed nature in each one of us, the
program leaders avoid responsibility for the unethical and harmful
practices and theories they promote and provide.*

— *Peterson Toscano, Ex-gay Survivor
and Performance Activist.*[35]

This and other behavior on the part of ex-gay leaders shows that the well-being of
their participants, or participants' loved ones, is not top priority. Therefore it is not
surprising (though still damaging) that there seems to be no accounting on their
part for all the harm that thousands of people have voiced. In fact, ex-gay enthusiasts seem resolutely oblivious to criticism. One thing has remained consistent: their
belief that God cannot tolerate homosexuality. To them it is a sin, and therefore
their motivation is to change it, whether or not it is in the best interest of their
participants (not to mention whether it is actually scriptural or not — more on
that later). As psychotherapist and ex-gay critic. Ralph Blair says, "The only people
who believe that change [from gay to straight] is possible are the people who think
change should be possible... That's very suspicious."[36]

CHAPTER 3

Religious Abuse & the Ex-gay Movement — Twins Hatched from the Same Egg

A Comparison

BEFORE WE GET TO the practical steps of my recovery, there remains a highly integral piece of the ex-gay puzzle that must be addressed. The most important discovery I made in my research and understanding of my recovery process had to do with the way the ex-gay movement functions. Briefly put, it is nothing new. In fact, the movement is a microcosm of a larger, more rampant problem in religion today. Actually, religion suffers from two related phenomena identified as religious abuse and religious dependency. To be clear, religious abuse happens when spiritual leaders or religious organizations abuse power to force their beliefs, opinions, behavior, and doctrines on people seeking their guidance.[1] Religious dependency, or what is often called religious addiction, compulsion, or obsessiveness, is when those seeking guidance use a religious organization or its leadership to avoid taking responsibility for their own actions and well-being.[2]

I had a suspicion that the ex-gay movement might have some commonalities with religious abuse and dependency, but I had no idea just how similar they were. As I began to read about religious abuse, I would often blink my eyes and glance at the title of the book to make sure I wasn't reading a book exclusively about the ex-gay movement. It seemed that what was described as a structured kind of power abuse within a given church, was describing point for point any number of ex-gay groups. Whole chapters of religious abuse books could apply perfectly to what has occurred in the ex-gay environment — really!

Comparing Ex-gay Organizations and Religious Abuse

Indeed, it clearly looked as though the ex-gay movement was simply an extension of the larger phenomenon of religious abuse. The various books and research articles I read on the subjects of religious abuse and addiction (see Bibliography) had similar lists of the features of religiously abusive environments. To show clearly the comparison, here is a general review of the most prominent features, followed by ex-gay survivor's personal experiences:

- The leadership is viewed as God's conduit of authority, to which everyone and everything (Biblical interpretation, pop psychology, science, education, reality) is subject.

    Anyone can have a positive and growing experience from authentic spiritual leadership. Unfortunately, all too often an abusive relationship surfaces when an unspoken deal is struck. One side of the deal is that most people would rather have someone else take on their problems so they don't have to be responsible for them. The other side of the deal is a leader who may genuinely wish to help, but ends up overstepping a person's individual responsibility by "solving their problems" rather than supporting a person to solve his/her own problems. Although this system can seem to work very well for a large number of groups, this kind of relationship cultivates communal dependency rather than individual responsibility.

    The leadership referred to the Bible, the 12 Steps and pseudo-science to reinforce their teachings and to strengthen their authority over us. When I questioned the leadership, they told me I needed to submit and trust them. The environment placed most people in a vulnerable state where we looked to the program leaders as authorities to lead us out of the mess they claimed arose from our sinful natures and poor choices. When any parent or loved one questioned the teachings, program leaders responded with program jargon, scripture or pseudo-psychological language. The leaders stood as the final authority, almost as gnostics who possessed hidden knowledge that they attempted to share with those still darkened by ignorance and inner rebellion. Ultimately I realized that the only ways out of Love In Action required that I either fully submit to the wishes and teaching of the staff, or I had to become a rebel, and in their eyes a failure, leading to a shameful dismissal from the program.
    — *Peterson Toscano, Ex-gay Survivor*
    and Performance Activist.[3]

    While in the program [Love In Action], I was astonished at the energy expended by the leadership to maintain control. Absolute obedience was expected, even demanded at times, and any questions or doubt brought swift deflection to God: "It's not us, but God who tells us to do this...." Continued questioning by a member brought accusations of disobedience and rebellion from the leadership and would eventually result in excommunication from the program.

— *Sean Greystone, Ex-gay Survivor.*[4]

- All things deemed as the "corruptible world" — i.e., different religions, "secular" cultures, the body, pleasure, human experiences, those who do not agree — are believed to be ultimately evil, are not to be trusted, and work against you and God.

With leadership in such an all-powerful position, any group and any individual who could possibly undermine that pedestal is simplistically seen as the enemy, and untrustworthy. Religiously abusive leaders have an "us versus them" mentality and they are not ashamed of it. This approach is maintained by employing the use of fear. It demands a strict loyalty. Unfortunately, fear and distrust can rarely be so selective, for if you imagine "they" are out to get you, you can imagine that anyone is out to get you. The tighter the group closes, the more isolated it becomes.

We did employ a lot of techniques that, looking back on it now I realize, were brainwashing techniques. We don't associate with anybody who disagrees with you. Don't read any non-Christian books. Don't go anyplace where non-Christians are hanging out. Certainly don't ever read anything that's pro-gay. If there's a show that presents gays in a favorable light turn it off.

— *Michael Bussee, A Founder of Exodus International and Ex-gay Survivor.*[5]

In the ex-gay programs I attended in New York City and Memphis, as well as the one I visited in Ecuador, we got the message that the outside world provided a direct and constant threat to our resolve to straighten ourselves out. In Love In Action, the staff enforced a rule that stated we could not enter "The Forbidden Zone," a large section of Memphis where one would find gay establishments, open and affirming churches and cruise spots. We maintained a bunker mentality with the belief that the devil and the World maintained a pro-gay agenda. Even the church we attended as a group did not provide a safe haven after one of the participants repeatedly met up with a parishioner for sex in one of the many restrooms.

The staff insisted that we not maintain contact with anyone who proved gay-affirming, even close family members and friends. We had no access to television and only limited access to one movie per week which had to be approved by the staff. (These included mostly family film or testosterone-laden action adventure films. No romantic comedies or movie classics. They even banned Bible films since the characters wore such revealing costumes).

— *Peterson Toscano, Ex-gay Survivor and Performance Activist.*[6]

I remember going to my youth pastor at church and telling him that my best friend "came out" to me. I asked for advice. What do I say, how do I respond to him? My youth pastor told me to stop being his friend and that it was dirty and wrong and there was nothing else to say about it. I was heartbroken.

— *Allyson (Hays) Snicker, Ex-gay Survivor.*[7]

- The abusive system requires participants to be viewed as "flawed." For most Christian settings this comes in the form of a shady, if not misused, concept about being "perfect in Christ." Sin is not only viewed as something you do, but something you are — a "sinful nature" that exists before you are aware of it — even before your birth. Convinced of being flawed at such a core level (perhaps being told at a young age) brings feelings, opinions, questions, sexuality, intuition, and even perceptions of reality under scrutiny, and distrust of self reigns. Now the enemy is inside you. Innocent and natural aspects of humanity are denied and suppressed as unwanted and evil.

The participant's aspiration is an utter dependence on God. Unable to trust themselves or the world around them, they are all the more dependent on the leadership as the only tangible interpretation of the Bible and the voice of God. The leadership might have in mind the participants' sense of contentment and peace in Christ, but most of the time the leadership's role is that of "problem solvers." What does that suggest about the followers? They are the problem. They are flawed. In extreme scenarios, leadership does indeed believe that the congregation is incapable of making their own decisions — lost without the ministers' "divine" guidance.

Through the Anglican church services, I imbibed an innate sense of sin-fulness, no doubt because of the oft-repeated prayers and confessions that promoted a sense of unworthiness. The overall emphasis was on the need for atonement for our sins and human wickedness. I did not understand why I was so especially bad, but I became certain I must be worse than most: nobody else ever seemed to need to talk about their sins. Whereas I never seemed to measure up to the standards required in anything.

— Jeremy Marks, Founder and Director of Courage and an Ex-gay Survivor.[8]

The feelings of defectiveness and isolation made me vulnerable to accept the very conditional and demanding love offered by religious fundamentalism.

—Jeffry G. Ford, MA, LP, Ex-gay Survivor.[9]

When I struggled to succeed, they continually pointed to some fault in me. I needed to dig deeper, commit myself more fully, or face up to hard realities that they believed I avoided.

— Peterson Toscano, Ex-gay Survivor and Performance Activist.[10]

New Directions was not the beacon of hope and love their public image portrayed them to be. If I was not being ignored, I was being shamed publicly by the leader which evoked in me feelings once again of being less than. Desperately needing to have approval I did eve-rything I was taught: I attended Bible study groups with healthy heterosexuals, tried to play sports, even sat in a chair the way that a man does according to New Directions. When all of this failed to destroy my "same-sex attractions" I briefly conceded defeat and allowed the feelings of being less than and not good enough to take over and sought out gay sex which tragically turned into gay bashing. With a broken nose, two black eyes and shameful secret (my story was that I had been mugged), I began to listen even more to the teachings of the ex-gay community and my fundamentalist church. I began to attend a new ex-gay program called Living Waters, which was much more charismatic and shaming than New Directions.

— Darin Squire, Ex-gay Survivor.[11]

• When real answers, trust and peace are allusive, instead of considering the system as flawed, the blame turns further inward. At the same time, success and acceptance fall dependent upon outward behavior and performance, while the authentic person is hidden, denied and neglected. There is not a sense of freedom to explore other avenues of growth; participants feel trapped, treading the same territory over and over again, although they may not be able to see it.

In most settings, if a method of growth does not bring about the results desired over time, we simply consider and try something else. However, in the abusive system, the goal of perfection traps participants into continuing to blame their own "shortcomings" and "weaknesses" as the reason the system is not working. "In an abusive system, you are told that you are 'the problem' for noticing that there is a problem."[12]

Innocent mistakes and common accidents are viewed with the same moral weight as conscious acts of evil. To deflect the reality that the system is not spiritually satisfying, focus is put on devotion to ministry. "Success," loyalty and spiritual growth gradually become measured by activities, diligence and time spent furthering "the ministry." Since doubt and questioning of the system are not encouraged, if not discouraged, participants are taught to suppress and ignore their inner thoughts and feelings while still keeping up appearances. "The ugly and messy relational process of meeting people's real needs gets sacrificed for a better looking but false peace. Many times, 'You just need to tell your problem to the Lord,' actually means, 'Just don't tell it to me,' or, 'Quit saying it out loud.'"[13] While "perfection" by workaholism has become the unspoken goal, at the same time it seems never to be attainable because the system perpetuates a constant victimization.

The message that you always get in the midst of this ministry is that you are not doing enough. If you admit that you have [gay] feelings, it's because you're not doing enough. You're not praying enough. You're not going to enough Bible studies.... So the message is always if you don't change it's because something is the matter with you.
— Michael Bussee, A Founder of Exodus
International and Ex-gay Survivor.[14]

The Steps, the Phases, and the hundreds of written moral inventories required many hours of concentration and will power. The effort dis-tracted me from the reality that "change" was not possible and was not happening, other than the negative changes resulting in depression, hopelessness and faithlessness. Instead my advancement through the Steps and our celebrated "Phase Bumps" (which took on the quality of some sort of tribal celebration with participants clanging pots and pounding the walls) gave the illusion that we experienced actual headway and growth.

Whenever we faltered in our resolve to sublimate our sexual desires and personalities, the staff and fellow participants urged us to work the program. Instead of questioning the failure or the methods, the staff compelled us to dive into the "therapy" with greater effort and intensity. When we did make progress in the Steps or Phases, the staff then lessened some of the many restrictions placed on our time and activities thus giving a false sense of autonomy. Once we failed again to meet program expectations, the staff placed us in an earlier Phase slapping on restrictions and sanctions to our time and hard-won privileges.

At times it felt like I lived in an elaborate board game where I got to move three spaces forward only to find that I somehow landed back in jail. I spent so much time and energy on the structure of the program and the hurdles I had to vault that I had little left to question just how ineffective the process proved. We labored towards the goal of graduation when we would stand before the community affirmed by the staff — victors of the game — examples to others that we could achieve success. Little did I know how much the staff deluded me (and I deluded myself) into believing that program success equaled some sort of real change.

— *Peterson Toscano, Ex-gay Survivor and Performance Activist.*[15]

- As time passes, most people within this system never acquire the deep satisfaction they work so hard to achieve, though they may never admit to it openly for fear of being disloyal. However, reality creeps in with signs of severe exhaustion, burnout, health problems, spiritual disillusionment, emotional fatigue and mental disorders.

  Responsible spiritual leadership helps bring about a deep, contented peace, despite the challenges of growth and unforeseen circumstances. Religious abuse, on the other hand, seems to have no end to its struggle and the sense of achievement is elusive. To survive, participants often experience extremes in coping mechanisms — irresponsible and dangerous behavior on Saturday night and then dogmatic self-judgment and repentance on Sunday morning. Others clamp down and suppress their inner person — emotionally, spiritually, sexually — to zombie-like proportions and therefore experience emotional breakdowns, outbursts of uncontrollable emotions, and physical manifestations such as rashes, ulcers, etc. Some participants deny reality and redouble their work ethic, literally driving themselves, physically and emotionally, to death — all in the name of "ministry." Most eventually admit to "failure," but not of the system; they view themselves as the failure which often leads to deep and chronic depression, emotional paralysis, lack of desire, inability to function socially or sexually, suicide, and more. Patterns of rigid legalism, radical denial, and severe schisms between inner and outer experiences are so ingrained that even if a person were to escape the abusive environments, these patterns continue as if with a life of their own.

> *They give you a rough time-frame. There's no set time-frame in terms of when you're going to be healed or delivered over to heterosexuality. But there is the idea that [within] three to five years you should start seeing a lot of progress. I was there for at least that amount of time and I wasn't seeing a lot of progress. Instead, what I was finding was more guilt, more dislike of myself for who I was. And I was becoming self-destructive.*
> — *Ned Lichty, Ex-gay Survivor.* [16]

> *I became very ill the last year — extremely ill from stress [and] fatigue. Because of all the years of repenting from my sins, and going to the "lifestyle" and back and forth. Actually I got so sick, I couldn't repent. I didn't have the strength to go through it again. I was just crushed like that for years. And I don't know how else to describe my struggle but I thought I was going to take a gun to my head several times because of the anguish.*
> — *Stefani Cort, Ex-gay Survivor.* [17]

> *One young man got drunk and deliberately drove his car into a tree. Another (a fellow leader of the ex-gay movement) told me that he had left Exodus and was now going to straight bars — looking for someone to beat him up. He said the beatings made him feel less guilty — atoning for his sin. One of my most dedicated clients took a razor blade to his genitals, slashed himself repeatedly, and then poured drain-clea-*

ner on the wounds — because after months of celibacy he had a "fall."
— Michael Bussee, A Founder of Exodus
International and Ex-gay Survivor. [18]

The above points, compiled from various books on religious abuse and dependency, never once mentioned the ex-gay experience. Yet, as you can see, point for point, they describe the ex-gay experience with amazing accuracy.

Ex-gays and Religious Dependency

In this chapter I have, thus far, focused on the organized abuse of religious power. Of course these organizations are all populated with people, and a person's dependency on religion plays a part in these dysfunctional structures, as well. Here are some key features of a religiously dependent person:

- A "religion addict" uses religion to avoid managing the realities of their life, and/or to fill a "void" they feel in their life — much like a person would use an addictive substance to anesthetize him/herself for the same reasons. Some of these avoided realities may include daily and mundane responsibilities, personal health, unwanted truths, challenging decisions, painful memories, unpleasant emotions, mourning losses, and more.

    Let it be said that those of us who were faithful to the church had a genuine spiritual experience at one time. I met Jesus as my personal Lord and Savior. She was born again. He was baptized in the Spirit. You were saved. These experiences were valid enough in our lives that they truly changed us. We saw a whole new dimension to life. We became pilgrims on a spiritual journey. Unfortunately, all too often this journey got reduced to attempts at regaining the spiritual high from that particular experience. I associated that high with closeness and "rightness" with God. I wanted to feel it again — permanently. Trying to relive the feelings of the past was equated with spiritual maturity. Of course, that high is anyone's prerogative to chase. However, a kind of addiction forms when I use the pursuit of that "re-experience" to avoid the other, "less pleasant" areas of my life.

- Religion as avoidance is used so regularly that it seems to take on a life of its own. The person might feel out of control, trapped and at the mercy of the experience.

    I had a certain amount of success regaining that original spiritual high, and I grew a lot from what information was around to be learned. But by then, I had equated my hard work and faithfulness to God with the feelings of "reward." "Maybe if I work harder, I'll get more good feelings of love from God." Of course, knowing which buttons to push to get which reward was a complete mystery. "I know God hasn't yet shown me the way, but I'll just keep praying until God opens the doors for me." I was going to be even more faithful and work even harder. A vibrant, spontaneous and interactive relationship with the Spirit was reduced to an addict/dealer transaction. Why did it seem that my interaction with God was often hit or miss? Because God is a living, changing organism, if you will, not a candy dispenser, but the only thing I wanted — the only thing I was capable or willing to receive — was a fix.

- Religion becomes the object of obsession, under which everything — including perception of reality — takes its cue. It is viewed as the answer to every problem, which is somewhat different from a case of substance addiction. Booze and drugs are not necessarily viewed as the "answer" to life, they're just (mis) used to numb oneself from life.

    This is much like a man being so obsessed with a celebrity that he believes they actually have a connection. This dictates his perception of reality, influencing his behavior and enabling him to becoming a stalker. The reality is that the celebrity doesn't know the man exists. When he is made to face this reality, it only appears to him as a threat. As an ex-gay, I was willing to ignore factual research because "God knew better." Often, when I would put religion on such a pedestal — higher than my sexuality and even reality — everything in my world would warp toward that overriding priority. This is much like when an anorexic looks in a mirror and only sees an obese person. If, hypothetically, my ex-gay leaders had said, "The Bible says grass is pink," I would have questioned my own eyesight before I would have questioned their interpretation. Not only was I using religion to avoid the real problems I was facing; religion was the answer to everything, so why focus on solving my problems when I already had the answers?

- Religious dependents have low self-esteem. When "bad things" happen, the obsession is not considered flawed, but blame is turned inward. The individual is subtly viewed as not good enough: "I am nothing without God." Religion is used all the more to avoid dealing with the interior condemnation, shame and lack of self-esteem.

    Not only does the abusive system squelch its members' creativity and individual thinking, but religious dependents can only view themselves as "unworthy" before God. By the way, worthlessness is not one of the fruits of the Spirit! I use to say, "I have God. I have the answers. Why aren't I getting the results I want? What is wrong with me? I must not be doing something correctly. God must not be pleased with me, otherwise he would change my sexuality. Maybe if I work harder. Maybe if I get Christian counseling three times a week instead of two."

- There is a seemingly worthwhile religious organization "legitimizing" the dependency, using religion as avoidance. This helps keep the "addict" in a constant state of victimization. In extremes, "addicts" turn over management of their whole life to the obsession/organization.

The example of an anorexic person is a great comparison. No, there is no official Church of the Immaculate Skin and Bones, but what of the fashion industry? Of course, clothes designers do not state that girls should starve themselves to look like the models in their latest collection. They don't have to say it. Their look and clothes speak louder than words.

What of capitalism? It is the "religion" that drives the world's prosperity. Doesn't it, as an ideal, have something to say about dependency? After all, what were former President Bush's "words of wisdom" to soothe America's sadness after 9/11? "Go shopping." What did that say to us in our time of shock and mourning? "You will feel better and you will feel more whole if you go buy things." Did that really make anyone feel better? Temporarily, perhaps. Did it perpetuate a sense of dependency, if only a kind of dependency on things to make us feel better? Yes.

Taking this feature to extremes, there are the cults, like Jim Jones' People's Temple, or the Ten Commandments of God Cult whose members turned over their very lives to their leaders by following them into mass suicide. Ex-gay ministries or reparative therapies are not motivated by malicious intent, as far as I can tell. I don't think the leadership is trying to hoodwink its members. They appear sincere and they want those involved to succeed.

Finally! Someplace where I could talk about God and talk about my sexuality at the same time! I kept myself on a spiritual high by seeking out pastors, counselors and leaders who would pray for me and minister to me. I attended conferences and special church services and found church members who embraced me as family. I thought that I had made so much progress. After all, I was looking more and more

feminine, and I wasn't feeling much of anything sexually, which I saw
as an answer to prayer. God must be healing me! I even spoke to my
church's youth group about brokenness and God's healing power. After
a few years passed, reality set in. And along with the reality, came
guilt, shame and a pervasive sense of failure.

— *Christine Bakke, Ex-gay Survivor.* [20]

• Since religious dependence is part of the equation of religious abuse, it shows the same results: signs of severe exhaustion, burnout, health problems, spiritual disillusionment, emotional fatigue, mental disorders, and more.

The ex-gay movement does not function to the extremes of The People's Temple and other cults. They have never suggested as a cure for homosexuality that anyone commit suicide. However, as their methods continue to fail, and when so many already guilt-ridden people equate themselves with that failure, it is not surprising that many have contemplated suicide, and some have succeeded. Being dependent on this abusive system, how can they not obsess with the possibility: "What if I am the 'bad apple'? What if there is no redemption for such a worm as I? Maybe God wants me to end it now rather than spend another moment as a heterosexual failure."

The long-term damage in the lives of us all has been incalculable.... It
has proved spiritually catastrophic, many having given up their faith
altogether; financially catastrophic, many of us having lost practical-
ly all we had, leaving a wholly inadequate provision for retirement;
and mentally and emotionally catastrophic, many ending up seriously
depressed with some people even becoming suicidal.

— *Jeremy Marks, Founder and Director of*
Courage and an Ex-gay Survivor. [21]

I hope you can see how a religiously dependent person and the religiously abusive environment work in tandem, especially in the ex-gay environment. Which came first, the compulsive behavior or the abusive structure? It is probably impossible and unnecessary to discern. I believe, however, that what makes this kind of abuse so insidious is that it is promoted by the "church," which so many view as an irrefutable organization. John Bradshaw believes, "There is no addiction that covers up the addict's core of toxic shame better than religious addiction."[22]

Here we are again. How many times in the past 2,000 years has the Christian movement run with the loving message of Jesus and got it wrong — to the extreme degree that people have killed themselves "in Jesus name?" I like to say that whenever people make Christianity out to be anything other than the love of God, they miss the point. Whenever the church adds anything to Christ's message of inclusive love, it's no longer Christianity. When the spiritual leaders of Christ's day tried to change the connection with God into a set of laws, they missed the point. When the early church made Christianity into the dominant political and governmental laws of the day, they missed the point. The Crusades missed the point. When the church put to death early scientists that claimed the earth was not flat, it missed the point. When American ministers less than 150 years ago misused the Bible to affirm slavery, they missed the point. When Christianity becomes a multi-million dollar, commercially-profitable organization, and happens to be a ministry — damn it — it misses the point. When the church requires people to think and behave identically for Jesus sake — it misses the point!

This is why it is so important that religious communities begin to address the rampant abuse caused by the misuse of their beliefs, and it's why I am spending so much time outlining these comparisons. The ex-gay movement is a microcosm of the unchecked and unrestrained abuse of religious power throughout Christianity and other fundamentalist religious groups. Let this be the time in history when this kind of abuse ends.

The ex-gay phenomenon has so many direct parallels to religious dependency that I trust anyone can see it, especially straight Christians who have felt the sting of religious abuse. There are a certain number of straight Christians who have been rather silent about the "gay thing" while their churches used the sexual issue to exclude individuals and ultimately make people feel unloved by God. You don't want to rock the boat. You might think, "The 'gay thing' is not my problem. I can't really relate to it." However, religious abuse is something you have felt intimately. You have felt unacceptable for whatever reason by the church, community, family, maybe even God, and you have found yourself devising ways to feel more acceptable, when in the end this was not about learning how to love others, or how to love yourself, or about knowing God. It was more about power — the love of power rather than the power of love. It was more about conformity, being stripped of individuality rather than being embraced for your uniqueness. For those of you who are seeing more clearly than ever before this comparison between ex-gay ministries and religious abuse, I hope this moves you to be just a little less silent. Maybe the next time a minister rails against how "homosexuals" are dragging America down into the depths of hell, you will see this manipulation for what it is — misguided fear and an abuse of the gospel of Jesus Christ's love. I also ask you to, please, do something about it.

Concerns about "Addiction"

To present the parallels between abusive religion and the ex-gay movement as clearly as possible, I have held a few of my own concerns and cautionary thoughts about religious abuse and dependency until this point. One of the concerns I have is the importance of recreation. In all this talk about abuse, dependency, and obsessiveness, it might be assumed that I am suggesting that any kind of escape is wrong. Not true! Given all the stresses and challenges in life, we need to take a break regularly. The body knows this — that's what sleep is all about. Not only does all work and no sleep make Jallen a dull boy; it can make me psychotic, to boot. Working too hard could even put me in an early grave. Escaping into a strategically-timed movie for a couple of hours can get me through the rest of the work week. This is not avoiding problems but simply taking a temporary break from them. Furthermore, I may not "need" a sappy and inspiring song to wake me up in the morning, but it sure the heck helps. This is not dependency. It's wise management. Taking a vacation to Hawai'i after I have worked very hard to complete an ambitious project, like finishing school (or finishing this book), is not frivolous. It's celebrating an important marker in one's life and is well deserved. All of these are good for our well-being. I will even go so far as to say that the majority of the population can use moderate amounts of substances such as alcohol and other stimulants to enjoy, recreate, and celebrate life. These people continue productive and fulfilling lives, and they don't get enough credit for managing them so well.

It's also important to point out that most of our abusive behaviors and addictions have their roots in survival. To endure the challenges of life, to survive unbearable circumstances, as in the case of an adult survivor of child abuse, a person naturally will turn to things that would help her forget or cope with the pain until she's more capable of dealing with it. Unfortunately, these perfectly good and natural survival mechanisms simply can get out of hand and take on a life of their own.

We've all used and misused power to one degree or another to get what we want. We've been in businesses, community groups, families and halls of academia, just to mention a few, where manipulation and abuse of power come to the surface one way or another. And we have survived. Additionally, there are times we take a course of action, like going to church or taking up a skill, to genuinely grow as human beings. Yet, somehow, we find we've gone down the wrong path. It might take a simple decision or it might take a decade to adjust our course or learn from our mistakes. All of this is to say that abuse, dependency, and obsession come in all shades and degrees. There is neither the perfect organization, nor the perfect escape. Although I may have outlined several key features to religious dependency and abuse, none of them are hard and fast rules. If they are taken as such, we would never be part of a community for fear of it being abusive. For every person who can in no way have a shot of liquor, there are several others who are able to drink alcohol. Holding tightly to a rigid set of "do's and don't's" may also be a way of not dealing with life realistically.

You may have noticed that in the above quote by John Bradshaw, "There is no addiction that covers up the addict's core of toxic shame better than religious addiction." he uses the label "religious addiction," whereas I try to use the label, "religious dependency." There's a reason for this. Truth be told, if the word "addiction" weren't such a widely-used label, I would not use the term at all for any of the phenomenon having to do with religious abuse and its participants. This is another concern — the vernacular use of the word, "addiction." It's a household word, and we overuse it for everything. "I'm addicted to TV." "I'm addicted to my '64 Chevy." If we like something enough, then we're "addicted" to it. If a woman grew up drawing buildings, and then goes to college and graduate school to become an architect, should we say that she's addicted to architecture? That's silly. We're using the term so much that we subtly cast a shadow on anything we receive pleasure and fulfillment from.

This reveals and enhances our subtle yet effective phobia against pleasure (more of that in later chapters). We use the term "addiction" so loosely that it's created a kind of debilitation all its own. Now, a man may have no kind of addiction whatsoever, but in this addicted-to-everything climate, he is probably in constant fear and on his guard that he might be addicted to something. He doesn't know what it would be, but he keeps a watchful eye, second-guessing himself and maybe even holding back the enjoyment he can receive from life on the off chance he might be — gasp! —addicted to it.

Some time ago there was a contemporary Christian singer who mounted a whole "revival" to win kids to Jesus, and the theme song and slogan he used was, "Addicted to Jesus." What? Isn't that like saying, "I'm an alcoholic for the Lord?" Addiction is not a good thing and applying the word so casually devalues its seriousness.

The other problem I have with this wide-reaching use of the word "addiction" is that it actually is now being used to justify irresponsibility. We're addicted to the word addicted! We use the very word "addiction" to avoid taking responsibility for our lives and behavior. "I just love chocolate bars. What can I say? I'm addicted to them (chuckle, chuckle). Can you hand me another?" "Playing video games is so addictive." "I just spent another hundred dollars on the Sell-your-brains-out Shopping Network. I'm just so addicted to that TV Channel." We actually use the idea of addiction as a way to avoid taking responsibility for how we act.

There is, however, a very important use for the clinical term "addiction." There are actual substances in this world that, if ingested, will in fact cause your body to want more of the same substance. They will actually change the chemical make-up of your internal system to cause you to crave more of the very same thing, so strongly that the desire may be beyond your control to resist — that's a clinical addiction. Take crystal meth, for example. Before a guy on crystal meth can regain control of his life, he will have to take the time to rid his physical system completely of the substance. Furthermore, that same person may have to permanently remove any contact or use of meth, if he is to maintain a healthy life. From my perspective, the word "addictive" should only be used for physiological dependence on these kinds of substances.

I am aware that obsessive behavior, like religious dependency, or compulsive eating, or habitually watching television, might cause you to feel as if you are at its mercy, especially after the habit has become a well-worn pattern. You might feel out of control when it seems that you can't stop going to church whenever the doors are open. But some of the belief that you lack control is your continued way of duping yourself so that you can continue avoiding responsibility for your behavior. This is not stated as a way to heap more guilt on you or me. It's is a way for us to realize that we don't have a foreign substance in our veins forcing us to crave more religion. Instead, I have the option to eat only one candy bar. I can turn the TV off. Despite being spoon-fed religion since the day I was born, I still have the capacity, strength and power of will to get off my pew-imprinted ass and walk out of the church's open doors if I so choose. This is a very hopeful prospect for recovering from the ex-gay experience and it's distinctly different from being controlled by a foreign substance in the bloodstream.

Another distinction that I think is important to make between chemical addictions and obsessive behavior is that, as I stated previously, to maintain a healthy well-being a person may never be able to put a particular substance in the body ever again. There are, however, behaviors that cannot be utterly removed from a person's life without damaging repercussions. Compulsive eating is a good example. You can't simplistically say to compulsive eaters, "Just cut out all of your food intake and you'll be fine." They would starve and die. These kinds of dependencies must be managed. And when it comes to our sexuality and our spirituality, I believe that these beautiful aspects of humanity are better managed than excised.

Certainly, many of us don't cozy up to the idea of managing our own life. Heck, that's what many of us have habitually used religion to avoid. Skills like responsible personal management (aka, taking good care of oneself), using moderation, wise decision-making, and even civility in public debate might as well be foreign words in our society. I still wonder why they aren't right up there with reading, writing and arithmetic, since as adults we have to employ any number of these skills daily. Yet I can't recall anyone ever consciously teaching me a thing about them. No wonder we spend so much time avoiding them. We have to deal with personal responsibility every day of our life, and we often don't have any idea of what that looks like. It's especially hard for those of us who have been taught from a young age that it is better to get on our knees and pray for answers than doing our own footwork to find answers. "What? I have to actually get out of my prayer closet and deal with life to make wise decisions?"

Oddly enough, when I finally addressed these human challenges — personal responsibility, lack of self-esteem, fear of rejection, self-hate about my sexuality — the power of my obsession seemed to defuse. When I took better care of myself, I didn't need to depend on religion or the ex-gay ministry to fix me. And this is my final concern about the over-use of the label "addiction." We love our "addictions." Even when we are no longer using them, we love to talk about them and how they took form, how much money we lost because of them, how they destroyed our lives, how we miraculously recovered from them and what support group we go to now. My concern is that all of this can still be a subterfuge if the real problems underneath are not resolved. There is too damn much emphasis on "addiction" — which is always a warning sign for a deeper problem. It's as if there's a sign by the road that says, "Watch for falling rocks," and all drivers seem to be able to do is look at and obsess over the sign, missing the reason it's there in the first place. My advice is to quit fiddling with the addictions and get on with livin'!

Abuses to Watch Out for

Although I will be dealing with the effects of and recovery from religious abuse and dependency throughout the rest of the book, here are a few initial tips that help keep me from falling into abusive environments:

- Do the messages (especially the subtle ones) of a particular organization give me a sense of peace, empowerment, personal responsibility, and love, or are they really about fear, "shoulds," rewards and punishment, and dependency?

  After all those years when I was coming out and still performing in conservative churches, I got good at listening for the unspoken messages. I would listen for themes in the sermon that indicated the pastor's motivations. Was he tacking "the peace of God" on the end of the morning service and was it a reward for walking down the aisle, while the majority of his sermon was on how bad the world is out there, and the only safe place is sitting in the pews on Sunday morning? Did the organization give me an overall sense of inclusion or exclusion, dependency or affirmation?

• Similarly, do the organizations I'm a part of really struggle with the balance of truth and love?

These are kinds of organizations that do not simply assume and profess that they have the truth and that they are loving. Instead, they have an ongoing determination to seek the truth in a given matter, whether or not it is aligned with the group's beliefs or comfort zones. Further, when a truth is determined, do the members of the organization strive to express it as lovingly and sensitively as possible?

One of my most dear spiritual mentors took me aside on more than one occasion and as gently as possible pointed out that, although I was becoming very good at speaking the truth, I was often unaware of how my enthusiasm came across like a baseball bat to the listener's head. It is an ongoing challenge to this day for me to speak the truth with love. So important is this idea that I penned the following song in honor of my late mentor, Kelley Combs:

> You say you want my attention. You want to bend my ear.
> My hearing has become so jaded I may not hear you loud and clear.
> In this land of fast talking, when a word bites and twists.
> Please, just take me by the hand. Look me in the eye and let me have it.
> No need to yell, I'm not the enemy.
> Don't tell me stories, just say it to me.
>> Gentle and honest, I'll hear every word.
>> Nothing's more calming, you won't go unheard.
>> You choose the topic, tell me the lowdown.
>> Gentle and honest, you'll hold me spellbound.
> When my head gets bigger than my heart, I need you to tell it like it is.
> When that truth stings and smarts, I need your voice to feel like your skin.
> Don't play me games. You'll fail before you begin.
> Just lay it on the table. I can take it on the chin.

Gentle and honest, it ain't that profound.
Nothing's more calming and how sweet the sound.
Your choose the topic, no need to beg or hound.
Gentle and honest, I won't let you down.
Don't tell me excuses. Don't beat around the bush.
Don't spit your words. Don't shove or push.
Gentle and honest, how good it can feel.
Nothing's more calming, when these two heal.
You choose the topic, don't hold back.
Gentle and honest, just give me the facts. [23]

- Related to this, I sometimes check the balances in my personal life. Black and white extreme thoughts and behaviors have become indicators to me that my well-being is out of balance.

  When I feel anxious or upset, and I can't put my finger on it, I access my balance. Inevitably, I realize, "Oh yes, I've been working non-stop for ten days; might I feel a little less out of whack if I gave myself some fun time off?" You bet. Are the organizations I'm a part of affirming this balance, or are they encouraging more and more extremes in commitment?

- I occasionally take stock of the elements and tools I use to maintain my well-being. Are they serving me or am I serving them?

  My elements of well-being can be anything I use to keep me healthy — from the way I talk to myself, to going to the gym regularly, to being a part of a spiritual community. Am I benefiting from them or am I enslaving myself to them? When I came out of the ex-gay environment, one of the first tools I let go of was memorizing scripture. All those vast chapters I memorized — their content was rarely nurturing to my soul, probably because I wasn't using them to feel contentment. I was using the exercise of memorization to distract me from dealing with unwanted realities in my life.

CHAPTER 4

Drinking the Kool-Aid

All about Denial

WHEN IT CAME TO KNOWING how to recover from religious abuse and my ex-gay experience, I can't really pinpoint a moment when I started, much less what I started on. I can remember that, somehow, I knew that the biggest challenge, and probably the most important challenge I had, was learning to accept myself unconditionally. I had some outlandish notion (sarcasm intended) that, if God could love me perfectly and unconditionally, then what excuse did I really have to hold myself in such contempt? However, there were some pretty big obstacles I had to dismantle before I could truly embrace this kind of self-acceptance, and the first obstruction was denial.

Why couldn't I see the abuse that now seems so obvious? Why couldn't I look deeper and begin to address the real problems? Besides all the aforementioned compulsions, dependencies and workaholism, sadly, I was also in denial. Baby, I have hung with ex-gays that were on a state of the art yacht sailing full steam ahead up "da' Nile," if you know what I mean. We were so afraid of an all-encompassing rejection that we would do anything — including lying to ourselves — to keep from it. Denial is a kind of deceit and a form of non-acceptance, but it's far more insidious (if not delusional) because first and foremost it's self-deception. I couldn't see it because, well, quite frankly, I was in denial. Denial can be defined as "an unconscious defense mechanism characterized by refusal to acknowledge painful realities, thoughts, or feelings." [1] It is another way of avoiding the realities of our lives, and it had to be dealt with in my recovery process.

It seems like a design flaw in the brain to have the ability to double back on itself, pretty much lie to itself and then with all confidence believe what was just fabricated. Yet, when circumstances are severe, as in an abusive situation or in times of war, limiting our field of vision in such a way can actually get us through incredibly difficult times. Indeed, I'm sure almost everyone initially accessed the denial state of mind as an innocent means to survive. I like to say, "Never underestimate humanity's capacity for denial." Ex-gays should receive doctorates in denial, because they are so proficient at it.

> *I considered myself "ex-gay" because I had ceased sexual activity, and I spent my time promoting "change" in others. When these changes did not occur, the people in my care frequently asked how long it would take for desires to change. I lied and encouraged them to keep praying and reading their Bible. When they asked how long it took for me, I avoided the question.*
>
> — *Darlene Bogle, Ex-gay Survivor.*[2]

Some years after I had come out, I was on the road in Houston, Texas. I had picked up the local gay rag and was thumbing through it. In the classifieds' spirituality section was a line ad that my eyes happened to catch. It said something to the effect of, "Tired of the gay bars, sex with strangers, and life feeling purposeless? We will accept you and help you find meaning in your life." I knew right away what it was pushing, and I wasn't about to let them get away with it. I promptly picked up the phone and called the number in the ad just to confirm my suspicion, but I had no idea that I would bear witness to the biggest earful of bull-shittin' denial I had ever experienced. It was also a walk down memory lane because I had once believed so much of what the young man on the line was saying.

To begin with, the gentleman started every answer to my questions with such precursors as, "Well, you know, that's all a matter of perspective…." I would ask, "Have you changed from gay to straight?" He would say, "Well, that's all dependent on your outlook…" I felt like saying, "Do you have your head up your ass?" He probably would have responded without pause, "Well, that depends on how you look at it…" I suppose it was a set of words to soften the outlandish statements that followed, but the intro seemed also to convey, "Here's how I lie to myself so I can swallow all this other stuff that doesn't add up."

Legitimizing Denial

I mentioned in Chapter 2 that as the ex-gay movement gets more press, what else can they do but adjust their mindset as well as their verbiage to bolster their denial in the face of such a lack of success? This is easily seen in a *Christianity Today* magazine article reviewing a study conducted by Christian psychologists Jones and Yarhouse.[3] The article states, "Exodus can describe 38 percent of its programs' participants as successes, changing to either a 'meaningful but complicated' heterosexuality (15 percent) or a stable chastity (23 percent)." I have to hand it to them, they certainly try to place even their own (awfully skewed) study in the best light possible. But it doesn't take much light to see that even this "positive success" is a statistically dismal failure. What they are not saying is that as much as 85 percent of those studied have not found any significant changes to their sexual orientation, since 23 percent remain gay yet chaste and 62 percent continue to have a homosexual orientation. Furthermore, the nebulous idea that gay people are now "complicated heterosexuals" sounds suspicious at best.

Dr. Patrick Chapman, a biological anthropologist, examined their study in more detail than I and found that "the only way ex-gay ministries and advocates can sell their message is by using imprecise and deceptive language, by obscuring or shifting what change in sexual orientation actually means, or by misrepresenting results. Unfortunately, these are all evident in the Jones and Yarhouse study." [4]

Jim Burroway of *Box Turtle Bulletin* also weighed in with his findings about the study:

> *In short, the Jones and Yarhouse study was funded and fully supported by Exodus and conducted by two researchers who were avid supporters of ex-gay ministries. They wanted to study 300 participants, but after more than a year, they could only find 57 willing to participate. They then changed the rules for acceptance in order to increase the total to 98. After following this sample for 4 years, 25 dropped out. Of the remainder, only 11 reported "satisfactory, if not uncomplicated, heterosexual adjustment." Another 17 decided that a lifetime of celibacy was good enough.* [5]

Of course, they have the right to emphasize the positive all they want. In fact, those who participated in the study were the ex-gays' "cream of the crop," specifically recommended for the study. But what about the overwhelming majority of ex-gays that "fail?" Not a word in the article about them. I call that denial.

Even attempts to legitimize reparative therapy as a viable therapeutic treatment for the "cure" for homosexuality constitute a fascinating exercise in denial. Take the organization, The National Association for Research and Therapy of Homosexuality (NARTH) as a great example. It sounds so professional despite the odd acronym. What amazes me is the extent to which the leaders and theorists of NARTH go in order to carefully and subtly downplay their religious bias and basic belief that God doesn't want people to be homosexual in the first place. It's hard to find any religion on their site or in statements like, "NARTH upholds the rights of individuals with unwanted homosexual attraction to receive effective psychological care and the right of professionals to offer that care." This statement is something any healthcare professional can agree with. What's not being said is that NARTH's "therapists" have a predisposed bias that homosexuality is sinful, and an agenda that it should be changed. In fact, their version of religion is what motivates the whole organization, but you wouldn't know this by reading their information.

Attempting to have a public image legitimized by the psychological community, the NARTH counselors are willing to downplay Christianity, downplay their religious beliefs, and downplay their relationship with Jesus. One could even say that they hide their "first love" to create more acceptability by the greater society. Does this reflect an unashamed and transparent relationship with Jesus? Is this a shining example of lighting their Christian candle and placing it in view, like a city on a hill for all to see? I don't think so, but are they behaving in a familiar pattern. You bet. As I have already explained, to be ex-gay I was willing to do anything to gain acceptability — bend the truth, lie to myself and others, betray what and whom I truly loved, behave one way on the outside and nearly die on the inside — all for the cause of being accepted by my community. It was a compulsive obsession to legitimize my acceptability. NARTH behaves the same way. Why do they feel they have to present a psychological demeanor and downplay what they really believe? If they are indeed right in their claims, what would be wrong with being up front and honest about its religious motivation? It's because they are desperate to be accepted. Their need to avoid rejection is stronger than the need to be true to themselves, and in this case even their spirituality gets sacrificed. Why do they allow themselves to contort in such a manner? Why can't they see it? Never underestimate humanity's capacity for denial.

Granted, some ex-gays and their supporters may not be in denial about what they are doing. Still I have to ask, if they are purposefully trying to package their religious views as legitimate psychological theory without making the religious perspective known, isn't that deceitful and manipulative? But again, when I ponder the reason they would do such a thing, the most basic response I hear is, "Please find us legitimate. Please accept us."

Denial and Projection

Have you ever noticed that what sometimes irritates you the most about other people, is that which irritates you the most about yourself? I have noticed this in my own unfounded judgments of other people. I could be ready to give someone the third degree when I am stopped short, realizing what's pissing me off the most is that I am just like those I want to accuse. So what happens when people are so repulsed by what they see inside, that they can't even bring themselves to admit it? Some people lash out, even violently, to condemn it in other people.

Not only is this denial, but it is projection, as well. Psychological projection, briefly defined, is a defense mechanism often unconsciously used "when a person's own unacceptable or threatening feelings are repressed and then attributed to someone else."[6] The reason I bring it up is that I have always wondered what the idea of projection says about people who so fiercely attack the LGBT community in politics and religion? Is it surprising that they sometimes get caught behaving in the very ways that they condemn? Why would they go so far as to be hateful about homosexuality, so negatively vocal about it, condemning it as sin, and finding so called "cures" for it, unless it is what they hate and fear about themselves — or at the very least, they have given an enormous amount of attention, energy and thought to it. Straight men don't do that. They just don't think about it. They think about having sex with women. Reparative therapists and leaders fighting to negate homosexuality must think about it a great deal. Maybe the only way they can allow themselves to think about homosexuality is by thinking about it as a horrible sin, but they're thinking about gay sex nonetheless. I call that denial.

The Verbiage of Denial

Back on the phone with that fellow in Houston, he showed an excellent command of euphemistic terms. I asked, "So are you still a homosexual?" His response, "Well I don't believe that homosexuality really exists, just heterosexually confused people." Wow. That denial was astounding. These days, whenever I am entangled in shifting definitions and confusing conversations with ex-gays I try to get as downright basic as possible. "So are you still aroused when you see a handsome man?" His response, Like Paul's thorn in the flesh, "I will always be tempted." I tried to get even more practical, which means I usually have to get graphic: "So do you get erections when you look at women?" His retort, along with his precursor, conveniently avoided the question altogether: "Now see, there's another, more godly way of viewing that. God wants my mind to be kept pure, so that I can be ready to meet the woman God has for me."

Whenever he referred to homosexuality, he was careful to use the term "homosexual lifestyle," which is another trick of terminology that encourages denial. Some groups have even gotten in the habit of calling gay culture not just "the lifestyle," but "the deathstyle."[7] This makes sense when sexuality is defined as behavior only. If all homosexuality is reduced to what we do and how we behave, well of course it can be changed. This is the Pavlovian motivation to an enormous amount of ex-gay activities, as well as one of the prime features of religious abuse. When ex-gays don't see fundamental changes in their attractions, the issue becomes one of modifying their behavior. They change their "lifestyle," which they have labeled "homosexual." Why else would the leadership encourage men to participate in baseball games and other sports, and provide make-overs for the women? This is why they condemn wearing certain kinds of clothes and why they teach people to sit in ways that would be more "masculine" or "feminine" (for the respective gender, of course). It may sound laughable if not, um, undeniable. But when you are in that desperate situation, and there is little actual change of sexuality, what else can be done but generate denial and "success" by changing behavior and calling it heterosexuality?

Ironically, the leaders' own beliefs about homosexuality betray them when it comes to viewing it as a lifestyle choice. If homosexuality were just a matter of choosing the right behavior, then why all the therapy, prayer and psycho-babble? Just choose not to have gay sex and then you're straight, right? Of course it's not that simple, and no one who has had any real part of this struggle believes that, not even ex-gays. They would like to believe it, but I call that denial. Besides, when you think about it, the ex-gay way of life, as futile as it can be, is really just another "gay lifestyle."

Ex-gay leaders also use the term "sexual identity" in a similar manner. They contend (and are partially correct) that a child can be given outside messages from dysfunctional families, media and peers, that inform the child about sexuality. They might say, "It's just a lie from the outside world, but on the inside the child is always heterosexual," as if homosexuality was a mask that people can simply take off — a persona, if you will. Trying to explain this even in the best light seems shallow and incomplete. Again, sexuality is not that simple.

Term modification, like making slang and coming up with a group's own lingo, is an activity to solidify different kinds of communities and subcultures. The ex-gay environment is no different with the modified use of words like "lifestyle," "success," "identity," and "heterosexually confused." Even the term "ex-gay," has become, for lack of a better term, the general label — but not for straight people who were once homosexual; instead, it defines those who find themselves attracted to the same gender but are attempting to become straight.

> *Their whole spiel to us was that before we joined the ministry, we were homosexual. The day we got into the ministry, we were Ex-gay — you were labeled Ex-gay without any change even taking place.*

That's what they drummed into us: "You are now all changed; you are now all Ex-gay.

— *Catherine Wulfensmith,*
Ex-gay Survivor [8]

Sadly, the "ex-gay" title seems to hinder rather than help. On the one hand, ex-gays are uncomfortable calling themselves homosexual because it's sort of an admission of failure and sin. On the other hand, they are hard pressed to call themselves "straight" because they know that's not what they are sensing inside and they don't want to lie, especially when lying falls under the category of "sin" as well. Damned if you do and damned if you don't. Unfortunately, this puts them in a kind of no-man's land, if you'll pardon the double meaning. They feel scared of the LGBT community because of all the horror stories they have been fed, and yet they don't really feel a part of the church because of the constant fear that at any moment they could be thrown out if they admit to their attractions. Everywhere they turn, they experience fear. I recognize the fearful isolation in the eyes of so many ex-gays because I felt so alone trying to deny my experience, too. Is it any wonder that some eventually contemplate suicide?

Denial's Future

Another pervasive technique that ex-gays use is what I call "future talk." My friend on the phone in Houston explained clearly, "A perspective that has helped me a lot is seeing myself as a new creation, someone that God is not finished with yet. I don't see myself as the man I was. I see myself as the man that I will someday be for God." Notice how he dwelt in the future fantasy of who he wants to be, to avoid the man he was in his present form. I remember as an ex-gay being so repulsed by who I knew I was inside, that I would spend as much time as possible imagining who I would someday be. Of course this assumed that I would be heterosexual. Talk about a fantasy life. I would spend hours visualizing my future self — father, husband (though I didn't do much thinking about sex with my wife), minister, and how proud I would make my family and God. I envisioned myself as more than acceptable. I was going to be popular and an example of Christ, winning over everyone I came in contact with for the Lord. As long as it diverted my thoughts from who I was in the present, I would try to live as much as possible in the future person God would make me into.

Denial of Abuse

I pointed out at the end of Chapter 2 that ex-gay enthusiasts seem resolutely oblivious to the damage they are generating. To me this seems the worst part of their denial. There is even some evidence that these programs of designed repression can reflect the similar features of sexual abuse.

> *Reparative therapy's harmful effects mirror those displayed by victims of sexual abuse, who have been dominated (usually as children) by an authority figure. They are given the message: "Your sexuality doesn't matter. My sexuality is superior." Those in the ex-gay movement are not overtly abusive, but their covert sexual abuse is nevertheless the same: "Something is wrong with you." Whether it's a clergyman in church or a parent who teaches children to be ashamed of their homosexuality, that's a form of sexual abuse.*
>
> — *Joe Kort, MA, MSW, ACSW* [9]

Keeping those "dirty secrets," or being taught that "we just don't talk about those sorts of things," is a key feature of both sexual and religious abuse. Furthermore, it does nothing to promote health, sexual or otherwise.

> *Closets are a place of death. So many gay people are forced to live in two different realities — the world where they are pretending, and then that closet world where they have all their fears, and feelings of guilt, anger and shame. I think that's why "don't ask don't tell" is so important to the military and to the church. They'll let you serve as church organist, or pastor or teacher as long as you don't tell. So once you don't tell you're cut off from all that confessing, all that conversation, all that interplay that makes you healthy.*
>
> — *The Rev. Mel White* [10]

I felt for the kid on the phone, and at the same time I wanted to beat my head against the wall from all the painful memories of going along with it for so long. Alas, for acceptance's sake, I had been in denial. When the phone conversation was finally over, I promptly called the newspaper and alerted them to the actual motives of the people who placed the ad.

In All Things, Acknowledge Denial

If you haven't deduced it by now, denial is simply counterproductive to recovery and self-acceptance. The very act of refusing to look fully at myself — even to go to such lengths as to lie to myself about it, indicates that I am not accepting that which I am hiding. Therefore, as I began to look with new eyes at self-acceptance, I developed a clever little ironical statement that helped me stay in the moment and helped me stay honest: Acknowledge denial. Although denial can start out as a way to survive, for most ex-gays it has outlasted its usefulness, and now it just gets in the way of our self-acceptance. When you are ready, as you learn to accept yourself more, put these words on bumper stickers, make them into refrigerator magnets, write them on the inside cover of your Bible, and whenever you can, acknowledge denial. Just get that B.S. out of you. Whether you say it to yourself, or tell your friends, or shout it out your car window, whenever possible, acknowledge denial!

CHAPTER 5

My Voice in the Crowd

Becoming My Authentic Self

"If ever a dogma spawned a theological mutt, it is the ex-gay movement. Filled with fear and loathing it is nothing more than an all-out war against love. It does not honor love. It is the catastrophizing of natural love. It is run by people who believe in moral absolutes but not in moral equality. They lack true Christian values—honesty, charity, love of neighbor, the charge to avoid deception and not bear false witness. The Ex-gay movement does not honor reality. It dishonors reality. In the ex-gay movement you are not allowed to have your own authentic human experience. Why? Because you have besmirched the planet by the audacity of your existence. You are not allowed to expand into the truths of who you are. It is constructed to dim the light of your existence, your spiritual intelligence and the desire of your heart. It claims to be a movement up the spiritual food chain but in actuality it is a movement down the spiritual food chain. In other words, welcome to hell now that you are convinced it is heaven. It is constriction, not expansion. Life is a journey to one's authenticity. The ex-gay movement does not allow for the authenticity of the human experience. It is a derailment of that journey."

— Dr. Sylvia Rhue, Director of Religious Affairs
National Black Justice Coalition[1]

ON A PARTICULAR OCCASION in my teens, I was in a line for a movie with my youth group from church. There was someone in front of us who had the verbal habit of saying, "I swear…" in just about every sentence. Mind you, he was not saying any curse words, just "I swear." "I swear that girl is dressed so hot. I swear it took so long to get here. I swear I sure say 'I swear' a lot…." My youth pastor, who was becoming visibly uncomfortable, said, "All that guy can say is 'I swear,' and the Bible says you aren't supposed to swear." The pause of silence in our little circle showed we were all thrown off. We all thought the Bible meant, "don't say the Lord's name in vain." Maybe he was referring to swearing as in, "don't make a promise that you are not going to keep." When he saw our confusion he dismissingly said, "It's just not a good word to say lightly. I don't want to use that word and be misunderstood. It would be a bad witness for Christ."

Huh? It was as if "a witness" was some kind of porcelain doll outside of me that the slightest guilt by association could shatter with no potential for reconciliation. It really didn't matter what I believed, I had to "act" like Christ. I had to protect that delicate image. How many times was I guilted into modifying my behavior, speaking on topics I knew nothing about, and even manipulating others to do things? Don't speed, don't interrupt, never tell a lie — not because they were the right things to do. No, I did it to avoid marring my Christ-like appearance so that I could win others to know Jesus. I was completely sincere, and completely deaf to whether I believed those things or not.

After all the lies and outward showing off of how God was supposedly changing me, I began to realize that a witness didn't function that way. A witness on the stand in a courtroom is there to simply relay what his experience was for a given event as honestly and accurately as possible. What kind of witness would I be if I didn't authentically believe what I was saying? But that didn't stop me from polishing up my outward appearance. I did and said all kinds of things without taking the time to know what I thought about them. Would that be a semi-lie? Now I see that this whole "witness for Christ" game is a feature of religious abuse, when the emphasis on outward appearance is more important than who the person is on the inside. Ultimately, all the time and energy I put into being a good witness (and fearing that I wasn't) was a distraction from what was in my heart, ignoring God's voice inside me, ignoring who I really was and taking myself farther and farther away from any kind of developing love for myself, for others, even for what was true.

It took a long time — about a decade — to rid myself of as much denial as I could find, and rid myself of the compulsion to lie. It was not easy, especially in the years I had accepted my sexuality yet was still making my bread and butter performing in conservative churches and private Christian schools. There were a few times when people would ask me, "So, where do you live?" and I would tell them that I was from San Francisco. I would watch the growing concern on their faces as they would think something like, "How is he a Christian in San Francisco? I wonder if he's…?" Then — right on cue — they would ask if I was married! I was living with a great guy named Stuart during this period and it felt like marriage to me, so I would say, "Yes, I'm married." A wave of relief would rush over their faces and I would think I had eluded their condemnation. But then they would ask, "Oh, what's her name?" And I would mentally grit my teeth — damn it! I'd say, "Ssss—Stephanie." Granted, I was between a rock and a hard place. Lying was truly a survival mechanism since my income depended on being acceptable in the church.

I'm not proud of those deceptions, not just because I was deceiving people, and not just because lies like this inevitably returned to bite me in the ass. The biggest reason I gradually stopped bending reality was that it made me feel just plain bad about myself. I could feel it when I lied, and it made me feel unhealthy (as corny as that sounds). I felt more miserable every time it occurred. It generated guilt in my already shame-ridden character and my emotional health was becoming far more important than tricking people into accepting me on false pretenses. Deception is a fascinating paradox because attempting to garner acceptance by deception only generates a greater realization that I actually do not have acceptance, since I have to lie more and more to get it. And if I have to lie about myself to gain acceptance, others are not truly accepting me. They are accepting the charade I let them see.

No Secrets

One of the best mental tools I used to break myself of my lying habit and enhance my recovery was to adjust my beliefs about secrets. I now choose to believe that there is no such thing as secrets, at least in my own life. Sooner or later, one way or another, especially in this Information Age, if someone really wanted to know something about me, they could probably find it. Of course, I'm not going to blurt out every detail of my life every chance I get. It is living in such a way that if my life were somehow to be laid bare, there would be nothing that I ultimately need to hide. If I could bottle and sell this kind of freedom, I'd be rich today. It is such a genuinely freeing experience to live, as best as possible, without secrets. Furthermore, it really pulls the plug on the habit of bending the truth.

For several years I corresponded with a man who lived somewhere in the Midwest. He was in ministry, had been married to a woman for many years, had kids and grandchildren, and he was in denial. He had for decades maintained a gay sexuality and in his mind the facade between his two worlds was as impenetrable as a prison. When he first wrote to me, he spilled his life in detail and seemed genuinely proud of how he maintained the dichotomy. "Oh, no," he'd write, "my family will never know the other side of my life." He was so self-assured, and did I mention that he was in denial? Interestingly, he wasn't so much in denial about his sexuality as he was in denial about his two worlds intersecting.

"Don't bet on it, buster," I'd respond. "If you have talked to me, you've talked to other people and the moment someone else learns information about you, that's the very moment you no longer have any control over said information." Such is the power, the fragility, and the devastation of secrets. Any one of the people he told, with a little effort, could contact his loved ones on the other side of his life and spill the beans. Who's to say it hadn't happened already, and he just didn't know it? That facade may be carefully maintained, but in reality, just one well-placed word — one little slip — would bring it all down. Besides, what a horrible and sad way to live, to never be truly open to anyone, especially to the ones to whom one feels he is closest.

Doesn't this suggest that the degree to which we feel acceptance is, in some ways, dependent on the degree to which we are willing to be honest and vulnerable? For example, how will I ever know if my best friend really accepts me fully, if I have not revealed myself fully to him? This is not about my friend. It is about me presuming that my best friend would reject me if he knew the real me. Who is not being accepting? I am.

Honesty, the truth, lies, denial, acceptance, dichotomies, vulnerabilities — sometimes it gets way too confusing — like trying to understand two teenagers sharing gossip, "Well he said that she said that her boyfriend thought that their mom was..." Even former President Clinton was so far into denial that he actually thought he could get away with saying, "I did not have sex with that woman." What was he thinking?

Let's complicate the subject a bit more. Dr. Robert Francoeur collected sexual profiles from hundreds of different cultures and compiled them into a four-volume compendium like no other: *The International Encyclopedia of Sexuality*. If you were to read this work from A to Z, you would find very little in common among the wide diversity of cultures around the world and throughout history, when it comes to sexuality. There are so many different ways to behave sexually. However, Francoeur found a cluster of features common to most societies: 1) people have personal beliefs about sexuality; 2) they behave in particular sexual ways; and, 3) their society has public beliefs about sexuality. Yet, without fail, these three features contradict each other to different degrees within a given society. All of us have discrepancies between what we think, what we say and what we do. When I learned this little tidbit of information, I had a crisis. If everyone is bending the truth and, furthermore, not doing as they say sexually, what the hell's the point of being honest? I was confused all the more.

The Ferret in the Football Field

I use the term "voices" to describe what was going on in my mind, as I described earlier with my parents' and my rebel's voices. How was *my* voice any different from all the others that had found their way into my head? I pleaded with my first San Francisco therapist, Michael, to tell me whose voice was really mine ("Fix me. Fix me!"), and he would always be silent. Out of frustration, my rebel would want to accuse him of being in the position of my parents — another authority keeping the truth from me. My rebel would hunker down in stubbornness and as a result there were hours of therapy spent primarily in silence. At the time, I felt like I was going nowhere. I wanted to blame my therapist for not being very good, but somehow I knew the silence was for a reason... which I had to figure out for myself. Lost in internal arguments, all the voices gradually... finally ran out of energy. I didn't know that only after all the voices fell silent would I ever be able to find my own. In these quiet hours a kind of fable developed that was a visualization of my predicament. I called it the Ferret in the Football Field, and I have the journal entry from the time it materialized:

> *My counseling appointment was phenomenal. I went in admittedly depressed. I started talking about how I constantly argue with myself. Whenever I want to enjoy an activity I can't feel good about it because there's always something that objects inside me. I keep criticizing and judging myself until I'm exhausted without any desire to do anything. Not even the activity I originally wanted to enjoy has any appeal after all that debating. This arguing seems to undermine my confidence. When it comes right down to it, I feel I can't be really confident about anything, because confidence might insinuate delusion or over-confidence. How does anyone know if they're completely confident or right about anything? Michael suggested that being right and being confident were two different things. Yeah, I get it. What's so bad about being confident? Immediately, I heard the voice of my parents questioning my motives, "If you are too confident you will run the risk of being arrogant and prideful." As soon as they started in, I fell into a vision of sorts.*
>
> *I found myself in a stadium and from one side were being yelled my parents' cautions, criticisms and condemnations. From the other side another voice yelled back. It was the rebel standing in the opposite set of bleachers shouting, "Fuck off!" and "Leave him alone!" As these two went at it both Michael and I observed that neither of these voices sounded much like me. I realized that the rebel was just a reaction to my*

parents, while Michael pointed out that maybe my parents' voices could simply be a reaction to me. But who are my parents yelling at, and who is the rebel trying to protect? Where was I in all of this?

As everyone's voices began to fade, somewhere down on the field between the two grandstands I noticed a hole burrowed a foot or two into the ground. And in this upturned soil, a small furry back exposed to the sun was what I best could conceive as myself. I hardly recognized me. It looked like a shy little frightened ferret. At first I thought it might be dead, but then I saw it shaking, raw and unkempt. Only after a long time of complete stillness did it show any kind of movement, but then it slowly came out of hiding. It began darting back and forth a few feet around the hole — the movement fluid and smooth. Watching all this I wanted to move in and embrace the real me, but any movement from an observer would only frighten the creature. It seemed that just a light breeze would send it ducking for cover. Could this have been one of the very first times this amazing creature ever had the courage to stand alone in belief of its own existence? I could only sit in silence, breathing shallowly in awe, and watching what I can only describe as the real me.

Looking back, I now see that all of this was my psyche desperately trying to find my own voice, which was long overdue. With this vision in place, I saw that I was a completely unique and distinct being, whatever the voices yelled around me. This creature could grow strong and adept. There were times I would imagine that ferret and I as one — fast, sharp (dare I say), cute and cuddly, yet with a bite. Other times, the ruckus of life would be just too predatory and nothing was going to coax that creature out of its hiding. Yet those were the times when I could be the adult, standing tall on the field, acknowledging the ferret's fear. I could protect it, guard it, and provide a space of strength for it. Over the years a lot of people, along with their voiced opinions, have sat in the arena of my mind, and I have listened to them all, for better or for worse, including my parents and my rebel. But the fights have ended. Even if the crowd gets too loud, that ferret is now confident enough to quiet the chorus. I can listen and allow myself to take in the information and decide what I think, how I respond, and what I do.

Authenticity

Eventually, I realized that my commitment to honesty cannot be reduced to what others think of me, or what a culture believes about sex, or even the particular words that come out of my mouth. Ultimately, my commitment to honesty is a radical step of self-acceptance. If I can be honest to myself, to others, and to my community, it is a kind of ritualized self-acceptance. Quite frankly, over the years the different words we use to describe this idea have become so loaded that I've searched for a better term. The term "truth" seems nearly meaningless these days. Whose truth? The ex-gays say they have the truth — and look how well that's turning out. The government says they tell us the truth and who believes them? The word "honesty" feels too much like something to pry out of someone else. "Why won't you be honest with me?" And, er, to be, well, truthful, "Honesty is such a lonely word," as the amazing bard, Billy Joel, sings. If you haven't guessed already, the word that has worked best for me over the years — who knows, maybe it's just the latest buzz word — is "authenticity."

Setting my mind to think authentically has been one of the strongest tools to help me compensate for the "Jesus first, me last" ways of thinking. Indeed, I believe that being programmed so early in life to put "Jesus first, others second and myself last," was the very thing that made finding my authentic voice such a challenge. To be authentic, I have to know myself rather intimately. This means it may take me a little time to figure things out, and I am not always as quick on the draw as I would like to be. It takes time to know oneself and, as I have already stated, that's why I think it's important to employ a professional listener (therapist) so that I can take just an hour or two a month to get to know the growing and changing me.

I remember challenging that Midwestern minister about his mortality and the possibility that only after his death would his two worlds learn of each other. He still seemed to think it would never happen (such is the nature of denial), but I've seen plenty of situations to the contrary. I've known others who said, "So what? After I'm dead I really won't care what others think of me anyway." This brings to the surface how shortsighted and selfish denial can really be. I can't imagine what it would be like for that minister's family to discover after he's gone that, for who knows how long, he had lied to them so resolutely. Sure, maybe he really didn't care, but for the rest of his family's existence, they would always feel betrayed, that they never knew their own father/husband, and that he never really loved them enough to be honest with them. And, essentially, they would be right. "He never really loved us enough to be authentic." How about slapping that on your tombstone?

Dan Haitt

After graduating from college, I remained in Santa Barbara to get on my financial feet as I began performing concerts full time. I was a man with a mission. My sense of purpose and ministry was to use my musical gifts to further God's love on earth. After a year passed I made plans to move up to San Francisco — a place I had always felt drawn to, even before I was aware of my sexuality.

About a month before I moved from Santa Barbara I had a birthday that a number of my friends celebrated for me at the (only) local gay bar called the Pub. Most of these friends were relatively new since it was after graduation that I had gradually come out in this little bar on the other side of the tracks, next to the porno shop. Since Santa Barbara was definitely a small (yet rich) town, everyone in the LGBT community knew each other pretty well. I had experienced acceptance from these new-found friends that far surpassed some of the kinds of limited love I had experienced from people I had known for years. Therefore this group was dear to me.

At the party, a lesbian friend of mine asked me a genie-like question: "It's your birthday. Ask me for anything and I'll do my best to get it for you — within reason." I was taken a bit off guard. What in the world do I ask for — a drink, a particular song from the DJ? Throughout the night, she kept asking me the question (this might have had something to do with her alcohol intake), even after I told her I wanted a kiss from the very cute bartender and he granted me a wet sloppy one — yum! As I was getting ready to leave, I spotted a guy named Dan that I had met before and I felt a spark between us. I was unsure just how mutual it was. In passing, I said to the lesbian, "I'd sure like to have some fun with him!"

He had arrived late in the evening after performing in a local musical. Within the theater hierarchy of the city, he had risen quite rapidly as a leading man. He certainly had the looks for it — a couple inches taller than me, great singing voice, nice average build, neither too lean nor too muscular, and a knockout smile that indicated a lot was going on in that head, although it seemed to be a challenge to find out exactly what that was. We made eyes a few times and said some casual hello's in the final few minutes of the night, but I couldn't read him.

I ducked out before the bar closed since I didn't want to be part of the post-bar man-to-man pairing up for who would be sleeping with whom — at least I didn't want to do it on my birthday. Just as I reached my car, I heard a voice behind me call my name. Turning around, I saw Dan approaching and heard him ask where I was going on my birthday. I tried to form an intelligent sentence but it wasn't coming out, and it didn't need to. As soon as he got close, his arms embraced me and he planted a sensual, deep kiss on my lips — all in one fell swoop. When we finally came up for air, he whispered in my ear, "Happy birthday, mister." I could tell that I was indeed getting just what I wanted and it wasn't going to be a large amount of sleep.

I spent the night in his bed — one of many before I left town. On the one hand, there was a certain amount of frustration because I was leaving. On the other hand, we both knew it, and that somehow created a safe microcosm of sexual freedom. Our connection ran deep, happy, fairly non-verbal and very sexy for those last few weeks. It was, however, bringing up an internal dilemma of a sex-ethical nature. If I knew that this relationship was limited to just a few weeks, and that afterwards there would probably be little to relate to without the sex, wasn't this whole connection self-centered frivolity? "After all," I thought, "How is the time I spent with Dan moving me toward my goals, or improving my relationship with God?" There were a number of mornings, after he had gone to his day job, when I would wake up and actually feel guilty that our sexual connection was perhaps self-indulgent.

The weeks ended soon enough, and I moved to San Francisco. We talked on the phone a couple of times, but it was as if we couldn't communicate unless it was with our bodies. I was actually grateful that he had seemed unable to really open up to me emotionally, because that made it easier for me to let go and move on. Months passed, probably close to a year, and out of the blue I got a call from Dan. He was talking a mile a minute — talking about his feelings, emotions, what he was experiencing in his heart. I kept wanting to say, "Who is this? Is this really that quiet guy, Dan, I shacked up with for a month?"

It was, and there was a reason for his new-found verbal expression. In the months since we had last talked, Dan had found out he was HIV positive (I was not too concerned about contracting it since we had always played with little risk). He had found out his status after getting really sick. Because of this, it had been hard to hide it from work, family and friends. Consequently, he had lost his job and a number of straight friends.

For Dan, this had been a wake-up call. It helped him take better care of himself — more so than at any other time in his life. Facing his mortality helped him value and enjoy life all the more. It also helped him find his authentic voice. Despite the challenges, Dan had blossomed, and I admired his courage. Surviving AIDS in the 1980's was truly the exception, but that didn't stop Dan and thousands of other victims from using the illness as an opportunity to make life better. This is why I share this story, out of dozens of similar ones I have experienced. It was an honor to sing at his memorial service some years later. There were so many people there who had known love and courage from the special person that was Dan.

Facing death with a loved one — holding their hand in the final hours and looking into the face of a friend as their spirit actually leaves their body — has changed me. It has healed me. It has cured me from the future talk about the person I will someday be. It has enabled me to truly be in the moment, for that's all we really have as a guaranteed experience. If these people can crack a smile and let their love of life freely flow from them, if these people have that sort of courage, then I, who apparently have much more time on my hands, can be my authentic self right here in this moment — if not for me, at the very least for all those who have had their very existence wrenched from them. And you know what? It feels great! I look back on my few weeks with Dan as pure gold — a rare and priceless gift, and not just because he's gone now. We both felt a genuine connection and we followed it. We could both be ourselves on a deeply sexual level, and we enjoyed it for what it was for the time we were given. I don't know how to be any more authentic.

Experiences like knowing Dan and others strengthened me to the point that I began the transition from performing and ministering in only conservative churches to doing the same in LGBT-affirming churches, as well as other venues like cabarets, clubs, and gay pride festivals. But before going completely public, there was a set of people with whom I had to be honest — my family.

The Biggest Coming Out of All

When it came time for Dad and Mom to find out about my sexuality, we really had to start at ground zero, or should I say ground negative ten. My parents have said they did not see it coming — that is, they did not have any idea while I was growing up that I was "that way." On the one hand, a boy who drew super heroes (mainly muscle-bound men), hated sports of just about any kind, played the piano, even defined himself as "artistic," and got his last doll — er, "action figure" — at age 13 seems to be a likely candidate. On the other hand, there is no doubt that my parents thoroughly loved me, and their love was blind. And when I consider what my parents' extremely horrible stereotypes of a homosexual were like at the time, I looked nothing like what they might have imagined. I suppose I had my compulsive lying to thank for some of my parents' unawareness, as well. After all, I learned my deceptive chops by practicing on them. So when the time came that I stepped out of the closet, they truly were in shock.

I had been giving some thought about coming out to my parents. Through Evangelicals Concerned, I had learned some strategies about it — for instance, I knew I wanted to approach this on the offensive. I wanted to be prepared with resources and educational information and be ready to help them through the whole process. I did not want to be on the defensive, where maybe they would find out accidentally, and not be prepared. One thing I decided to do was to come out first to someone in the family that would be some kind of support, not just to me, but to my parents, so they would not feel entirely alone. I took this step while on a camping trip with my mom's side of the family. Here's what I wrote in my journal:

> *I want them [my family] to know and accept me. I doubt if either will ever happen. So then I pull up my bootstraps, "Okay. I'll seek community somewhere else." But it is so hard to find the kind of family that took a lifetime to establish. And I don't want another family. I want this one to accept me.*
>
> *Today my aunt and I took a walk. She is the most level headed and probably [the most] educated of the generation before me. As we walked I tested her with a couple of questions to see if she was trustworthy or not. She was. I slowly and nervously let myself out of the closet, and to my hopes and dreams, she accepted me. She wasn't overjoyed or excited, but she wasn't "Oh. I'm so sorry," either. When I asked her what she thought, she said, "Who am I to say?" Wow. What character. What wisdom. What acceptance. In all areas that I talked about with her, she could understand and realistically accept me. I was, to say the least, blown away!*
>
> *I knew that the extent of her telling others would go to her husband [my mother's brother] and no further. By the end of the day she told me she had told him, but he treated me without a glint of difference in our interaction. His love and acceptance (and my uncle has a lot of it) did not change at all. What a relief to have someone in the family that knows and accepts me.*

Another part of my strategy was to send out little hints casually about the subject. On past visits I had mentioned a friend or two, and in passing I would say, "...David, who happens to be a homosexual..." After all, I lived in San Francisco. Surely Mom and Dad would assume that I knew some gays and lesbians. I guess I had forgotten from whom I get my tenacious curiosity, and in this instance, theirs was my undoing.

There are times in life that seem to progress with more gut-wrenching than any soap opera could ever wish to develop, and coming out to my parents nearly broke all drama-o-meters. It was only days before I was to give a concert at the church I grew up in. I had my share of being "never a star in one's own hometown," and I was going to show all these people I loved so dearly what college had done in making me a performing music minister. I had even pulled in a couple of my girl friends to sing backup on a few songs. I drove two hours to my parents' home on a Thursday afternoon and the backup singers were driving in on Sunday night just for the concert.

"Son, How Do You Know So Much About Homosexuality?"

This is what my mother casually asked me when we sat down to her great home cooking. Suddenly I found myself between a rock and a hard place. I wasn't going to lie about it anymore, but I was definitely not ready to come out — not now, right before the concert. I tried to blow the question off as unimportant without lying, but they saw right through it. Needless to say, by the time dinner was through, Mom and Dad were asking me point blank, "So are you telling us you're a homosexual?" And their panic was on the rise.

Several hours and a few nightmares later, we were all a mess. Wailing and gnashing of teeth paled in comparison to how my parents were behaving. I remember highlights in the negative of that evening. I remember watching what I could only describe as these dark and distorted stereotypes surfacing in my parent's minds and the sheer terror of their son being one of "them" flashing across their faces as though real pain was being inflicted on them. I would try to educate. I would try to stop them from blaming themselves, or blaming the college I had attended — at one point they were sure I had been molested. I would try to dispel their myths of what a gay person was and let them know that it was going to be okay. Then another thought would flood their faces and it was more than I — more than anyone, really — could keep up with. It was as if my parents were engulfed by one trauma after another and there was nothing I could do but watch. How could they possibly respond in a loving manner when they were experiencing such a tidal wave of fear and shock from their misinformation (and lack of information) regarding homosexuality? I remember at one point my mother realizing that I might never have children, and her sobbing words were, "… and you're so good looking." That really surprised me since I don't remember ever getting such a compliment when she was in her right mind. Everything they believed me to be was falling apart and they could not hold back the "horror."

Mixed into the revelation and the sadness was argument. I can't say that my mother uses her emotions to manipulate a situation in her favor, at least not consciously. I'm not sure she has the mental dexterity to be that malicious (which I realize is a back-handed compliment, but a compliment nonetheless). But I will give her credit for not being able to hide her internal emotions — ever. Unfortunately, she could be so emotionally forthcoming that hurting Mom's feelings, either purposely or accidentally, seemed like "the" cardinal sin in our house. As I was growing up, it was one of the reasons I'd rather lie than be honest about something that could make my mother upset. I might as well have cut her with a knife than hurt her feelings. It was as if her emotional pain was just as real as physical pain, or more so. The hurt in the room that night seemed out of everyone's control.

The evening finally culminated in the harshest statement she has ever said to me: "This is worse than when your sister died." I couldn't believe she said it. To try and deflect some of the utter rejection I, as usual, denied it and tried to justify it away in my mind with excuses, like, "Oh, she's just upset. She really doesn't mean that. She's trying to manipulate me into changing, etc...." But it had hurt me so deeply that my survival instinct finally kicked in. That statement quite honestly sounded emotionally life-threatening. I called the conversation "over" and said that we needed to take a break and get some sleep since it was already late into the night. It was the first time that I did not feel at home in the very house I grew up in, and that only heaped on more feelings of rejection.

Fortunately, I had friends in town, a gay couple whom I called and basically said, "I've come out to my parents. I cannot stay here tonight. I'm coming over right now." — without so much as a chance for them to respond. When I set foot in their house these two muscle-bound lumberjack men enveloped me into their arms. I was in such shock that the two of them insisted I sleep between them, safe and warm where nothing evil could reach me. God bless them.

The next morning when I returned, not surprisingly, mom and dad hadn't slept much. As I have previously stated, I give my family credit for being tenacious in their creativity and curiosity. Yet the dark side of this characteristic is what I like to call "scab-scratching." If there's something that isn't quite perfect, we just can't leave it alone. And so it was with my sexuality.

Something that took me by surprise was that Dad was going to call his pastor to cancel my concert. "We can't knowingly allow a homosexual to get up in front of our church." Youch! That was a harsh blow and further diminished whatever bit of confidence I thought my parents had in me. Somehow I felt like a coward to leave it up to my father to make the call, so by the end of Saturday I called the pastor and cancelled the concert without giving any reason except that it was an emergency and it couldn't be avoided. I felt that I had come so close to doing something special for my church family, and now, not only was I forced to bail on them at the last minute, but the humiliation around the whole situation was so potent that I almost never set foot in that sanctuary again, aside for a funeral or two. "Never a hero in your own home town." I hate it when clichés are truly spot on. Yet a friend tried to comfort me by saying, "Jesus had that problem too, ya' know."

Damage Control

In the following weeks and months several experiences occurred that were memorable, although I've forgotten their exact order. We had phone conversations which consisted of more arguing and crying — lots of arguing and crying. A couple of childhood friends from church called. One I remember called to tell me to repent. Another called to try and offer support, but she was pretty ignorant about the subject. Yet she loved to pass on the latest gossip. She told me that some of the people in church were advising my parents to, in effect, excommunicate me. I feared the kind of advice my parents could be getting. Would they agree and take a "tough love" approach, thinking it would snap me back into straightness? I was afraid that, in reality, a tactic like that would only distance them from me even further.

I knew of an evangelical ministry specifically for parents who find out their kids are queer. I deeply empathized with my parents and I knew this organization could help them, but I also knew that if I offered this as a resource they would not trust it. I knew they would ridiculously think that it was some kind of trick to brainwash them, as if listening to me would somehow corrupt them. That's just how extreme the situation was. How ironic that, when I finally was honest, they wouldn't believe a word I said. I was now on the other end of "us and them." In the religiously abusive system, I was in cahoots with Satan and could not be trusted. I was trying to think of a way to get the information to them second-hand, when my parents called and said they felt somewhat better because they had talked with a woman at a ministry for parents in their situation. Whew! It was the very same ministry I was hoping to mention to them.

I was relieved, but this was the first of a long line of events where I knew what my parents needed. I'd hold my tongue because if the information came from me it would be invalid in their eyes. Then my parents would do exactly what I predicted. It's not my intention to sound "holier than thou," but can you blame me for grabbing at any kind of reassurance that I was making good decisions? My parents were all but rejecting me. That didn't do much for a son's confidence. Furthermore, they were unwilling to trust what I was saying. At least I could take some solace in the idea that I could see and predict what they were going through. In an odd sort of way, I felt we were somehow on track.

They asked me to go to this ex-gay program, or meet with that person, or read another book — all of which I had already done in one form or another several years earlier, and because they had not been included on my journey of discovery, somehow it was just not real to them. It was not good enough to simply take my word for it. I realized that they had to go through all the painstaking education, all the feelings of isolation, all the sexual and spiritual ethics just to come close to what I was experiencing. What a pain in the ass for them. What a pain in the ass for me, and no, I didn't want to do it. I knew that the whole "coming out" process probably entailed far more work and information than they could ever comprehend.

When Mom and Dad called to tell me they had talked to that particular ministry, I could tell they were not going to kick me out of the family. I could hear in their voices that they wanted to love me, even though it was sounding like "love the sinner and hate the sin." Ultimately, I have to hand it to them. There have only been a few family events when life has really, really been dire. And on those occasions, my parents have come out on the side of love. So when I heard that from them, I knew I could take a break. I told them I needed to stop the communication for a while — not forever, but for a while. As best as I can remember, there were some long periods during this part of the journey that I had to recover and heal from all that had occurred. It was just too painful to feel the fresh sting of my parents' rejection, which was only emphasized by the concert's cancellation, as if the entire congregation that was my life-long family had rejected me, too. I think the longest period I went without communicating with them was three months, which doesn't sound like much, but it sharply contrasted with our talking on the phone every couple of weeks.

I couldn't imagine anything more difficult than coming out to my parents. Even coming out in a ministry newsletter to my several-thousand-member mailing list was nothing compared to coming out to my parents. It was around this time that I really shifted into "recovery mode." I had wounds that were going to take some time to mend.

Although it has not been easy, being my authentic self is a constant reward all by itself. I am no longer dependent on what others think of me, or on who I think I should be someday. Sure, I still have goals and dreams I work toward. They motivate me to be creative and even to write this book. However, no more is my happiness at the mercy of how quickly I complete a project. Right now, I am Jallen and I am happy with myself in this moment because there's no one else I have to be except me. Another friend who has passed on used to say, "If I was a better person, I would... oh, wait a minute, I'm not a better person, so never mind." Although I certainly aspire to be a better person, this little saying speaks to how important it is to recognize, enjoy and honor my authentic self as I am right now.

There's a theory that straight guys who truly are secure in their masculine and feminine sides aren't phased by putting on a dress as a costume, because ultimately they really don't care what others think of them and whatever they are wearing.

Although my explanation of this theory is over-simplified, I mention it because I grew up with an odd version of it. I avoided dressing up for Halloween or a masquerade party, because I felt that my true self was lost behind a façade all the time — so there was no joy in creating a façade just for fun. In my mid-30's I finally felt secure enough in who I was, that I started getting a kick out of pretending to be someone else. My authentic self no longer had to hide, so it was fun to dress it up in a skirt once in a while. Now I look for opportunities to make my own crazy outfits and to try on different personas, because I know who I am and no outfit calls that into question. I'm comfortable being outrageously fabulous — inside and out!

CHAPTER 6

What Ex-gays Cannot Do

The Challenge of Unconditional Love

*I don't believe in a God who would create you as you are and then set
you up to be hated by God.... I believe in a God who creates variety.
No two people look alike genetically, physically and emotionally. We
are very unique as people. And I believe that being gay or lesbian
is simply a part of the natural variety of creation. It's nothing to be
ashamed about. If you learn to love yourself the way God does, you can
live a happy and full life as a gay or lesbian person.*

— *The Rev. Elder Nancy Wilson,*
UFMCC Minister[1]

I MENTIONED at the beginning of the chapter on denial that probably the biggest challenge I had in my recovery process was to learn to love myself unconditionally. Indeed, I believe acknowledging denial and embracing authenticity are activities that build a foundation for recovery. That foundation supports unconditional acceptance. I must emphasize the intentional activity of learning to accept oneself fully. For me, this was not just another thing at the bottom of my "To Do" list, which could add to my guilt for never getting to it. This was not just a mantra whose meaning faded with repetition. After all the years of self-hate, and after all the religious abuse that indirectly (and directly) supported this self-hate, learning to love myself unconditionally moved very close to the top of my list of recovery tasks. I was increasingly aware of, and ridding myself of the remnants of, ingrained self-hate, and I was focused on finding tangible methods of self-love. Ways of self-love are so important that they will turn up throughout the rest of this book.

Perhaps self-love is one of those life goals that will end only at my death bed, because it seems that everyday as I grow and change I have to learn also to accept and welcome the person I am evolving into. At the very least, accepting one's self fully is not a one-time decision that we are then done with. Self-acceptance, and eventually creating acceptance in general, is a daily challenge in this world. This chapter specifically focuses on the elements that further produced this foundation for recovery.

Therapy

Most ex-gay survivors I meet have a real love/hate relationship with therapists. Usually, this is a result of them having bad experiences with Christian, quasi-counselors that had very little, if any, actual training in psychotherapy or sexuality. It's obvious that therapy is valuable to me and I continue to use it to this day. I like the analogy of servicing a car. I suppose I could wait until my car breaks down on the side of the road and I am in dire crisis to fix it. But my options would certainly be limited in that scenario and the stress would be high. I would much prefer to have my car serviced on a regular basis so that, for the most part, I can avoid breaking down in the first place. Therapy works that way for me. Although I could always talk to my friends, they were not necessarily trained professionals in interpersonal relationships or to "servicing my engine." I neither expected nor wanted my friends to be my engine mechanics.

After college, when I moved to San Francisco, I began to look for a new therapist. The overriding goal was to find a therapist who was going to function not just as a mechanic, but as an emotional mirror for me (yet another metaphor). Sure, I'd want his insights. I wouldn't even mind a kick in the pants every once in a while. But I had learned that the kind of therapist that worked best for me was a person (a man was my preference) who could reflect back, to the best of his ability, what he was seeing in me, so that, for just an hour or two a month, I could take a good sober look at myself. I wanted a therapist's ability to reflect what he saw, to be stronger than his need to agree or disagree with my choices or lifestyle. This is precisely what I would request when I was interviewing potential therapists. This was my self-motivated recovery. The more clearly I could look in that mirror, the better I knew what I had to work with and how to make decisions. The more clearly I could look in that mirror, the more easily (although uncomfortable at times) I could see parts of myself that needed adjusting, and at the same time accept myself unconditionally.

Sizing Up the Challenge

Another step toward recovery from self-hate was comprehending all that I was up against. I learned that in our society we are confronted with hundreds of choices a day. Many of these choices say, "Do this, buy that, try this and you will be more acceptable." In essence, these statements beg over and over again the question, "Do you really accept yourself as you are?" In fact, most of them aren't asking. They use every trick in the book to tell you, if not beat you over the head with the idea, that "You are not acceptable unless you buy our product." No wonder we are such a society of consumers who at the same time suffer and buckle under the weight of low self-esteem.

In addition to all these messages, the LGBT community has its own set of obstacles to maneuver through if we are to dispel self-hate. It is no understatement that as part of a sexual minority, when it comes to self-acceptance, the odds are stacked against us in many ways. We all have our stories of how we first realized we were different from the sexual norm, and these experiences are rarely happy. Maybe it was the name-calling that branded us outcasts — faggot, pansy, sissy, momma's boy, lesbo, bull dyke, queer, just to name a few. Maybe you dreamt and visualized how wonderful it would be to make your friends and family proud by marrying that perfect person of the opposite gender. The only problem was that all the people you were attracted to were the same gender as yourself. Maybe you overheard a conversation when someone said, "All fags are child molesters," and although that didn't describe you, somehow you felt stereotyped as "deviant." Possibly sexuality was never talked about, and the silence was as condemning as any words spoken about sexuality. If you were the rare exception who brought your sexuality out in the open — maybe you just didn't know how gender-non-conforming you were as a child — it most often was met with painful and utter rejection, even violence from those around you.

Experiences like these taught us to conform. Not only did we have the regular peer pressures that came with growing up, and the constant tickle of a consumer culture stimulating our discontent, but society, in many other ways, instructed us to force our sexuality to fit in. We had to work harder to conform ourselves than most heterosexuals do. It was pretty much impossible to find any acceptance — inside or out — in this veritable onslaught of pressure to acquiesce, to put it mildly.

Oddly enough, we live in a climate that works very hard to keep us from what everyone wants most. It's like going to a dark and noisy bar to get to know someone — the very environment works against us. And what does everyone want most? Conformity seems to scream one thing — "Be acceptable!" We want to fit in — to have a sense of belonging, and if we have to sacrifice our sexuality to get it, so be it. To consider that our culture might have the wrong information and that there was in fact nothing wrong with me, was far beyond what I could comprehend. My innocent and naive brain, trying to understand the complexity of acceptance and sexuality, naturally deduced that if I simply changed my homosexuality, I would then be worthy of love. It seemed that there was no other choice, but it was anything but simple.

For some, having a strong self-esteem despite all the outside messages to the contrary may sound like a simple and even unconscious task that any healthy human being with a good self-esteem can do almost naturally. If this is you, let me shake your hand because I'm very happy for you, if not envious. However, have you met a lot of people like this who live in our society? Just about everyone struggles with self-acceptance at different times in life. And I have yet to hear anyone say that Fundamentalist Christian ex-gays are healthy human beings with good self-esteem.

I've just outlined two or three kinds of complicated social structures that I (and most of us) had to maneuver through to feel acceptable as a young person. But wait. Those structures seemed minuscule when compared to the religious and theological obstacle course that I faced to gain some sense of acceptance for my immortal soul — thanks to the messages I received from religious abuse. All of it hinged on the messages about my sexuality. I thought the only way I would be acceptable to God was to be heterosexual. So even though I hoped and prayed that the ex-gay experience would indeed make me straight, the overriding motivation was to achieve acceptance from God. This can not be understated. Who wants to feel rejection, particularly from God? To imagine utter and eternal exclusion from the God of the universe was more than I could bear.

I Love You, but...

There was another question I asked the Houston ex-gay minister on the phone (from the chapter on denial). "So does God love me unconditionally?" I'll admit, it was a set up. "Oh, yes. It does not matter what you have done or where you've been. God accepts you, but..." I interrupted, "What did you just say?" He repeated, "God's love is unconditional, but..." He said "but" every time he mentioned God's love. He even did it after I pointed it out to him. "Oh, I'm sorry. God loves you unconditionally (pause), but you see, that doesn't mean Christianity is a free ride." His answer conformed with a little survey I've done over the years when I talk to ex-gays. They put a "but" after God's love every time. A lot of Christians do it, and I'll bet it's consistent with the religiously abusive lingo.

For the record, unconditional love has no "but." It's unconditional, for Christ's sake. This is a lovely example of insidious denial: ex-gays and a lot of Christians can profess acceptance and take it back within the time it takes to say three or four words. Furthermore, it seems almost impossible for them to see it. Even one of their most popular catch phrases says it in so many words: "Love the sinner, but hate the sin." I ask you, how do any of us hate our behavior and at the same time manage to love ourselves unconditionally?

As I began to embrace love without conditions, I began to see more and more holes in "ex-gay theology." Whether you believe in God or not, something that needs to be driven home (and that the Christian community needs to hear) is that ex-gay dogma is not congruent with most Christian doctrine and especially not with the teachings of Jesus. It became clearer and clearer to me: the idea that my behavior could gain God's acceptance is contrary to what most Christians believe about salvation and the unconditional love of God. Most Evangelicals believe that it is not what we do or even who we are that puts us in "right standing" with God, but the sacrificing of Jesus' own life that opened a completely free and accessible avenue of relationship with God. Therefore I already had God's unconditional love. I couldn't do anything and I didn't need to do anything to earn God's grace and love. In terms of Christianity, I already had full acceptance because of what Jesus did about 2000 years ago. It had already happened. This is just how unconditional God's love is.

> *I can't, for the life of me, imagine that God would say, "I will punish you because you are black; you should have been white. I will punish you because you are a woman; you should have been a man. I punish you because you are homosexual; you should have been heterosexual." I can't for the life of me believe that is how God sees this.*
> — *Archbishop Desmond Tutu,*
> *Nobel Peace Prize Laureate* [2]

The Bible states that "nothing can separate us from the love of God."[3] This was one verse that stuck with me all those years. Even though the ex-gay propaganda upstaged this idea considerably, when the dust settled, when it came down to just God and me, this message of love endured. I don't write this to proselytize. I really want to make the point that the ex-gay movement, when examined theologically, runs contrary to Christianity. And, as has already been pointed out, it is synonymous with religious abuse. Oddly enough, I already knew it was unnecessary to earn God's love; yet, my attempts at becoming straight evolved into just that. No wonder it felt like I was banging my head against the wall: I already had what I was desperately trying to get. I just couldn't believe it. What is worse is that I was made to feel unacceptable by the very leaders that were to be spreading the good news of Christ's unending love. This is how damaging religious abuse can get.

I constantly battled feelings of worthlessness, self-hatred, and guilt.
The doctrine of God's unconditional love was useless to repair the
damage done by the doctrine of homosexual sin.
— *David Christie, Ex-gay Survivor.* [4]

Christians are to exemplify the unconditional love of Jesus. Yet ex-gay promoters are in basic conflict with this love because their premise is that God only finds a very specific kind of sexual attraction and love acceptable. I was once in their shoes, too. I believed that God loved me unconditionally even before I was conceived, "but" that didn't stop me from nearly destroying myself, attempting to win God's approval. That's denial for you. Christianity, myself, and even the greater homophobic society at the time — we were the ones requiring more. We were the ones who couldn't accept my sexuality as it was. As I allowed unconditional love to gradually seep into my consciousness, I began to realize that somewhere inside I knew all along that God's love was different. It was unconditional. I can't remember how I knew, I just knew. God's acceptance was always there down deep inside — deeper than any other root could burrow.

I always believed God was love — pure love, and I still believe it even though my perception and understanding of God have changed drastically over the years. These changes do not negate what I once believed about spirituality. God — the one who spoke with my deepest inner voice since infancy — that God has been with me all along. Even if my perception of God might radically change in the future, the God of love that I have already encountered is still probably the most consistent love I have ever experienced.

God's Love Became the Example

For some, using God as an example of unconditional love brings back too many painful memories of religious abuse. In my recovery process, however, the best example of complete acceptance was this pure form of love. If God's unconditional love endured all I had been through, I wanted to learn from that example and find a way to accept myself in the same way. It was not a familial love: "Well, you're kin so we have to accept you." It was not a needy love, either: "That poor sap is whining for me to save his ass again." It was a recognition that I am lovable and worthy to give and receive love just the way I am.

I remember saying to myself many a time, "Look, Jallen, if God Almighty can love you unconditionally, then you can cut yourself some slack, as well." And I really didn't mean it in an ass-backwards, self-deprecating sort of way. This was an enormous step toward the positive and away from the religiously-sanctioned, abusive years of emotionally beating myself up from attempting — and failing — to be "perfect" in God's eyes by denying my sexuality.

This kind of love often didn't make logical sense to me; yet there were times I truly experienced it. Accepting the "nonsense" of God's unconditional love meant that I could treat myself lovingly even when I didn't feel that I deserved it. What wonderful nonsense! Freedom and joy came from accepting the fact that I would probably never understand love and self-acceptance completely. I didn't have to entirely comprehend it. Love was to be experienced. So I let my mind think it was nonsense, and at the same time I embraced myself unconditionally. If God could give me grace without logic, I wanted to follow that example. Regardless of what I wanted to change, or how I was born, or what childhood experiences I had, or what the Church said, or the kinds of parents I had, right in the moment I could experience unconditional love. There were no strings attached, and I didn't have to understand it. I could just receive it.

The leap of faith it took to believe in God's unconditional love was the same leap of faith it took to believe in my lovability. Yes, this opened me to the possibility of being fed more bullshit from misguided and manipulative spiritual leaders. Is this kind of leap risky? You bet. Yet this time it was distinctly different. I was not the passive victim constantly suppressing myself and taking others' word for what was true. I was not depending on the leadership to be God's love. This was a direct connection between the purest form of love and myself — no go-betweens. I followed the example, I took the risk and trusted myself, and I was not disappointed.

In my journey to love more fully, one thing I have learned is that there certainly is no lack of opportunity to put love into practice. The performance-based patterns that were often the guiding principles of religious abuse were hard to put down. Even in writing this book, going through my journals, and listening to old music, I caught myself being hard on the person I once was, as if my stern feelings in the present would somehow change history. It was so hard for me to give the Jallen of the past unconditional love. It was another opportunity to love that kid who was striving so hard to gain God's approval, especially when he had done the best that he could at the time.

In the last two chapters I reviewed my process of surmounting the most challenging of all steps in my recovery process — learning to accept myself unconditionally. I explained how the "Jesus-first, me-last" approach distorted and sidetracked my young development of individuality and responsibility. I pretty much hid in a hole, like my ferret, from all the noise coming at me. To help me recover I acknowledged denial, using therapy as a mirror to look at myself as clearly as possible. Taking a good look at myself a few times a month helped me to quit lying, and to live without secrets. Building on these steps, I was able to get a sense of my authentic self, stay in touch with it, and let it naturally be reflected in my outer persona. I used God's love as a metaphor to heal my individuality as an adult. Learning to be the loving and courageous protector of my authentic self has filled in the missing pieces of my personality, and I feel stronger and happier than ever before.

CHAPTER 7

Taking My Spirituality Personally in Every Way

My Spiritual Journey

There's nothing wrong with a fifth grade understanding of the Bible, as long as you're in the fifth grade.

— *The Rev. Dr. Laurence C. Keene,*
Disciples of Christ Minister [1]

A COLLEGE BUDDY of mine called out of the blue and wanted to take me to lunch. In the five or six years since we had graduated, he had married, had a couple of kids, and become a music minister at a Pentecostal Church. I suspected why he suddenly called me — he had read my newsletter in which I announced that I was gay. He showed up for our scheduled lunch, and we walked over to a greasy spoon that was known for its breakfasts but turned out to be really bad for lunch. I knew where the conversation would go, and I knew that it would do nothing to bring us closer together — probably the opposite. Still, he was a friend and he was buying, so I gave him the time.

We ordered from the menu and started catching up with each other. As our meals got worse, the conversation got more tense. By the time I put down my shoe-leather burger with one bite out of it, he was trying to keep his voice down: "It's plainly in the Bible what God thinks about homosexuality." If I had a good burger every time I heard that, I'd have died from high cholesterol by now.

Scripture

During my coming-out process I spent a lot of time going over the different debates regarding what the Bible says or does not say about homosexuality. I looked closely at the "clobber passages," (the four or five spots in the Bible that the ex-gay movement and conservative groups believe speak against homosexuality). There is plenty of solid exegesis about these scriptures that explains it much better than I can (see the Bibliography for relevant books and articles), but since it was important for my recovery I want to list here in a nutshell what I found.

The sin of the people in Sodom and Gomorrah,[2] popularly suggested to have been homosexuality, resulted in God utterly destroying their cities. Yet the Bible doesn't state specifically what the sin was. In fact, in a couple of casual references to the cities' demise, it says that their downfall was inhospitality.[3] They were so inhospitable that the men would come out in force and gang rape strangers that came to town — hence the homoerotic overtones. Yet this is a far cry from God condemning all homosexuals, especially when plenty of perfectly straight military men of the day would sodomize the captains of a losing army as a means to further humiliate the fallen. That's not gay, that's rape.

The verses in the Levitical law that say, "Thou shalt not lie with another man...; it is an abomination"[4] are couched within a whole slew of laws that even the most zealous Jew rarely obeys. Christians break most of the laws without a thought. Why? Because the laws are not relevant to their relationship with God. I have no problem with that. Evangelicals seem to have no problem violating dozens of them. Yet they are emphatic that gays and lesbians should obey this one law in order to be acceptable to God.

As far as the first two chapters of Romans go, the author seems to be describing a well-known gentile cult at the time that would go to sexual extremes to appease their gods. In addition, the passage states that these people turned their backs on God and purposefully choose activities that worshipped self-indulgent images. That did not describe any of the homosexuals I knew. To this day, I know thousands of gays and lesbians who have not turned their backs on God. Furthermore, what rarely gets mentioned is that in the very next verses (chapter 2) it plainly says, "Whoever judges these people, they will be judged." The whole point of the passage is not to judge others. Yet what are fundamentalist Christians, by and large, doing? Casting judgment: "Homosexuals are not worthy of inclusion."

The couple of references in Paul's letters[5] give lists of who's not going to enter the Kingdom of God. The couple of words that are now interpreted as "homosexuals" have had numerous translations over the centuries. There is almost no other use of the two words in the original language, so it's next to impossible to get a real idea of what they meant. In fact, one of the words was not interpreted as "homosexual" until the early part of the 20th century.[6] Furthermore, when these passages were originally penned, neither Greek nor Hebrew even had a word in their written language (as far as we know) for a person who is exclusively attracted to the same gender.

When I did my homework on these passages, taking into consideration the time, the culture, and their belief system, it was clear that the possibility of ongoing, loving homosexual relationships was beyond their understanding. In all of the teachings of Jesus, not one word is uttered about the subject. It would be like their society comprehending the possibility that someday people's lives would be saved by transplanting a lung from one body to another. However, just because they couldn't yet understand it or imagine it, that doesn't make it wrong.

One of the most profound ways my world has expanded in my adult life (and the moon has followed me around less and less) was by giving me a better understanding of the past. It is said that if we don't learn from the past we are doomed to repeat its mistakes. People had vastly different lives 2,000 years ago. We know a lot more now about the goodness of sexuality beyond the purpose of procreating. It seems to me that God is capable of taking this into consideration. I certainly don't think that God stopped talking when the last period was put at the end of the Bible.

I was stunned to find that five little passages in the Bible were the sum total of evidence against homosexuals. It was not my sense that God was holding these few, vague little verses over the heads of gay people and saying, "No, no, no, I'm not gonna let you in." Over time, as this sank in, I became so disillusioned by all the wasted energy, all the money and time devoted to changing homosexuals, when there's barely any Biblical evidence to support it. Compare that to the enormous portions of the Bible that address compassion, generosity, justice, and inclusion. If only today's mega-ministries with their millions of dollars and resources would spend as much on embracing the outcast as they do on judging the LGBT community.

Different Interpretations, and That's Okay!

The lunch conversation with my friend ended as many others had — our interpretations of the Bible were different. Dare I say, he had more of a beef with me than my hamburger bun did. Every time he raised his finger to make another point, I had to maintain my composure and simply reiterate that we interpreted the Bible differently. Same as it ever was, amen. I could rest on that point, unfettered until he was blue in the face, if that's what was called for.

Let me state this as plainly as possible: If someone ever says to you, "You're not interpreting the Bible correctly," they are actually saying, "You are not interpreting the Bible the way I want you to interpret the Bible." Let these statements serve as a big red flashing warning light of religious abuse. I've even conversed with people who have had the audacity to respond with, "It's not my interpretation. It's God's interpretation!" Here's what I believe: every time a Christian says something really stupid, an angel falls over laughing. After every statement like, "It's God's interpretation," there must be a whole flock of angels laughing their asses off.

But I realized one important thing from that lunch conversation. Every person interprets the Bible for her/himself. It's unavoidable. Each one of us views the Bible and actually the whole world through our own set of lenses. We can view the same sunset and each of us has a different experience. This is not a negative thing. On the contrary, it's positively amazing! I think most Christians believe God made us this way, and it's a good thing. As a matter of fact, if I were to take other people's word for what the Bible says, I could hardly call that a personal relationship with God. I began to realize that personally interpreting the Bible and a "personal relationships with God" go hand-in-hand. After all, what was the very first feature that was outlined about religious abuse? A group takes the word of their leader as the voice of God, rather than finding out for themselves what God and the Bible mean to them.

Even by Evangelicals' own standards, if God has made every one of us unique, and if God wants to be intimately involved with each of us, why then should we believe God has the identical (one could say, cookie-cutter) relationship with everyone? That doesn't sound all that personal to me. And if each of our relationships is intimate and special, why would we think that everything in the Bible should apply to each and everyone of us identically?

I began to realize that most Christians already accept that we live with different views on the Bible to one degree or another. Don't get me wrong; I'm not suggesting that Christians should be flippant and careless with their beliefs. Rather, I think most Christians have a desire to try and understand, as best they can, the origins and teachings of their religion. Yet, at the same time, there are hundreds of different denominations that believe slightly different versions of the Bible. So what? Does it really matter in the end? Do Christians believe that God has withdrawn his love because we don't all agree (perhaps some do)?

On the contrary, a Christian's connection to God is through Christ and nothing else. The Bible also suggests that the way you know a person's genuine motives is not by their religious knowledge, or their upholding the letter of the law, or how right their theology is. No. "You shall know them by their fruits." (The double meaning is ingenious!) And I have seen way too many "Christians" treating the outcasts of society not with love and inclusion, but with disdain and exclusion.

Looking through the lens of religious abuse, I now can see that some of the most vocal arguments about insisting on right theology were essentially religious leaders insisting on conformity. In other words, they insisted that everyone should believe their way. For example, if someone had the courage to challenge the leadership's interpretation of Scripture, I would often hear them say, "If we compromise one verse in the Bible, then that opens the door to compromise anything it says."

Why? Is the Bible some kind of house of cards? Is God so fragile that one little change brings the heavens a-tumblin' down? There are stories in the Bible where people changed God's mind and stories when God struck deals with people. Furthermore, even the most fundamentalist Christians don't follow everything in the Bible. How many parents do you know who stone their kids for being rebellious? Yet that's what the Bible says to do.[7] Further, these "compromises" don't keep the very same Christians from firmly (and literally I might add) believing the rest of it. What's the big deal? Probably, I am just not interpreting the Bible the way they would, and their hyper-conformity constitutes religious abuse.

Another popular tactic by ex-gay leadership was the "Satan is deceiving you" scare, which often came on the heels of an "if you don't see Scripture like I see Scripture" statement. Believe me, this held a lot of people in check, including myself. It undermined our self-esteem, our intuition, and our sense of self-confidence. It kept me in a constant state of fear and distrust. It created further dependency on the leadership as the voice of God. Now I can look back and see how abusive it was.

I have spent literally years struggling just as hard, if not harder, than most to understand the mind of God on the subject of homosexuality. After all, God has told us if we seek then we will find. If I'm going to have any amount of faith and trust that God has my best interest in mind, does it really make much sense that after busting my butt seeking God's heart I could be so dreadfully duped by the devil? Why would God have me do all this work in drawing close to the Spirit and at the same time allow me to slip off to hell in a hand basket without even knowing it? Does that sound like God's way of doing things? "Seek ye first God's reign on earth with all your heart and God will allow Satan to completely trick you for all the days of your life"? To quote some fundamentalists, "There's absolutely no scripture to back that up."

Bible Worship

Biblical literalists are people who know the truth absolutely, so they are not able to engage in a conversation. They are only able to engage in a pronouncement. Biblical literalism, far from being a classic Christian approach, is in fact very modern. It belongs in the early part of the twentieth century. So we had almost two thousand years without Biblical literalism. It's a modern invention.

— *The Right Rev. Richard Holloway,*
Bishop of Edinburgh (Ret.) [8]

As time went by, I became more and more aware of the fact that many a conservative church was using the Bible and the name of Jesus like a weapon to drive people, especially gays and lesbians, away from the loving arms of God. My guess is, basing a relationship with God on faith and love is just too vague for literalists. Possibly, they latch onto the next best thing — something tangible to grab onto — certain words in the Bible — and build everything on that. I wrote the following song to convey some of my thoughts about literalism:

Lover, lover far in a distant land
You will tell me you love me as much as you can
So you take to the paper and write me a letter
One that you'll send right away
So you send me a letter that says that you love me
For that's all that you wanted to say
> *You can see me getting the letter by mail*
> *And the pleasure a letter like that can entail*
> *So I sit in bay windows with sun streaming in them*
> *So excited as the letter begins*
> *I read the letter that says that you love me*
> *I read it again and again*
But our love is too strong. You can't take the distance
So you choose to come live with me
You sacrifice all. You sell all you own
You leave your home town so together we'll be
> *Now you sit beside me. Now you can look in my eyes*
> *Now you can love me for all time*
> *But I sit in bay windows with sun streaming in them*
> *I push you away and I quote*
> *I'm reading the letter that says that you love me*
> *For that's all that I wanted to know*
I'm worshiping the letter that says that you love me
For that's all that I wanted to know
I'm worshiping the Bible that says that you love me
For that's all that I wanted to know[9]

Indeed, I believe that some of the religious abuse today is simply a result of Bible worship. It is all too easy to create conformity within the religiously abuse environment, because "all we have to do is follow the rule book." I can't tell you how many religious leaders I have heard say those very words. Isn't that the 11th commandment? However, I can follow everything the Bible says to do and it still does not mean I have a relationship with God. We can learn a lot from what is in the Bible. We can slap on it whatever label of inerrancy we like, but that does not change the preeminent factor that if we make Christianity out to be anything else than God's unconditional love, we are missing the point.

"Breaking Up" with God

My point and the purpose of this chapter in the light of recovery is that I had to take some time to figure out for myself what I really believed about spirituality. Not just in a manner reactionary to my past: "They believed that, so I'm gonna believe this." That's just like the mental voices in the stadium analogy. If I had not decided what I believed ahead of time, my lunchtime friend could have given me a lot more indigestion than that sorry burger. I'm not saying that you have to be a theologian to recover from the damaging effects of religious abuse, but I am saying my healing process was definitely helped by taking considerable time to decide what I really believed spiritually, whether it ended up being some form of Christianity or not. This was the path that I took to heal my soul and recover from the wounds inflicted by religious abuse on a spiritual level.

I know there was a lot of "God talk" in the last chapter, and now this chapter is about sorting through my spirituality. Be aware, this step in recovery is not some sneaky way to get you back in good graces with the "God of your childhood." This is not some manipulative trick to soften a "hard heart" so that the prodigal will come home. But it crossed your mind, didn't it? I'm glad it did. Evaluating what I believed as a chapter topic set warning alarms off in my head, too. Rest assured, you may get to the end of this chapter and realize you don't believe in anything spiritually, and that would be okay in my book, so to speak. You have to determine what your self-directed recovery is to look like. But since we are looking back into the past to better understand what happened, it's important to look at our beliefs — past and present.

Much of my own spiritual evolution was centered around my perception of, and relationship with, God. I outlined in the previous chapter how God's unconditional love became a template for me to accept myself. If you're still cringing at the very thought of reading this chapter further, let me suggest an analogy that I think will lend further understanding as to why I'm proceeding down this path.

My first primary relationship ended after three years. I did the "breaking up" and I probably did not do the best job at it. Stuart stopped talking to me.

He had every right to manage his part of the relationship any way he saw fit, but this made it difficult for both of us to create closure, in my opinion. I had never experienced trying to wrap things up with someone who was a closed door in nearly every way. I felt unresolved and incomplete. It felt like there was someone in the world that I had not been able to make peace with, and that was unsettling for me. After a couple of years of respecting his silence, I heard that his immune system was shutting down due to HIV, and he died before we could establish any further communication. Stuart was someone I deeply loved and after his death I had to deal with creating closure for myself in regards to our connection. I don't think there was anything else I could have done to smooth things over with Stuart, but I wish there had been more opportunity to say thank you and goodbye.

When it came to my recovery, sometimes the best I could do to create closure was simply to stop whatever it was I was doing. After all, if I really wanted to stop playing games, I had to give up the possibility of winning and simply walk away. Sometimes that's closure enough and that's as much closure as I was going to get. Some of my religious experiences were so damaging that when I left, or when I felt forced out, my spiritual strings were untied and left blowing in the wind. I think some of those undone strings were so raw — like tattered nerves — that they were painfully triggered whenever the slightest breeze stimulated them. The memories and pain were so real that the smallest reminder could stop me in my tracks, paralyze me, and I would feel unresolved all over again.

Maybe you can't go back to many of those circumstances to create better closure. People and circumstances have irreversibly changed. But I would suggest that a spiritual life is not so. You can alter your perception of God to be the kind of being who is very willing to create closure. You may not even believe in God's existence anymore. But you once did, and it obviously was a significant part of your life if you went to the trouble of going to an ex-gay group. So I would suggest an experiment. During the rest of this chapter on spirituality, consider suspending your belief or disbelief about God, and simply imagine that God is the lover who, after a time of silence, has returned, desiring to create better closure with you. I know that all you might remember are words of hate, pain, and feelings of betrayal. God's listening ear could be the very thing you need for closure. Despite the emotions you may need to get out, I have found some real personal value in doing my best to leave a loved one on good terms, even if it's some kind of simple ritual that allows me the opportunity to say goodbye, such as, "God, I think our connection is at an end, and I don't want to leave this relationship hating you."

The "Healthy Parent" Model

Here's a vision of God I recorded in my journal from my college years:

*In the distance and through a white haze are two huge doors. When
I get closer, the air clears and the doors slowly open outward with such
strength that the air seems to rush inwards, drawing me in too. Inside
is a huge palace of shining gold and all that is elegant. I lightly walk
down the large hall that is lined with giant pillars on either side. The
room is warm as a womb.*

*At the opposite end of the room is an enormous throne, and who sits
on it? None other than Jesus Christ. He is the classic image of the Savi-
or, and he is bigger than life. He is dressed in a robe, with a broad smile
beaming through his beard. He is glad to see me. There is no doubt now
that this temple is my heart. At about the center of the room, I kneel
down with my face to the floor and my hands outstretched. I worship
God with all my strength, mind and heart. But soon Jesus stops me and
says: "I am so very pleased with your worship, but you don't have to do
it at such a distance. Come closer."*

*I am scared and shocked to think He would want me closer to him,
but I do not pass up the moment. I walk to the steps and climb them like
a baby crawls up stairs. At His feet I bow but my eye catches His movement. "No," He says, "not there." His strong arms open up to welcome me
into His lap. My breath is lost in the overwhelming acceptance, and my
fear just drains away. For an instant, I am frozen, but His arms remain
steadfast. I scramble up His knee and sit amongst His frame. My heart
might as well stop, for I am completely sustained by our connection.
I spread my arms across His chest and hug what I can reach. His large
arms close around me. I feel as if I have become one with His presence.
I hear the words: "This is the kind of worship I desire from you."*

Although kind of corny, it still is a beautiful image of how God was like a
parent to me. During that period, I needed to know God was there for me,
and loved me — not just at a distance, but as tangible as pair of big strong
arms. This was amazingly reassuring because of the distinct possibility that
my parents would eventually push me away because of my sexuality. There
was no doubt that God accepted me, no matter what. Something that has
always stuck with me, and I find is suggested in the Bible, is that everything

around us is a reflection of God — parents included.[10] But I perceived God as the model of a perfect parent. God was The Parent to me. Over time, as I meditated on what an ideal parent meant to me, my understanding of God changed.

I asked myself, "What is the role of the perfect parent?" A parent is a protector and nurturer for a child that cannot fend for itself, and cannot survive on its own. Initially, it can't even feed itself. The parent is the child's lifeline. Here is where most people end the analogy of God as a parent. Worship services are filled with people begging and pleading for God to protect them and nurture them (which, by the way, is not worship). With the fervency of hungry and neglected infants, people raise their cries to God: "I need. Please help. Rescue me. I can't live without you." Literally millions of people have functioned in this kind of relationship with God for generations. To be sure, we all need a little help upon occasion, and there's nothing wrong with asking for what we want.

However, as important as the Nurturing Parent is, there is another aspect of parenting that is just as important. I write of the healthy parent as a Mentor, Instructor, and Liberator. I'm not referring to setting the captives free. A parent's ultimate goal for having and raising children is that the children will someday step out on their own. This model does not have every detail of the child's life planned out. What kind of parent would God be if she were like a doting mother, with every little moment of the child's life planned down to the minute? Kids are going to grow up whether a parent likes it or not. The question is, will the parent teach and encourage them to survive and even flourish in the world on their own? Eventually, the goal of a parent must be to let go of their creation. There are many instances in this over-populated world where I see parents treating their kids with neglect and abuse. I shudder, thinking, "What were these parents thinking when they decided (or didn't decide at all) to have children?" But God, the Master Parent, has in mind the goal of responsible freedom for us from the start.

God's unconditional love provided the safety for me to learn to stand, walk, become strong, gain a wise sense of the world, and eventually The Parent let me run right out the door. Comparing this model to how the majority of church culture functions today, I see a movement of huddled, adult children refusing to leave their parent's home, and it amounts to religious abuse. Instead of joining the world out there, they beckon the world to "come inside our house." God's house, while it can be a positive refuge, has become the flop house of spoilt trust-fund kiddies who refuse to leave or grow up. I have been to churches which, quite literally, have built entire malls around their sanctuaries, including fast-food restaurants. Sure, they feel very safe within the environment they have created, but as God's children, we weren't raised to hide, conform and live for safety. No wonder I look at some of these "Houses of God" and can't figure out what game they are playing. I don't see God in their eyes, much less love. It seems they see God only as an Answer Parent, who is pestered by three-year-olds with questions that will not quit: "What's this? Why's that? When's this? Who's that? Why? Why? Why?" I imagine God gets to a point of saying, "I'm sick and tired of you kids (some of whom are many years into their adult lives). All you do is ask me for this and ask me for that. I gave you a brain. Use it. Jeez, you can't brush you teeth without nagging me for permission to do so. I taught you better than that. You just won't use what I've given to get out there and live your life. So you keep the house. I'm retiring to somewhere I can get some peace and quiet!"

Stepping down from my soapbox, and back to my journey, I began to see that God, as an ideal parent, was not equipping me to simply beg for crumbs of mercy at God's feet or even in God's lap. God was not bestowing all these great gifts only for me to be constantly asking for permission, "Um, God I took a step out of the house, is that your will? Um, God, I smiled at a stranger today. Was there a way I should have smiled better?" Sheesh! I finally got the point. God's spiritual boot was firmly on my butt to get out the door and live my life abundantly. God wasn't going to do it for me.

I found that as time passed, I risked going farther and farther out that door (hmmm... could this be what faith is?). Funny thing is, I got the sense that the less I kept asking for God's approval on every little thing, the more opportunity it gave The Parent to say how well I was doing and how proud God was of me. It was as if my unnecessary begging for things I already had in abundance, never gave anyone, much less God, a chance to get a word in edgewise. That was an amazing switch that often led to tearful realizations of a deeper sense of unconditional love and gratefulness. I had The Parent who thought the world of me. I could get out there and take risks on life and bare my soul with my gifts in whatever I did. If I fell on my face, which I did a number of times with the grace of an ostrich, I could return to my God for healing, a pep talk, and a hug from those big strong arms. But the more I got out there and gave from my heart, the more my Parent would sit back, beaming with pride, and say, "That's m' boy!" All those years I was trying to win God's approval, and God kept thinking, "Jallen is performing so hard to win my approval, he can't hear my voice telling him he's already got it!"

Co-creator

The model of God as the ideal parent evolved even further. I have watched children imitate their parents — for better or worse. These kids would do anything to walk in their parents' footsteps, and their faces show the deep satisfaction when they are given that opportunity. Let's say a child comes home from school with a finger painting. The child takes the masterpiece and shows the parents. Now the parents may not notice the artistic potential, and the parents may overlook the hand technique or the color pallet. Yet the parents are overjoyed at what the child has created. They take the painting and display it on the house art gallery — the refrigerator door. They all stand shoulder-to-shoulder, admiring the finger painting.

Likewise, I began to notice a kind of fulfillment when I was in my creative groove, composing or performing a song. I felt like God. Don't press that blasphemy button yet. Hear me out. I was learning another model of the nature of God as a creator — The Creator. I might even say, God wrote The Book on it — silly joke, I know. What this means is that when I am creative, I am imitating God. I am doing what God does. Tell me, what could be more fulfilling?

Even one of the creation stories has God asking Adam to exercise this creativity as Task Number One.[11] God parades all the animals before Adam to see what he would name them. Not only did God challenge Adam's creativity, but the story indicates that God was genuinely interested in what Adam called each creature. I always imagined some crazy American Idol-like audition line where God would bring a creature into a well-lit spot, saying, "And this one…?" Adam would sit on a rock, tapping his chin and squinting his eyes until, "Platypus!" God would hoot a big, "Woohoo!" and give Adam a high five. "How about this one…?" After a while Adam would just try to get God laughing: "I'll call it a superciliaried hemispingus!" And both of them giggled so hard they rolled around on the ground with tears running down their faces.

This kind of relationship is so often overlooked. We usually approach others on a face-to-face level. We talk to people, and they talk to us. However, there is another approach to relationship in which we relate to others shoulder-to-shoulder, doing something together. It was a great feeling to be creative like God. And I learned so much about God when I was being creative.

Beyond Comprehension

I began to find it almost entertaining when many Christian leaders spoke as if God was in their pocket. How many times did I hear Christian extremists say, "God told me he's coming back on such-and-such a day"? I was baffled at how many people take a brief stroll around Scripture, make some interpretation, and then say, "God's promised me something and God's gotta come through on all his promises." Why? Even if God did make you a promise, God can do whatever the hell God wants. Tell me, if God should decide to keep this promise and break that promise, who's going to stop God? Are you? Is Satan? God is God, and God answers to no one, Goddamn it! Who did these people think they were when they presumed that God had to come through for them? Furthermore, who did these people think they were dictating what my relationship or others' relationships to the Divine should or should not look like? Oh, that's right, I wasn't interpreting the Bible the way they were, and it was all religious abuse.

To be honest, I still feared that the more I loosened my grip on who I thought God needed to be, the more God would slip away from me, but the exact opposite happened. The more I relaxed my grip, the bigger God got — to the extent that I could see God's reflection in more models and examples than I could ever comprehend. The freedom that came with not having to comprehend all of it was exciting and euphoric. I'll never forget the day I really understood that God was just as wonderfully feminine as masculine — as well as neither and everything in between. The realization was so freeing that a song erupted out of me in just about one sitting.

I see God like a frantic young painter who finds time to paint everyday.
Over and over he paints self-portraits. He paints them in you and me.
More than this. That's not all. I forget God is God.
  I see God like a manly shepherd who guides his flocks by green plains.
  Even though the flock's his livelihood, he knows each one by name.
  How dare I describe God with pictures like this?
  Whatever I think of is less than what God is.
  So I see God like an Egyptian queen, who rules as far as you can see.
  Dressed in robes of righteousness, she rules with justice and peace.
  More than this. That's not all. I forget God is God!
I see God like a motherly swan that glides across the lake on the waves.
Drowning her chicks she teaches them to swim. She guards them under her wing.
How dare I describe God with pictures like this?
Whatever I think of is less than what God is.
I see God like a splashing dolphin who swims next to me in the waves.
Always keeping an eye on me. Its language is a mystery.
More than this. That's not all. I forget God is God!
  I see God in the face of a parent, in the face of a eunuch and child.
  God's spirit will dance and prance through nature.
  I see God in your eyes.
  More than this. That's not all. Don't forget God is God! [12]

Fear and Decision-Making

Over time, I ventured farther into creative experiences which, in turn, made me feel more courageous to explore, yet at the same time stronger in my connection to God. However, there was still my longstanding fear that somewhere out there "well away from God" was a place that would be too far. I describe this as a location, but it was more like a state of mind. I think it was a morph of the fear that Satan could still deceive me. Certainly there had to be limits to God's patience. There had to be something I would do, some point of no return that would make me lose all grounding in God — such is the nature of fear. I find that a lot of Christian motivation to "seek God's will" is really about a chilling fear of being out of God's will. That doesn't sound like a connection based on love. In some ways, I knew these were outdated messages from old belief systems, but like mildew in cracks it seemed impossible to get rid of all of it.

Make no mistake, this was a real fear, and it mainly held me back in making decisions. In therapy, I was well aware of a longstanding problem with making any kind of decision. Why? For fear I would make the wrong choice. I was so afraid to make the wrong choice that I would often rather have reality make it for me, something that reality would always do if I waited long enough. One could call this fate, but to be more clear, I'll use an example. Let's say my ex-gay friends invited me to a Charismatic Retreat Weekend where everyone attending would get away, get filled with the spirit and get further "straight." I could tell it wasn't for me, but I didn't want to hurt their feelings or have them to think I wasn't a good Christian. Therefore, instead of just saying no, I delayed. Putting the decision off was convenient because it meant I could avoid responsibility for making the decision, "Oh, too bad. The car is full and there's no room for me to get a ride." I have no choice then. Reality made the decisions for me.

I could almost have fooled myself that this was a great way to go through life, if it hadn't been for two things. First, unfortunately, although reality might have forced my hand, I was still the one who had to live with the consequences. Dang it all, I still had to take responsibility for where my life progressed. Second, and worse, I still lived in fear. Having reality force me into my next phase in life did nothing to elevate the deep-set fear that I could be going down the wrong path. In fact, often my decision avoidance would increase my fear because suddenly I was forced down a path that could have just as well been worse for me rather than better. Like painting myself into a corner, I no longer had a choice. And I truly did not know how to rid myself of this fear-based problem.

I believe that there are times in a person's life that can be described as conversions, but I think I see them more broadly than the specific "born again" experience, although certainly many of us have had that kind of valid conversion. I think these experiences can happen on purpose and by accident. I think we can walk right into conversions with eyes wide open. I think these times of transformation can also happen to us, as if something from outside of us moves us to a new place in our maturity. I suppose it's where we get the phrase, "turning over a new leaf," but I think this emergence, if you will, is not just an attempt. It's more decisive. It is a point of no return — the ending of one thing and the start of another. Often these conversions are stressful and do not make sense at the time. Only in hindsight can we see the pure genius of these "spiritual" experiences, and they border on nothing less than miraculous. Such was the way out of my fear of making the wrong decisions.

It was a period that lasted about three or four months in which I just felt out of whack. Something wasn't quite right, but I could not define it. I'd go to therapy and often cry. I felt that there was this weight on me that needed lifting, but I couldn't name any particular burden or stress. I finally surrendered to whatever was taking place in me (possibly an important step to take when nothing else seems to work, but that's another chapter). In some kind of spiritual dialogue with God, I said, "Alright already. I don't understand what's going on. I'm taking care of myself. I don't feel ashamed or that I'm avoiding something. So God, whatever is going on, I'm in your hands. If there's something I should be doing to remedy this, just let me know. I am at a loss." In that act of letting go, I trusted God just a little bit more. Within a few days, the dark cloud lifted. Almost immediately I realized what had lifted with it — fear. Whatever fear had been growing in the cracks was washed away by that transformation. To this day, I truly do not know how it happened in those few months of angst. All I know is that when it was over, every bit of fear regarding God and my spiritual walk was gone. I guess it was time for it to go. That period of transformative "darkness" somehow removed the fear from my emotions and from my body.

Radical Faeries

With this fear removed, I began to take steps toward a particular community I had been curious about for a long time: Radical Faeries. I had a growing desire to encounter my spirituality, not just as a mental exercise or religious tradition but more in my body and in the world around me. I sensed that Radical Faeries could help me in this process. Furthermore, feeling that I had gleaned all I could from traditional church, I longed for a kind of community that understood the value of ritual and, at the same time, celebrated diversity and authenticity. Would these folks understand that? Would these Faeries accept me with my religious background?

For some time, I had seen a specific kind of art around town. It was a combination of photography and computer-manipulated art, but this artist, whoever s/he was, truly took the computer to the next level as an artistic tool. It had a queer, psychedelic, counter-culture, back-to-nature, cosmic look to it and I (as well as many others) gravitated toward it. Little did I know that the artist was someone I had seen around town for years. Once aware of each other, Stevee Postman and I became close friends. Not only did his art give me insight into Faeries, but Stevee, a Faerie himself, became mentor and hand-holder for me as I explored their world.

Becoming visible around the 1970's, Radical Faeries can be briefly described as queer hippies, receiving their name originally from the gay activist and father of all Faeries, Harry Hay. But their heritage goes deeper than a few decades. Faeries have taken their direction from gay mystics throughout history — from ancient pagan and Greek rituals involving homosexuals, to the two-spirit medicine men of native America. Faeries weave their spirituality with the threads of many diverse sources. That said, I know some Faeries refuse any definition. Some see their role as the constant contradictor. One of my favorite definitions is, "If you think you're a Faerie, then you're a Faerie!" They enjoy communing closely with the natural world and, from their fashion sense to the names they choose to call themselves, they are some of the most creative people I have ever encountered.

I remember my first gathering with them at a retreat center in northern California. I was still singing full-time and transitioning from conservative churches to gay-positive venues. I was a little nervous because I heard some of them describing me as a Christian, and I wondered what that would mean to them. Would they reject me? Was there a place for me in this environment, although I was in serious doubt of calling myself a Christian anymore? Toward the end of the gathering one friend approached me and said, "You know, I heard you were a Christian, and I was uncomfortable about it at first. But now that I've gotten to know you, I think you're all right." His statement brought me great joy — perhaps the kind of joy a Christian is proud to feel.

I had an amazing experience at that first gathering, and it sparked a whole new depth of spiritual growth for me. At the time, Stevee had begun work on designing an entire tarot deck using images of Faeries to depict the different cards and their meanings. This was no small feat, since there are 72 cards in the deck. I was deeply honored to be one of the first batch of models photographed for his deck. He placed me on the card that is traditionally titled "The Last Battle." Sound strange? I wondered what it meant, too. No, I wasn't the anti-Christ ushering in the reign of Satan. The Last Battle symbolizes none other than the final decisive moment before going in another direction. It is the definitive decision to change. The point of no return. Stevee renamed this card — the one in which I am pictured with huge, blossoming, blue butterfly wings — "Emergence." I look at that card and its image as a glorious depiction of my spiritual experience at the time when my persona left the cocoon of fear. I spread my wings to venture into all that was to come.

Over the years, the Faeries have become an integral part of my extended family. There are still aspects of certain rituals that rub me the wrong way. And you know what? They don't care. They accept and enjoy whatever ways I feel like participating and contributing. How refreshing, compared to the religious community I grew up with and the ever-present fear of falling out of the line of conformity. With the Faeries I have witnessed true healings, spiritual visions, ecstatic dancing, meditative communions with nature, worship and respect of the One(s) beyond our comprehension. This is my kind of church. They are part of my family, and this is where I authentically experience God. I mentioned that it is a tradition to choose a Faerie name to identify oneself. In honor of that keen little ferret in my vision, I chose the name Weasel, reclaiming it as a positive title.

> *...I suspect that for me the way is like the weasel's: open to time and death painlessly, noticing everything, remembering nothing, choosing the given with a fierce and pointed will... The thing is to stalk your calling in a certain skilled and supple way, to locate the most tender and loving spot and plug into that pulse. This is yielding, not fighting.*
> — *"Living like Weasels," from Annie Dillard's*
> ***Teaching a Stone to Talk***[13]

My Spiritual Geiger Counter:
A Lack of Fear and a Sense of Humor.

Just as a person may be a very careful driver after having a horrible traffic accident, I am now very sensitive to the experience of fear. The emergence from fear has made me highly aware of when it is used manipulatively. I believe that God is love and there is no fear in it. In fact, I bank on that. The presence and/or absence of fear is a kind of spiritual Geiger counter for me, and this tool has been very helpful in my recovery process. When I make decisions, when I hear ministers lead their congregations with sermons, or when I watch politicians work in office, I ask myself, "Am I experiencing a significant level of fear as a result?" or, "Are these people using fear to manipulate others?" I see this fear in so many ex-gay groups today. They seem to be riddled with defensiveness, strategic justifications and mistrust. There seems to be an overall dodginess because, I assume, they can't risk trusting even themselves. It's as if this fear overshadows any real joy, any lighthearted happiness, and any hearty sense of humor.

That's been another really healthy and healing element to my spiritual journey: finding a sense of humor in all of it. I've known a number of theologians who include a sense of humor about religion on their list of indicators of healthy spirituality. You have to admit that some of our religious cultural experiences are pretty knee-slapping funny. And laughing sure is better than crying about it.

Humor helps me most by keeping me from taking myself too seriously, and let me tell you, I grew up in a church that took itself way too seriously. The way this seriousness got translated was in terms of an obsessive need for purpose. Everything had to have a reason, and if I couldn't find a reason, I would create one because I was so afraid that I was "out of God's will" or "wasting God's time." Everything had to be done to the glory of God because people were "dying and going to hell," so we couldn't waste any time having fun. Even fun had to have a bigger spiritual purpose.

I saw this obsessive purposefulness in Christian music, when every word had to have a deeper meaning. It was so important to be able to hear every word because I had to figure out the message. I remember that I could bet my life on this set of lyrics from a song on the radio: "Carry a laser down the road that I must travel." What a creatively modern use of a metaphor to explain bringing light to the world. Wow! Did I feel silly when I learned the words were actually, "Kyrie eleison down the road that I must travel" (Kyrie eleison being Greek for "Lord have mercy"). Just how spiritual was I in missing those godly words? I still cringe in embarrassment, and friends still laugh at my blind, or should I say deaf, assuredness. "Carry a laser..."?

That's what humor is for: laughing at ourselves. While working on this book, I dug out a lot of old christian music to help me recall and reflect on my experiences. Some of the lyrics are so trite. Some of the messages are severely guilt-ridden in a happy-pappy praise-Jesus pop sort of way. There are times it sends chills up my spine and the hair on my neck dances. Mostly, I have found myself typing away on the computer, giggling and grinning at all the memories. I can enjoy the music and the nostalgic sounds while the guilt-ridden messages have little effect on me. There are so many experiences in the Christian and ex-gay world that I can look back on and cringe, "What was I thinking?" But I can also look back at those same experiences and forgive myself, knowing that I was doing the best I could at the time. Furthermore, I can have a really good laugh about it: "What was I thinking? Indeed!" Laughing at days gone by helps me also see all the good and fun I had, and see that I have indeed made progress.

What My Spirituality Is Like These Days

The theologizing may be getting out of hand, but this has been my spiritual journey. To move forward with my life, I had to make spirituality my own or it wouldn't be authentic. I knew, for sure, that faking it was not spiritual. It was just lying. So to be authentic, I think it's important to tell you where I spiritually am now, although I suppose it will gradually change in the years to come.

As you know, my parents raised me in the Southern Baptist church. They used the Bible, religious tradition, and the incarnation of Jesus Christ to give me what they felt was the best understanding, purpose and relationship to spirituality. This environment, even though limiting in some ways, was great for laying a spiritual groundwork. At a young age I gained a respect and context for things truthful, loving and spiritual. My parents' and my church's tendency to cling to strict traditions and rules ultimately worked against them, generating in me a passion for creativity, diversity and freedom for expressing my truth.

I still hold to many of the morals and beliefs of the God/person, Jesus Christ. When asked if I am a Christian, I am hard pressed to say yes, because what a Christian is today is in so many ways a far cry from who Christ was thousands of years ago. However, I have no problem responding, "I believe in the teachings of Jesus Christ."

My definition of spirituality is the awareness of the "Mysterious Something More." It is an awareness of everything we encounter that defies explanation, or that seems to exist beyond our five senses. It is that which gives us a sense of awe, and that which tells us there is something more. It is observing aspects of nature — a sunset, the ocean, birth and death — and perceiving that something more than just biology and physics is occurring. It is scientifically knowing how the body works, yet being unable to explain how we develop emotions, creativity, a soul and, well, our spirits.

Since spirituality is a mystery, I am naturally, if not tenaciously, curious to comprehend and interact with it. Ironically, my best guide to the "great unknown" is that which is known — the truth. For example, when a light dashes across the night sky, I might think it's a UFO or an angel. But if I find out that it was an airplane (or just the moon over my shoulder), the truth has informed the unknown. If I choose to still believe that the light was anything other than a plane, I am not being spiritual, I am simply deceiving myself. I write this not to reduce spirituality to a fact-finding mission, but to simply say that I try to keep my spirituality and the truth inseparable. In addition, my spirituality is not a cold task of explaining everything away, but a comfortableness with the unknown, an acceptance of my place in the grand scheme of things. Religion — the attempt to standardize an understanding of spirituality — has its challenges since we are all so different. Yet, there seems to be no limit to "The Mystery" or the truth. In other words, the more I know, the more I realize how little I know. This keeps me humble, at least in my heart.

I want to believe I have some kind of interaction/relationship with The Great Unknown, and therefore I tend to imagine it having an identity. This I resolve to call, for lack of a better term, God. However, God is certainly not limited by my comprehension, and certainly not limited to one set of religious beliefs or standards. Just as I try to keep "The Unknown" and the truth paired, I try to balance my spiritual life with my daily, practical life. For example, as I was growing up I would do many things because I would some day "receive my reward in heaven." Now, truth be told, I don't know if there is such a place as heaven. I hope there is some kind of afterlife. However, I don't view God like a karmic banker who, because of what I do today, owes me big time with interest in heaven. My spiritual journey is so personally valued that even if there is no afterlife, my connection to God has been worth it all. I love others not because it will give me a bigger mansion on God's golden Main Street; having the ability, the gifts and opportunity to love others and to genuinely be loved is reward enough. What a daily adventure, enjoyment and challenge it is to find God in all aspects of life. I see the world full of both mystery and truth, and I am curious — like a kid in a candy store — to be in relationship with the wonder of it all.

I am happy to report that there are now a number of large denominations that have nothing to do with ex-gay groups. These churches strive to affirm the health, responsibility, and well-being of each person's relationship to God. Although it has not been my path, don't forget that these churches could very well be an opportunity for great healing. I know a number of ex-gay and religious abuse survivors whose recovery has been truly supported by these groups. As my good friend Dirk has reminded me, it is amazing to "open my heart to experience genuine acceptance and affirmation found in a healthy, open, questioning, ambiguity-embracing Christian Church." Thank God they are out there and they are growing in number.

Do I take my spirituality personally in every way? In a healthy sense — yes! I'll take full responsibility for my end of a relationship with God. I think after all this time of sincere searching, I have become so familiar with my spiritual connection that it has truly become a part of me — communion at its best — and what others think of me ultimately makes no difference. They can judge and attack me any way they like, but they are not responsible for my spiritual life. I can listen to their criticism, legitimately consider it, and continue life accordingly. This is my relationship with God, and I will never let the fundamentalist church or theology put it at risk again. Their walk with God is theirs, and in their own words, "I alone will answer to God in terms of how I live my life." I view modern-day Pharisees with a sense of humor. After all that I've been through, it's hard to view them any other way. My response to them (as if I even need to respond) is to teach them, as best I can, how I would like to be treated — with respect and as unconditionally as I can muster.

As ex-gay and religious-abuse survivors we were duped not by God, not by Satan, but by religious leadership who abused their power to conform a relationship with God to what they thought it should be. And either I was too young or too scared of utter rejection to know better. Well, I know better now. I'll bet you do, too. Although painful memories can still come up, I hope you grasp that whatever shape your spirituality takes, it is yours to discover, explore and enjoy. From my perspective, I would hope your spirituality grows and changes just like a deeply sincere relationship. I hope it is nurtured with love like a perfect Parent who sits on the edge of a seat — proudly chomping at the bit — excited to see what you will do next.

CHAPTER 8

Our Obsessively Negative View of Sexuality

The Source of Much of the Problem

IN ADOLESCENCE, I STRUGGLED TO UNDERSTAND the hormones raging through my body. I figured out how to masturbate, and I somehow got the message that it was a sin. This brought enormous inner turmoil between what felt good in my body and what I believed I should not do. I had learned in church and history class that people used to get married just entering their teens. I wondered, if I was having all these horny thoughts and yet our society had people marrying much later, then was our society out of sync with the way God made us? If I couldn't have sex until marriage, where was the sin in naturally enjoying what God had given to me? Time and again I would try to stop masturbating. In fact, in some of my earliest journals I had a code — a mark I would make on the calendar to tell myself when I last masturbated — I would see how long I could go. Of course, that was a game without a winner because it would only remind me of when I failed.

I heard (yet another) sermon about making commitments, and getting serious with God. The speaker suggested this: when making a promise, drive a stake into the ground so that every time you see that stake it will be a physical reminder of your commitment. So I fashioned a wooden stake from a leftover wood scrap in my dad's workshop. I went into the oak forest that lined the river next to our house. When I was growing up, this forest was a natural wonderland I spent my time playing in. I felt like a cross between Tom Sawyer and Peter Pan, swimming in the river and climbing the trees with nothing but cut-offs and sneakers on. In the Sacramento Valley, people like me were called "river rats." I took the stake to a particular spot — one so secluded that I had masturbated there on a number of occasions. This time, I drove the stake in the ground and said, "No more!" I don't know how long I abstained, or if it even helped. I do know I stopped going to that spot in the woods, because the only thing that stake made me feel was ashamed.

Our Sexual History

It wasn't until after college, when I joined Evangelicals Concerned, that I felt comfortable enough to ask tough questions about the church and sexuality. Not only did E.C. open my mind to various interpretations of the Bible; it also provided me the tools to integrate my sexuality and spirituality. Much of what I will present in this chapter had its beginnings in the safe place E.C. provided me. To be more specific, a particularly beautiful man and scholar, Jack Pantaleo, opened my mind and gently guided me through my integration process. He will be quoted often.

To view a fuller picture of how healthy sexuality and spirituality work together, I had to assess how and where I got all these primarily confusing and negative ideas about sexuality. To do this, the scholars in E.C. pointed me down the historical path. Would you believe that sex and the church have had a long and tumultuous relationship? This in itself gave me a clue as to where society got a lot of its negative messages. Indeed, as Jack would say, "The church and sex make very strange bedfellows." And after studying this history, I can add my two cents: "That is an enormous understatement!" The church's understanding of sexuality throughout history has not been helpful in establishing a sense of healthy sexuality.

Sure enough, one of the most outspoken critics of sex was in fact the Christian Church. I did not do this research to simply blast the Church about all the bad things it has done in the past. I really was looking to understand how we got our ideas and ethics about sex. Since most of them can not be found in the Bible, how did we get them? To be sure, whole libraries have been written on this topic of church and sex. I am going to cite just few high points, or should I say low points?

Augustine

Augustine can be primarily credited with bringing body-phobic beliefs into Christianity from another religion (Manicheanism) around 400 A.D. Jesus was a body-positive guy who gladly broke the law to give a loving and healing touch (we'll look at this later). Unfortunately, Augustine believed that anything perceived by the five senses was evil — especially sex. He became what I call the first Bible thumper, because he banged his book louder than anyone. At least he banged his version of the Bible. Truly, Augustine was the most popular theologian for a thousand years. That's like one pope's influence times 20. As a result, what he believed gradually became church doctrine and filtered into the secular law of the western world.

The term "original sin" was, in many ways, Augustine's brainchild. His take on the story of Adam and Eve's fall from Eden was all about sex. Augustine developed the belief that Adam and Eve having sex was the sin that got them thrown out of Eden, and every time anyone has intercourse we pass that "original sin" on to every generation.[1] Are there any scriptures that substantiate this theory? Not one verse. Yet Augustine was the right man at the right time to negatively influence all that came after him.

Thanks to Augustine's influence, as well as many others', even intercourse between husband and wife was believed to be a necessary evil for only the purpose of procreation — and even then, it was to be done without passion and was severely restricted. For example, sexual intercourse was forbidden by some church leaders for three days after the wedding, during a woman's menstrual period, during her pregnancy, and for several weeks after childbirth. Further, some church codes also forbid intercourse on: Thursdays, in memory of Christ's arrest; Fridays, in memory of his death; Saturdays, in honor of the Virgin Mary; Sundays, in honor of the Resurrection; and Mondays, in commemoration of the departed. Even Tuesdays and Wednesdays were partially restricted by a ban on intercourse during feasts and festivals.[2] I quote the humor of Jack Pantaleo: "With such severe restrictions, times when intercourse was permissible could only be figured out by a mathematician. Most other men visited prostitutes."

Oh, yes, the Church's view that sex between husband and wife for only the purpose of procreation was an easy rule to follow because prostitution was viewed as the lesser of two necessary evils. Thomas Aquinas, one of the many followers of Augustine's teachings, compared prostitution to a sewer: "Take away the sewer, and you will fill the palace with pollution. Take away prostitutes from the world, and you fill it with sodomy."[3] At the time, the word sodomy was used for a wider range of sexual activities than it is today. But wait — it gets even crazier. In the years between 1100 and 1550, there was actually a church brothel in Avignon, France, where "the girls spent part of their time in prayer and religious duties and the rest of the time servicing customers. Christians only. No Jews or heathens were permitted to cross the threshold."[4]

Keep in mind, these are our ancestors. Furthermore, most of our founding fathers came to the New World to practice their own brand of religion, often ultraconservative, away from the evil, godless Europeans. As comedian Robin Williams said, "How uptight do you have to be for the British to tell you to get in your little boats and go away?"[5] There's a reason they're called Puritans. It's not surprising that we still suffer from religiously tight asses — and I suppose this could be categorized as a disease of the body as well as the soul. These events in history may seem far removed from and inapplicable to today's standards, yet the underlying message is often the same as Augustine's: "The act of intercourse is fundamentally disgusting."

We can look back on many events in the church's history (this is truly only the tip of the iceberg) and wince at how far many Christian groups were from the loving gospel of Jesus, and how far they were from the truth, especially concerning sex. To some degree, they were doing their best to comprehend the world with severely limited information. Yet today, to those who stand by their "divinely inspired" sex ethics, I challenge you to consider that if the church could have really missed the mark back then, isn't possible that the church could be missing the mark regarding sexuality now? Is it really that far-fetched to suggest that we still have a lot to learn about sexuality and spirituality? But wait, as if the previous events hadn't made it hard enough, sadly there's more...

Victorian Health Gurus

Ever heard some of these: Don't play with your willy or you'll go blind, or you'll get hairy palms, or you'll have ten years of bad luck, or you'll go to hell. We joke about silly sayings like these, but it wasn't too far in our past that ideas like these were published as facts — really. Believe it or not, many of America's sexual misunderstandings come from physicians and health writers within the past 250 years. They promoted their sex ethics by "substantiating" them with so-called scientific proof. Many of these physicians described sexual pleasure as "disgusting" and taught that it did grave harm to the body. Where have I heard that before? Could it be Augustine? Many 19th-century doctors believed that intercourse was acceptable only if it was done without passion or emotion. For example, it was believed that birth defects were caused by parents deriving too much pleasure from the sex act. The defects were said to be visible signs of the parents' shame.[6]

Dr. Benjamin Rush, one of the signers of the Declaration of Independence, was "the dominant medical figure in America at the end of the eighteenth century." He taught that careless indulgence in sex would lead to (among other things): seminal weakness, impotence, tabes dorsalis (degeneration of sensory neurons), pulmonary consumptions, dyspepsia, dimness of sight, vertigo, epilepsy, loss of memory, and death.[7]

In the early 1800's the leading expert on human sexuality was man named Sylvester Graham, who believed that highly-seasoned food and rich dishes caused sexual desire. Therefore, he prescribed a diet that would cut down sexual desire. One such food was unbolted wheat, which got to be identified with a restrained diet and called Graham flour.[8] Now I know the real reason I as a boy was fed Graham crackers in Sunday school!

But Graham was not the only one to jump on the bland wagon. Dr. John Harvey Kellogg invented corn flakes to control the sexual appetite of Americans, and to "cure original sin by reducing the force of sexual passion."[9] Kellogg founded and directed the Battle Creek Sanitarium in Michigan where he developed a theory which was widely accepted as fact — he was an expert, after all. His theory was that masturbation led to insanity. How did he determine this? He noticed that his inpatients masturbated, so of course that must have been what drove them mad.[10] With this "scientific method" he discerned other sickening side effects from masturbating: "It also caused sleeplessness, failure of mental capacity, unnatural boldness, mock piety, lack of breast development... in females, use of tobacco, pimples, biting of fingernails, epileptic fits, bed-wetting, and the use of obscene words and phrases."[11] Son of a bitch! That's where I get it!

You have to wonder if these "expert" influences are still evident on the food industry today (their names still grace every single one of their products), just think of how much negative influence they have had, and still have, on our understanding of sexuality. If the common Christian could see that these beliefs about sexuality in our very own ancestries were "ass-backwards," is it beyond the realm of comprehension that maybe some of our sexual views — fueled by our fears — could be somewhat off the mark today? Are Christians so righteous in their sexual stance that they are incapable of mistakes?

The Sanctity of The Family

"Modern churchmen sometimes speak of 'the family' as if it were a Christian invention, but their predecessors were more inclined to blame it on the devil."[12] It's true. With Augustine and other early church leaders believing that any kind of sex was sinful — even for procreation — it's not surprising that marriage was a kind of concession for the "weaker" man to get by (women were not considered back then). Certainly any man who aspired to do the church's work was not to marry at all, since it was only seen as a fleshly distraction. This view that sex and marriage are beneath a spiritual leader has been the church's stance for the majority of the past 2,000 years, and it still is the standard in some denominations. They may not shun it now. It may be acceptable for "commoners" (lay people) to marry. But the sex-negative message is unavoidable: sexuality really isn't a part of a true man of God.

Furthermore, the arrangement of the "nuclear" family as it is now — father, mother, and 2.5 kids, living under the same roof, with the primary glue being mutual love and commitment — has only been in existence for about the past 150 years. This is a generous estimation. Before that, women were valued mainly as the child-bearers for the purpose of continuing the male lineage, and providing, quite literally, working hands to help in the family business. A woman unable to bear a child was grounds for annulment of the marriage, whether or not the problem might have been sterility on the husband's part. Furthermore, children have acquired legal rights in the past 80 or so years. Before that, parents could treat them any way they liked. Marriages were not sought as an expression of love or commitment, though I'm sure it happened. Marriage was a way to stabilize the family's future and financial security. Therefore, parents arranged their children's marriages much like contracting a mutually-beneficial transaction between two businesses.

This was also why polygamy was perfectly natural in some eras and even in some religions, such as Mormonism. The more wives a man had, the more children he would have, and the more stable was his future and the future of his descendants. It is these historical variations and adjustments to the structure of the family and marriage that make contemporary fundamentalists' claims that today's arrangement is the only valid, God-approved kind of family, severely shortsighted, if not just silly.

With history like this, how has today's familial model been raised to such God-like status? I believe one element in achieving this is the idealization of romantic love. It is what our society believes "makes the world go around." We hear it in our music, in our movies, on TV, in our writing, our commercials, our churches, and our relationships. In our society, what higher goal is there than finding "the right one?" Indeed, as the larger society has gradually continued to evolve in its understanding of relationships and connections, the only way the conservative Church gets away with enforcing aspects like chastity until marriage, is by raising the idea of the family unit to a God-ordained standard. It has been so closely equated with God that it's not unusual to hear ministers put "the family" on a higher pedestal than the Church itself. And what drives every one of these connections into existence? Not financial gain, not future security (I'm sure many Christians would say God), but the giving and receiving of romantic love.

Mind you, I've got nothing against romantic love or the family. In fact, I seek them out in my life, as well, but what is the church doing promoting it so zealously? To be sure, romantic love and unconditional love are similar. Most of us would probably hope that romantic love can develop into unconditional love. But the two are not identical, and if the conservative church has not gone wrong in so closely relating the family unit (as they see it) with God, it has gone severely wrong in elevating romantic and familial love to a higher place than unconditional love. Isn't that a violation of their first commandment, "Thou shalt have no other Gods before me"?[13] At the very least, it is once again a distortion and abuse of Christ's message.

Of course we see this hierarchy in the debate about gay marriage. The conservatives' restricted version of the family is far more important to them than embracing the outcast. After all the money, energy and unfounded hysteria that many churches have put into attempting to keep marriage the way they want it (between one man and one woman), is there ever a peep about compassion, justice, or equality under the law? Is it any wonder that thousands of people have been disillusioned when so much of the church has clearly lost its original message of Jesus' love?

Ultimately, I fear that the mainstream conservative church's idolatry of the family will only further its demise. Putting the family and romantic love on such a pedestal hurts even their own. In many congregations, adults who do not have that special someone, are corralled into the "singles ministry," which is nothing more than a way to do match-making for Jesus. To some degree, I find nothing wrong with that. People want to meet a potential partner who has the same beliefs. But what about all the people who don't find a spouse? What about all the single parents? What did Jesus say about taking care of the orphans and widows? How can a person feel whole and healed when they are always made to feel that they are not yet complete, simply because they are single?

What about the people who do not fit comfortably into one gender or the other? How does it feel to sit in a service week after week with the pastor preaching, defending, and glorifying romantic and familial love, and know that all of this does not include you because your genitals or your identity doesn't fit neatly into male or female? What about the Bible story of the eunuch who is honored as the very first convert to Christianity, assisted by Philip? [14] (A eunuch was someone who had their genitalia removed, usually in service to their king — talk about dedication.) Yet, how welcome would the very first Christian feel in such a family-worshipped church? It is simply a disgrace to the unconditional love of Jesus.

Sure, there are occasions when religious leaders tag onto the end of their accolades of married life, "Of course, it's God's plan that not all of us are meant to get married." Wow! Doesn't that make a single person feel just great? Doesn't that make a divorced woman feel good about having to move herself and the children safely away from the abusive husband? Seldom is consideration given to all the people who do not fit into that very specific mold, because our cultural aspiration of romance and having a family is believed to be pretty much inerrant. Once again, the church has traded the unconditional love and inclusive teachings of Jesus for an exclusive false god whose names are romance and family. I'm sure this harsh criticism would be denounced by many a fundamentalist as "blasphemy!" Blasphemy of what: God, or romance?

Capitalism

One more time I have to address this element that, in addition to its effect on self-esteem as discussed previously, contributes to the state of our sexual affairs. America's negative obsession with sex is fairly unique in the whole of the contemporary world. Yes, there are other countries that have been indoctrinated by our missionaries. There are cultures that take their lead from American consumerism, fashion and pop culture. But all of this is a pale reflection of what has become the juggernaut of popular American consumer society. Despite the historical negative perspective I have highlighted, sex is exploited as a tool for advertising products with overwhelming success. This is no longer surprising. Advertisers will use literally anything to sell a product. Why not sex? However, I am mostly concerned that the subtle sex-negative messages get ingrained in our brains even when we are rarely conscious of it.

Take, for example, a simple commercial for soap. It sets up a 30-second scenario about a guy using a particular brand of soap, and as a result, women are very attracted to him. On the surface it seems harmless, and it might even be clever. Nothing out of the ordinary, right? What happens when we go through our day and literally everywhere we see advertising saying, "Buy this and you will be liked. Buy this and you will be sexy. Buy and you will achieve everything you've ever wanted." What's not obvious is that these advertisements constantly imply that you are not acceptable the way you are. You have to buy this product, look a certain way, drive a spiffy car (and the list goes on and on) to be liked, popular, and acceptable. To get you to buy their product, they have to create the message that you are incomplete unless you use their product. Multiply that by hundreds and potentially thousands of advertising opportunities through any given day, and what else could we possibly feel than utterly "less than"?

It is all false. Even if we could "buy into" everything that is being told to us (people certainly try), would we reach real happiness? Even if we could buy what was being waved in front of our faces, would we achieve sexy popularity? Sadly, no. If only it were that easy.

What we are left with is an insidious insatiability. We don't even know what we want; we just know that we got to have "something" in order to feel better. It is truly the messages that "bigger is better," and "I need more to feel better." Sexuality does not escape this discontent. All too often our sexual satisfaction is dependent on someone or something or a set of circumstances outside of ourselves. So what is the culmination of all the aforementioned sex-negativity with this general sense of unfulfilled consumerism? You get more of the same — lots more of the same. You get obsessively negative sexuality.

Our Sexual Cookie Jar

It seems that by the time puberty sets in, our "knobs" are pre-set and locked in for sex-negative obsessiveness. It can be seen everywhere in our society. Just about every expletive is a sexual term, from mother-fucker to cock-sucker. Sexual and bodily slang usually has negative and violent connotations — bonking, spanking the monkey, the penetrator, she's got teeth down there, and on and on and on. The entertainment world portrays sex predominantly in risky and violent situations. What's the second most popular activity in a Mad Slasher film? Sex. When sexuality is brought up informatively, like on the news or in the classroom, the subject is almost drowned out with words like "disease," "addiction," "harassment," "don't ask," and "don't tell." The smallest hint of a sexual scandal makes headlines, and it can send a nation into hypocritical hysteria.

Maybe sex-negative obsessiveness started out as a trickle, but it has long since flooded our understanding to the point that almost every aspect of sexuality is drowned in fear, shame and greed. We hear these messages from all sides — the media, the church, the government, schools, friends, family, and from our own voices. I use a simple exercise in my teaching in which I have a class shout out any and every sex-negative message they have been taught or heard or believed. The voices start slowly, and as they begin to catch on, we could literally spend hours making this list. I always have to cut it off after about 15 to 20 minutes, or it just gets too depressing. Think it's not that bad? Then read some of the results that have been listed time and again in these brainstorming sessions (I've taken the liberty of categorizing them, although plenty of them overlap):

- SEXUAL SELF-ESTEEM (or lack thereof): I'm too small. I'm too big. I don't look like a supermodel or a buff athlete. Everyone else is normal except me. If you are a woman you really don't derive pleasure from sex like men do. The body is something shameful and therefore should always be hidden. I'm not good enough because… I'm not a sexy enough because… (fill in the blank).

- BEHAVIORAL MESSAGES: I'd better be good in bed or I'm a failure. If I get in a sexual situation, I won't be able to perform adequately. Sex has always got to be hot, hot, hot! If I don't please my partner, I am a failure. I should have an orgasm every time. It's not sex unless there's penetration. Anything other than the (heterosexual) missionary position is perverted. I can just wait until my wedding night to understand my sexuality, and everything will be fine. I'm not going to carry a condom with me because I'm not going to have sex. Gay people have shorter life spans because of their promiscuous lifestyles.

- LABELS (Sex is…or the word "sex" can be replaced with "masturbation" is…): dirty, nasty, sinful, risky, disease-ridden, evil, scary, abusive, disgusting, harmful, slutty, gross, perverted, deviant, godless, carnal, deceptive, destructive, violating, cheap, anything but love, (or, to the other extreme) always true love, of the devil, equals death, and so on.

- MORALIZING: You "should" wait until you're (heterosexually) married to have sex. In some circles the opposite: after a certain age, something is wrong with you if you have not yet had sex. All homosexuals are child molesters. Monogamous relationships are the best relationships. Open relationships will eventually fall apart. Sexual intercourse is only for the purpose of procreation. LGBT people are not a real minority. If you are single, something is wrong with you. Leaders should set an example by not being sexual. My partner should meet all of my sexual needs.

- EDUCATIONAL: If children are taught "the facts of life" too early, they will be sexually scarred. Don't touch yourself down there. If you teach people about condoms, they will only have sex more often. Abstinence is the only safe sex. Sex is a private matter and therefore should not be talked about.

- RELIGIOUS: Sexual sins are worse than most other sins, and homosexuality is the worst of all. Homosexuals will get what's coming to them, like Sodom and Gomorrah. God can't bless you if you're gay. You will go to hell if you're gay. You will destroy the beautiful person God is making you to be if you have sex outside of marriage. The only God-ordained sex is between a man and a woman in holy matrimony. It was Adam and Eve, not Adam and Steve. Furthermore, the reason Adam and Eve were thrown out of the garden is because they had sex. If you "spill your seed" you'll end up in hell. If LGBT people raise children, the children will be scarred for life. If you divorce, you are forever incomplete. LGBT people are corrosive to the family. LGBT people will bring the collapse of American civilization. Being gay is not God's "perfect will" for your life.

Interestingly, it seems that the more sex is cast in an "evil" shade, the more intriguing it becomes. It feels good to be bad. Could our negative views about sexuality only serve to make us more obsessive about it? Of course. Are negativity and obsessiveness all that diametric? Not to me. I recall the day I realized I was more focused on homosexuality after I joined the ex-gay ministry than before. I resisted my natural attractions so ferociously that all I could think about was gay sexuality. (This aligns with the behavior of denial and projection mentioned in chapter 4.) Sex-negative obsessiveness has been a societal attitude that allows the ex-gay environment to thrive. It is reflected in religious abuse as well. The ex-gay movement is reflecting our greater society's fear of and obsession with sexuality in general.

This negatively obsessive phenomenon is what I've termed "The Sexual Cookie Jar Syndrome." It seemed that an all-American suburban analogy was appropriate. Imagine, if you will, sex as a fresh-baked batch of cookies that, oh, let's say Mrs. Brady has placed in a cookie jar on top of the refrigerator. Looking down her wagging finger with a smile she says, "Don't you have any of these cookies until after your dinner." But how can we resist? We can't escape the aroma. We're hungry as it is. So, against the "rules," with deception and risk, we stuff our faces with stolen cookies. Of course, they taste even better because they were as forbidden as the fruit in Eden, but we also have a growing awareness of something in the pit of our stomachs besides cookies —guilt.

This metaphor reflects our society's approach to sexuality on many levels. To begin with, sex is established as a reward. Good straight people that marry get sex as a prize. It also reinforces our sexual naiveté, because "Mommy" simplistically hands out sex for dessert. She sets the parameters without any opportunity for us to learn healthy eating habits, or take responsibility for our actions. We're "helpless victims" at authority's mercy, even if we're adults. Furthermore, the metaphor reflects the potential for increasing paranoia. Since we've "cheated," we don't "deserve" to get any now, or after dinner, so we have to keep our behavior a secret. This metaphor reflects the potential of increased obsessiveness. If we're found out, we're sure to not get any more, so now is the time we had better eat more…and more, and more. Mixing negativity with a pleasurable experience becomes a vicious cycle because we naturally want more pleasure, but we also get more negativity in the bargain.

Binary Thinking in the Extreme

Sex-negative obsessiveness seems to enhance and affirm binary decision making. Theologically, this can be called Dualism, and I want to emphasize how it can limit our ability to make informed decisions. You probably noticed that several of the messages listed earlier were opposite extremes. Some people believe that sex is just a physical act that can be done without love, while other people think it should only be the greatest expression of love. Binary thinking would enforce that it is one or the other, but not both, and certainly this dichotomous thinking would never consider the possibility that there could be a myriad of options as to how sex and love interact.

Sure, a few decisions in life may only have two choices, but most of our decision-making is severely inhibited by assuming there are only two opposite and extreme answers. What little our culture teaches us about decision-making doesn't help either. We are a society that praises the squeaky wheel. Whoever and whatever is the most outrageous clip of the week is what the media focuses on, the subtle message being, "Extreme obsessiveness is applauded, while a moderate consideration of a diversity of understandings does not boost ratings."

The inhibitions of binary thinking can be seen in other aspects of our society. Read this next word and see where your mind goes: bathhouses. Yes, a certain percentage of bathhouses in the world are exclusively devoted to sexual activity (notice how easy it is to assume this sentence is a negative statement). However, there are a great number of bathhouses that cater to the "family crowd." For centuries, the bathhouse has been an important, social aspect of a number of cultures and communities, especially where hot water is not readily available to every household. Still today many societies take the whole family for a relaxing time in the warm waters, playing in the pools together and lounging in the steam rooms. Often the bathhouses are subdivided into men's and women's areas, but not all of them, and most of them do not require a stitch of clothing. But in America, this kind of bathhouse is all but gone. Where does our mind go when we think of bathhouse? A beeline right to sex. The message that is being implied is this: Nudity, bodily pleasure and comfortableness in one's own skin always leads to sex.

Binary thinking is a tactic used by religious abusers and the ex-gay movement. You're either with the program or you're against it. You're either bad or good, right or wrong, black or white, holy or evil, sexual or spiritual, heavenly or hellish, gay or straight, male or female. The list could go on, but never will it account for all the wild, rainbow diversity of our universe. When LGBT people stand up for equality under the law when it comes to marriage, what does the Religious Right say every time? "Next thing you know, they're gonna be wanting to marry animals!" They dive right for the extreme with negative hysteria. As I pointed out in the spirituality chapter, what do fundamentalists say when we consider possible interpretations to the Bible? "If you change one verse of the Bible then you might as well throw it all away!" What? How much more extreme can you get? Binary thinking does not help our understanding of sexuality, or the Bible, or the world, because in so many instances there are many more options than just two.

When it comes to sexuality — a beautiful example of humanity's diversity — it's a miracle that our culture gets beyond missionary position. Even gays and lesbians have trouble looking beyond the "opposite" labels of gay and straight. Yet the Kinsey Scale was not created with just two points, zero being straight and six being gay. It is a continuum with infinite orientation possibilities. You don't even have to choose a spot on the scale if you don't want to. This is why it is important to consider that some of the ex-gay "success stories" might be bisexuals. These people might truly have a wider gender selection of who they can feel deeply attracted to, because they are closer to the center of the continuum — attracted to both male and female. Yet this does not fit into the ex-gay binary way of thinking, since to them gay is sinful and straight is righteous. So when a bisexual man is able to bond intimately with a woman, the ex-gay world calls that a success, for he was once "gay" and now he's "straight."

Worst of all, when you have reduced your options to just two, it's almost impossible to avoid placing shame or negativity on the side that is deemed less acceptable. One has to win and the other has to lose. So does that mean young is good and old is bad? Or that white is better than black? Of course not! I was taught that the body and the spirit were at odds; therefore, I stigmatized one of them and glorified the other, when neither of them should have been treated in that manner. I tried to stay on the "good" side (the spiritual) until the "bad" side (the body) finally demanded my attention. It screamed, "Take care of me, pay attention to the body because it's sick," and I felt all the worse because I was forced to deal with my fleshly side, when it was actually trying to help me. I gave it just enough attention until it stopped pestering me, and then I ignored it again "for the glory of God."

Double Standards

This swinging back and forth, if taken to its negative obsessive extreme, opens the door to binge behavior and double standards. This is a natural outgrowth of being taught that we only had two options and, of course, one is bad and one is good. There are plenty of people who, while in the process of "coming out," live a prudish, celibate life and then swing to the other extreme, going on a sexual binge. Depending on the behavior, neither of these extremes is necessarily wrong; it's that these folks don't feel good about themselves in either position. Furthermore, degrees of sexual desire can ebb and flow over time, but if sex is only used as the release valve on the pressure-cooker of a sexually anorexic lifestyle, this pendulum behavior can go on for decades.

I lived two lives: By day, I was a mild-mannered seminarian. By night, I was a roaming animal, willing to do nearly anything to be satiated. the tension between these two lives eventually led me to emotional breakdown and despair
— *Ron Poindexter, Ex-gay Survivor* [15]

Back and forth: In the closet and back at church, out of the closet and at the clubs in West Hollywood. In the closet, attending revivals and leading worship, out of the closet and having an affair with a female co-worker. I was leading two separate lives and I was miserable.
—*Allyson (Hays) Snicker, Ex-gay Survivor.* [16]

Then there are those who swing so far into the extremes that they are a walking double-standard. How many hate-filled fundamentalist pastors and right-wing politicians who scream the evils of sexual "impropriety" (to put it mildly) have to get caught, quite literally with their pants down, before we realize that obsessive sex-negativity does no one any good? Their behavior is so desperate and risky — if not, at times, just plain stupid. It's as if they have left any sense of responsibility, not to mention their intelligence, on the pew of the church, and therefore they make destructive and foolish sexual mistakes that result in their demise. No one is benefiting from this kind of thinking or behavior. This is not wholeness; it is compartmentalization in the extreme.

What Can Be Done?

This juggernaut of obsessive negative sexuality often seems overwhelming. These sex-negative messages and patterns reinforce themselves and filter into all the different aspects of our sexuality. It's a heck of a lot of work to unlearn these long-held, limiting beliefs that no longer serve us, but unlearn them we must. It's about time we "toss our cookies" and retread our shame-filled patterns with positive, fact-based sexuality.

CHAPTER 9

Sexuality and Spirituality — Twins Hatched from the Same Egg

Solutions to the Problem

WE TEND TO HAVE SO MUCH negative "baggage" around our understanding of sexuality that we can't see clearly what it actually is. Once I had a pretty clear idea about all that I had been fed about sexuality, I set out to understand what it actually was. The following is what I learned.

It Is Not That Simple

We joke a lot about queer origins. "His mother was the man of the house so he turned out to be a fag." "She was a tomboy who played too much sports and now she's a big ol' dyke." "He listened to too much Barbra Streisand growing up." As for me, when I learned about Greek mythology I wanted to run around the backyard in nothing but a loin cloth made out of a hand towel. To this day I love the feel of a silky sarong.

With the lack of factual sex education in this country, there are still people who actually take these "cock-and-ball stories" quite literally and end up severely over-simplifying our sexual development. Furthermore, these oversimplifications fuel the reparative therapy movement which, as I have previously outlined, believes that if a gay man who had a passive or absent father is given a "proper" father figure later in life, this will significantly enable him to become straight. It sounds so logical, right? And it couldn't be farther from the truth.

Our sexual makeup is complicated to the degree that no one thoroughly knows how it develops. There are some pretty good hunches, though. The nature theory believes that our sexuality is mainly developed genetically before birth, and we're not talking about one minuscule gene that turns us gay; we're talking about millions of strands of genes that when pieced together on end and layered, somewhere in the first nine months of growing, somehow point our desires in a particular sexual direction. Wow! Does that sound simple? I don't think so. The idea of finding a single gene that makes us queer just ain't gonna happen.

The nurture theory believes that within the first four to seven years of life our experiences shape our sexual selves. This is the popular theory with reparative therapists, who think that if you just have the right "family values" everyone will grow up straight. It's strange, though, how often they ignore the tens of thousands of people who do grow up in the "picture-perfect family" and yet are gay and lesbian. I'll write it again, and you can read it out loud this time: "It's not that simple!"

Consider the classic example of the toddlers playing on the floor, eyes level to their mother's high-heeled shoes. A flexed calf and raised ankle eloquently balanced on a red leather-bound four-inch pump might be the first symbol of beauty and security for a rug rat. There are plenty of people who have this childhood memory and now get weak-kneed whenever a woman seemingly glides across a room in stilettos. Yet there are plenty of people who have the same memory and aren't necessarily aroused by pumps. They'd rather dress in them. There are still others who have the same memory and could care less about what a person puts on their feet. How can the identical experience not create the identical response? Because (all together now), it's not that simple.

Another common oversimplification is that of gender. Reparative therapists think that gender "should" always correspond with a particular sexual attraction, hence their softball games for male participants and makeovers for the female participants. Yet it is no secret that there are straight men who are great hair stylists, and female athletes that far surpass any man. What about the people who have the genitalia of both sexes, or the ones who have none at all? When we really take a look at the wide and wondrous diversity of humanity, we find gender as diverse as sexual preference, and the two do not always neatly line up. Sorry to be redundant, but it is not that simple, and enforcing a religious conformity only serves to increase shame and exclusion.

Sociologists John Gagnon and William Simon are known for introducing the concept of sexual scripting in their book, *Sexual Conduct*.[1] They propose that a person goes through life operating from an internal script which informs them how to behave. This script begins at conception and is constantly being written by everything that happens to us, everything that happens in the womb, everything we learn, experience and believe. Though we can comprehend patterns and pieces of it, one person's script is as complex and unique as their individuality, and pretty much incomprehensible in its totality. So our attractions may be started by nature and continued by nurture, and they are constantly adjusting and growing. There may be trends in our scripts that become outdated and therefore filtered out over time. There can be themes in our scripts that are so strong that we couldn't change them if we tried.

The debate of sexual origins all too often seems motivated by a desire to manipulate the outcome. For me, that hints at an agenda of unwillingness to deal with the present. As a sexologist, I'm not concerned with where our arousals come from as much as I am with wanting people to accept themselves and each other with love and mutual respect. And that includes responsibly managing and enjoying their "turn ons" as best they can. So even though understanding our sexual development is anything but simple, it is not a prerequisite for sexual pleasure. What a relief! If that were the case, the human race would have died out long before we had any fun at all.

What Is Sexuality?

I think it was beneficial in my recovery process to gain a better understanding of sexuality. What fascinates me about the "Cookie Jar Syndrome" is not how well it reflects our beliefs about sex, but how little it really has to do with authentic sexuality. Have you ever tried to answer for yourself the question, what is sex? It's not easy. In fact, it could be wagered that defining sexuality is just as mysterious as defining spirituality. The best way for me to define sex is to use a metaphoric approach to give us tangible examples of what sex is like.

One popular metaphor is that sex is a kind of commodity. To a degree, I believe this to be true. Why else would prostitution be referred to as the oldest profession? Regardless of what people morally believe about sex work, for centuries women and men have offered their sexual skills in exchange for capital. But sexual "property" is not limited to sex work: sexual predators also view their victim's sexuality as an object to be consumed. Oddly enough, today the "virgin-till-you're-married" movement treats sex like a commodity, as well, as if virginity is to be completely guarded and saved for that special person you will wed for life.

Yes, sex can be a gift you give someone special, but I think the commodity metaphor has significant weaknesses that promote misconceptions about sex. If it is a kind of internal commodity, like minutes on a sexual phone card, then all too often people tend to believe that it has a limit. Indeed, plenty of people believe that when they have sex with another, they give a part of themselves away without the possibility of ever getting it back. However, not everyone believes sexual energy is in limited supply. Sex writers Easton and Liszt make a distinction between tangible limits and ideas without limitations: "Time, for example, is a real-world limit; even the most dedicated slut has only twenty-four hours every day. Love is not a real-world limit: the mother of nine children can love each of them as much as the mother of an only child."[2] Although this is not referring to sexual love, it is a helpful example. Maybe all of this can be summed up with the idea that sex, like love, is more about quality than quantity.

For a long time, I have used a definition from my mentor, Jack Pantaleo: "Sex is the heart's deepest longing for authentic connection." Though it lacks a metaphor, what I like is that it allows sexuality to be present (just like intelligence or emotions) in a wide range of connections, without any agenda of having sex. I can give a friend a hug and look her in the eye. I can take time for myself by relaxing in a steam room. I might take the hand of someone who is in need of consolation. These are all examples of being physical, sensuous, even sexual with people I am connected to. Even though the degree to which I connect varies widely, the commonality is that I want all of them to be authentic, and our bodies are involved in the experience.

Sex is also defined as a form of communication. It definitely has a "give and take," just like verbal communication. It can be shared silently with one special person, or it can be shouted from the mountaintop and whoever wants to listen can benefit from the message. Further, viewing sex as communication means it's a skill that over time you can develop until you can speak in different languages. It's about what's being said and how effectively it is said, regardless of the time allotted. It's a communication that speaks more deeply than words. Sexual Linguistics 101, anyone? I have learned that I am indeed responsible for what I say, and I have learned the skill of choosing words wisely. Sex is not the phone card, but the conversation.

An aspect of sex that doesn't get enough recognition is that sex is adult play. Some may feel it is important to "put away childish ways," but my maturity has felt like "adding to" my childhood, rather than "trading in" my childhood for adulthood. There are very few ways in which our society allows adults to play — maybe through sports or the arts, but these are always justified by the need for physical exercise, healthy competition, or a serious need to express oneself. Yet sex is a unique activity during which adults (when procreation may not be the focus) can cut loose, get in there on all fours, and have crazy fun. That's really putting the "twist" in the game Twister. When sex is defined this way, that which we make so complicated seems rather simple and good.

These are the definitions that have been relevant to my sexuality. Sometimes it's a mix of all of the above. There are times that my sexuality is all about intimacy, trust and intensity. There are other times that it is all about play. I like having that kind of variety in my pleasure.

What Is Sexuality to You?

I'll be honest: when I wrote, "I find it beneficial to gain a better understanding of sexuality," I was not entirely forthright. Although that's important, I find it most beneficial for one to gain a better understanding of one's own sexuality. As with most aspects of life, sex can mean a lot of different things to different people. Just as I had to go through a process to discover what spirituality meant to me, I had to go through a process to embrace sexuality for myself. And if there's anything I learned from Sexology, it's what the father of all Sexology, Dr. Alfred Kinsey, discovered after interviewing literally thousands of people about their sexual experiences: we are all different, our sexuality included.[3]

Sexuality is one of those wonderful aspects of life that is completely yours to do with it as you see fit. My point is that nobody else is more responsible for your sexual satisfaction than you are. Sure, we are all severely influenced by the culture and pressures around us. There was a time I handed everything about sexuality over to ex-gay leadership and I was far from satisfied or content with it. There have been times I have left my sexuality in the hands of a spouse, and my sexual satisfaction was dependent on the ups and downs of his satisfaction. When I take responsibility for my own sexuality, I am guaranteed a far greater degree of satisfaction.

When I work with couples who want to improve their sex life, I often find that one partner's sexuality has become completely dependent on the other for satisfaction. Yet research has shown that the better a person knows and understands his/her own sexual pleasure, the easier it is to create sexual pleasure with a partner.[4] I tend to believe that if you don't approach sexuality on your own terms, you will not be completely satisfied. Don't let this sound like a chore. Let it be an exciting adventure of discovery, like being given the gift of a whirlwind trip around the world. The big question is, will you hop on the plane or not? It's up to you. I know this seems to leave sexuality in a somewhat loose format, and I think that's a good thing. All too often I work with clients who have attached so many specific and additional messages onto sexuality — commitment, self-esteem, status, obligation, shame, and more — that sex ends up being anything but pleasure. I think it's best to have a semi-flexible idea of what sexuality is so that there's growing room and space to gain new insights and explore many facets of ourselves.

Just as I recommend that a person access a therapist for delving into aspects of personal history and emotions, I suggest that employing a sex therapist or coach could be greatly valuable in gaining insight into the particulars of your own sexuality. Believe it or not, many psychotherapists and medical doctors have little sex education, and therefore they are sometimes biased, and ill equipped equipped to help you the way a trained sexology professional can.

Integration

My mentor Jack says that ex-gays are often "spiritually obese while at the same time sexually malnourished." I would venture to suggest that ex-gays are sexually anorexic, which means they have a number of key behaviors that a person with an eating disorder has: the lack of self-esteem, the distorted view of self, the bingeing and purging though in a sexual manner.

> *My ex-gay experience did nothing to foster a sense of wholeness within me. Instead it did just the opposite by separating two very important parts of my being, faith and sexuality. Only after integrating these two, did I find a genuine sense of health and contentment.*
> — Sean Greystone, Ex-gay Survivor. [5]

In my recovery process I began to recognize this imbalance, and I was motivated to allow my "pendulum" to swing less between the utter extremes of sexual and spiritual behavior. I realized that there was a balance I had to find between the two that would feel whole and integrated. Once again, my mentor, Jack Pantaleo:

> *Sexuality and spirituality are twins hatched from the same egg; they are different parts of the whole. They play together, laugh together, dance together, and breathe life into one another. Sexuality does not live in the bedroom any more than spirituality lives in a church. They are both integral to every part of life, whether we're making chocolate chip cookies, watching football, or making love.[6]*

The words "integration" and "integral" come from the same root word as "integrity." Perhaps this gives us a clue about persons of integrity. They are ones who are able to take all the aspects of life and integrate them together as one being. All the parts — emotions, body, soul, sexuality — work best when working together. People of integrity are no more repulsed or obsessed by sexuality than they are repulsed or obsessed by their hand or leg.

I'm annoyed now when someone says, "The body is just a shell that encases your true being." Just a shell? Watch your tongue, mister. In fact, you wouldn't have a tongue if it wasn't for that body of yours. It's not a shell. It's The Shell. So much so that the Bible calls the body a temple. My belief is that this dumbing down of the body is a product of our sex-negative rhetoric.

Ex-gays do not hold the monopoly on compartmentalization. There are a lot of spiritual practices that suggest another extreme that the mind is the enemy of the ability to be present in the moment. Definitely, we live in a culture that's primarily "in our head" most of the time. Certainly, we are way too "heady" a society. Many unaware people equate their whole identity — their very being with what they think of themselves, and nothing else. However, to stigmatize the mind as an agent of interference is just as dichotomous as suggesting that the body is evil. The mind is our amazing personal problem-solver and it helps us comprehend everything that comes at us.

Integration is not a balancing act. It's a recognition that divided walls no longer serve us. Integration is a gentle dismantling of those walls. It's allowing an ease of flow between our body, mind and spirit so that they naturally work together. As that pendulum slowed, I realized that spirituality and sexuality are not at extremes at all. I am completely spiritual and completely sexual all at the same time. The mind, soul and body — at least in this life — are positively inseparable. We can hypothesize all we like about out-of-body experiences, but that does not diminish experiencing the limitations and the wonders of our bodies. Sexuality and spirituality (as well as other elements of ourselves) aren't meant to be compartmentalized. The recovery/integration process was allowing myself to let go of all the sex-negative indoctrination and return to a more innocent self, where the mind, spirit and body were one. When a baby is born, she is not split into pieces with her mentality over there, her spirituality here, and her sexuality somewhere else. She is just a laughing, crying, eating, snotty-nosed, defecating being. As she grows and learns, she discovers and labels the various aspects of herself. And it is up to those who teach her — and to her own determination to grow — whether she will learn to love herself as a whole, or whether she will lose her sense of wholeness and be taught to hate the pieces.

The seamless interplay of spirituality and sexuality is really nothing new. Dr. Jenny Wade in her book, *Transcendent Sex: When Lovemaking Opens the Veil*, interviewed hundreds of people regarding their sexual experiences and how they found themselves swept away into different spiritual realms regardless of their religious, societal, or educational backgrounds. In fact, some consider sex to be the ideal activity to bring all of our different elements into perfect harmony — mind, body and spirit.[7]

Looking back, I am amazed to see that when I accepted my whole self — sexuality included — only then did my "walk with God" take on the kind of depth that really felt satisfying. When I was fighting my sexuality, it felt like I was walking in the desert. When I accepted myself as a whole, it felt as though I was living in the lush tropics. It was as if I had stepped out of the black-and-white, barren landscape of Kansas, to find myself in the technicolor wonder-world of Oz. I went from images on the page to 3-D movies.

To try and express this in my music, a friend and I joked that I ought to write a song that says something like, "I didn't find Jesus in church but in a gay bar." As silly as it sounded, after thinking about it, the idea seemed quite appropriate. I originally wrote and performed it as just that — "I met Jesus in a gay bar" — until the day a man said, "I like your music, but what's that song about meeting Jesus in K-Mart?" Uh-oh! So I changed the song to, "I met Jesus down at Stonewall," the Stonewall Bar being the symbolic birthplace of the LGBT civil rights movement.

Now the church bells are ringing, The members wear their best
In the pews they are waiting for the holy guest
The pastor knows the sermon, The choir stands in rows
There's a sense of something missing 'cuz the guest of honor never showed
I saw Jesus down at Stonewall, And he didn't seem the least upset
I saw Jesus down at Stonewall, That's the place we finally met
   I can hear the conversation, I can feel his heart unfold
   What would churches think that the Christ has come to my watering hole
   I saw Jesus down at Stonewall, One drink short of losing respect
   I saw Jesus down at Stonewall, Love can grow where you least expect
Now I always see him down there, He'll always draw me near
When I ask him why he stays, He says there's too much hate between the sacred
and the queer
   I saw Jesus down at Stonewall, And he didn't seem the least upset
   I saw Jesus down at Stonewall, That's the place we finally met
   I saw Jesus down at Stonewall, One drink short of losing respect
   I saw Jesus down at Stonewall, Love can grow where you least expect [8]

Integration has been a major goal in my recovery process. Certainly, there are times I swing heavy to the sexual side, and that's fine with me. After all, I spent the first 25 years or so of my life clinging to "spiritual things" and despising "the flesh." I was starving for touch. I was starving for sexual intimacy. I was inexperienced and afraid of anything having to do with the body. So if I felt the urge to "Eat up, me hearties, yo ho!" for a while, that's what I did. I am now happily aware of the wonderful and fluid interplay of my sexuality, spirituality, and mentality. Rest assured, I found my balance, and I know you can find yours. Here's more of what I did to get there.

Get Informed

As an ex-gay survivor, I was told "the truth" so often that I grew fatigued from choking down another morsel of "Godly wisdom," especially when I so often used it to beat myself up. Even more pronounced was the fear instilled from ex-gay leadership that reading the "wrong information" would somehow corrupt me beyond repair. My natural curiosity was undermined because I didn't know if simply seeing a movie or reading an article would utterly deceive me. This, of course, is one of the major messages from a religiously abusive environment: "I am not capable of making decisions (about sexuality) for myself." That's hogwash!

As I wrote in early chapters, when I was coming out there was very little published on the topic of sexuality and spirituality from an LGBT perspective. (Is this statement the information age equivalent of saying, "I had to walk ten miles in the snow to get to school"?) Fortunately, over the years, there has developed a wealth of information in books, websites, college courses and workshops to further our understanding of integration, wholeness, sexuality and spirituality. Don't think that I'm even hinting at being selective in what information to consume. Unlike the ex-gay's discriminatory selection of research and reading materials, I say, read it all. Ingest as much as you can get your hands on and determine for yourself what sexuality is and is not. It took practice for me to set aside the fear from those old messages and access all the ways I could inform myself and it sure felt awkward at first. However, it gradually became fun. Everything in my day-to-day life started to become an opportunity to better understand the world without fear. It was like eating new kinds of food, learning a new computer program, watching a foreign film and even going skinny dipping for the first time.

The Body

There is plenty of talk about the brain being the biggest sex organ; in many ways it's true. If you can visualize a sexy scenario, your body naturally responds. Yet you may have guessed by now that getting informed about sexuality is not just an intellectual pursuit. In fact, it is an experiential pursuit that most often requires the body. I work with a lot of clients whose thinking keeps them from experiencing sexual pleasure. Indeed, if I try to mentally understand and control every aspect of my sexual experiences, I will often limit my body's natural ability to enjoy the moment. Pleasure is not a logical equation to be solved by the mind. It is an experience of the body. To let your mental running commentary be the driving force in all of your experiences can restrain your pleasure. There may be an experience that defies words. So why be preoccupied with words? Just try relaxing into the experience your body is having.

I well remember the years of indoctrination that said my body would lead me to destruction. I remember the teachings convincing me that emotions and feelings were never dependable (which will be addressed in the next chapter). I remember the confusion created when positive, pleasurable experiences were undermined by my belief that the body was deceptively untrustworthy. As Peterson Toscano says of his ex-gay experiences, "I was truly at war with myself."[9]

But the body is trustworthy. Let me illustrate with another personal insight that my mentor, Jack Pantaleo, gave me in the form of an exercise. He suggested that I listen to my body and make a list of the things my body experiences during sex. Not concepts. Not ideas, but what my body was feeling and experiencing during sexual excitement. Here's a partial list of the items I, and others, have listed: euphoria, increased heart rate, a great sense of peaceful satisfaction, a lot of energetic excitement, tingly sensations, light-headedness, sweaty palms, butterflies in the stomach, dry mouth, misty eyes, strong emotions, sometimes it is hard to use words to describe it…. I hope you will make a list of your own, as well.

Then Jack suggested making a list of the things my body experienced during what I might call an enlightened experience or spiritual high. Once again, he wasn't asking for ideas or concepts, but what was going on in the body. Here's that list: euphoria, increased heart rate, a great sense of peaceful satisfaction, a lot of energetic excitement, tingly sensations, light-headedness, sweaty palms, butterflies in the stomach, dry mouth, misty eyes, strong emotions, sometimes it is hard to use words to describe it….

Holy incarnation, the two lists are identical! The very thing religion might cast aside as evil and corrupted, is an aspect of humanity that understands the spirit/sex connection very well. The body comprehends its unity even when our mind has long ago dismissed it as ludicrous. Our body is that dependable.

Therefore, in my recovery, I needed to reacquaint myself with my body. Nude beaches and lying bare in the sun felt great. The sun on my skin — all of it — became a kind of dare to accept my body "as is." It was the only body I was going to get and I wanted to know it thoroughly. I took time in front of a mirror — bare naked — to get to know my body. I noticed how the veins worked in my hands and the symmetry of the hairs on my arms. Could I admit to the natural beauty that every body possesses and that it was in mine, too? Was my body telling me to diet or did I just need to stay fit? I was able to admit for the first time that I could be somewhat content with what I had. I would shut my eyes and listen, searching carefully for the sound of the blood pumping, keeping me alive. Could my body give me signals of ailments deep inside? Initially, the body was foreign to me, yet, it was a companion that I could talk to like a friend, "Come on there, buddy, hop to it!" Now, it's just me. There are still occasions when I am truly uncomfortable in my skin, but those times grow fewer. My body is one of the most amazing gifts God has given me. I doubt it no more.

As a conduit for experiencing and gathering information, the body doesn't just have one way to take in information, but at least five ways (sight, hearing, taste, touch and smell) and probably a few more we don't comprehend. If we are deprived of one of our senses or have limited mobility, the body has the capacity to compensate to miraculous degrees — it's that good!

Touch

At the sight of bad news I just want to run and hide
Life can hurt
And my self-worth just dies
There's nothing to say I just need to have you close
So help me please I really need to know
> *'Cuz you say you love me I hear it*
> *When you smile at me it shows*
> *When you love with actions I feel it*
> *But when you touch me I know*

I'm ashamed to need touch—it's a statement of our times
And when I isolate
I create that lie
It's such a lie
So here I am
Don't hold back
I know the depth of feeling flowing from your hands
> *'Cuz you say you love me I hear it*
> *When you smile at me it shows*
> *When you love with actions I feel it*
> *But when you touch me I know* [10]

How do we get into our bodies, embrace our sexuality and escape what sometimes seems to be the maze of the mind? One sense in particular has helped me — touch. In my recovery process, I recognized an awkwardness with touch. I felt a nagging resistance just to giving someone, even a close loved one, a hug. When someone touched me, I would often freeze up, even when the person was reaching out with care and concern. Just about any touch would trigger a "mental storm" of negative thinking. And I would find myself right back in the mental maze again. "Have I crossed a line? Am I doing wrong? Will the person I am touching misunderstand my intentions? Is this going to lead to sex?" These were some of the leftover negative messages I had believed for so long.

Wanting to do something about it, I enrolled in a massage class. Here was an environment in which I felt safe to touch, be touched and practice at it. Looking back, it's not surprising that I blossomed. It seemed that my years of piano technique — acutely learning to sensitively touch the keyboard — primed me to be sensitive to the stress and tension in another's muscles. Even though the fear-based resistance in the ex-gay and religiously abusive environment was established first, over time and with practice I retrained my body to compensate, and I am still learning ways of freeing myself to give and receive touch more fully.

> *It has taken me years to give and receive touch without feeling guilty or afraid. These are hard lessons to unlearn, but I have unlearned them in the company of friends who love me.*
> — *Ron Poindexter, Ex-gay Survivor.*[11]

Though many ex-gay survivors share similar "touching" stories, the vast majority of our society as a whole remains tied down by fear-based misinformation regarding touch. I'm aware of two common misconceptions about touch. The first is that the need for touch is a sign of weakness. The "need" for anything sounds wimpy to our society. This silly idea has led to a chilling isolation of most of our male population since "real men don't need anything." Therefore, "I'm no sissy, I don't need touch." I try to think of touch like sustenance. Is the need for food a sign of weakness? No. Well, neither is the need for physical contact. On the contrary, touch makes us healthy. Ashley Montagu's classic book, *Touching*, relates studies of animals and humans who died or wasted away when touch was deprived in infancy.[12]

The second misconception is one I've addressed previously: touch always leads to sex. If you consider all of humanity's physical contact, you'll realize that only a portion of it leads to sex. Touch is its own experience. Sure, before sex there is usually touch, but that's because touch is pretty incredible all by itself. It's not unusual for people to reach levels of orgasm without involving the genitals whatsoever. Like the body, touch is that good!

Another important aspect of touch is having personal, physical boundaries. Fortunately, this has never been a challenge for me. I rarely seemed to have a problem with establishing the who, when, where, and how I want — or want not — to be touched. Unfortunately, the ex-gay and religiously abusive environments have sometimes eroded whatever sense of boundaries a person has. Some survivors feel that they never have the right to say "No" because that will come across as rebellious or it will limit what God can do through them. Furthermore, there are a number of ex-gay and religious-abuse survivors who have also been victims of physical and sexual abuse. For these folks, the delineation and respect of boundaries is very important. Here is where understanding the specifics of your own sexuality is essential. If, for example, I know that being touched on my arm triggers strong, negative sexual memories, then that is where I need to draw my boundary and protect that area so that I feel safe. Establishing and being in control of a "comfortable boundary zone" is part of being responsible for your healthy sense of sexuality.

Whole books are written about, and therapists devote their entire practices to, helping people recover from the damaging effects of physical and sexual abuse. If you are one who has been violated in such a way, I strongly urge you to access the many avenues to support and recovery for this specific kind of abuse.

I find that a lot of people know general information about touch and boundaries. The biggest challenge in becoming more tactile is often getting beyond the initial awkwardness. Briefly, here are some ways to sink your fingers gently into it:

- If physical/sexual abuse is in your history, talk with a professional therapist who can help you understand and work beyond your triggers.

- Find a safe place. Find an environment that will respect your boundaries unquestioningly, and be safe enough that you can touch and be touched.

- Ask first. If there's any doubt as to how touching will be received, verbally try it out first: "Can I hold your hand?" "May I give you a hug?" "I could really use a hug right now."

- Get a professional massage, or find a massage buddy. Get together with a partner and agree to take turns giving touch. Clearly establish your boundaries verbally before the massage begins.

Communication

Although touch is a powerful means of communication, it is not necessarily the most precise way to express oneself to another. One of the best ways to understand my sexuality was simply talking about it. I have already mentioned several times how the "silent treatment" regarding sex has left a negative, lasting effect on our society. How can we counteract that? By talking about it. There are many ex-gay and religious-abuse survivors who have never confided in anyone about their experience. When they start to speak up and tell their stories, they find out that they are far from alone. They unblock the experience by verbally releasing those painful memories. When you are ready, talk about it.

Experience: Enjoying Moderation and Experimentation

Ultimately, no matter how much you contemplate it, sexuality is most enjoyed by experiencing it. I know that for most ex-gay and religious-abuse survivors this can be petrifying, and there are several reasons for this. For one thing, most of us were used to taking the word of our spiritual leaders for granted, and we embraced their sex-negative teachings. We were assured that if we followed the rules, we would be content and at peace by doing the right thing in God's eyes. So when everything seemed so predictable, the possibility of an experience that unfolds in the present moment — who knows how it could end, or what the outcome will be? — can be frightfully intimidating, to say the least. The unpredictability of experiencing reality can be so scary that some ex-gay survivors turn right around and head back into the faux assuredness of the abusive system, especially when it comes to taking responsibility for a healthy sex life.

Secondly, probably the biggest reason sex can be scary is that it is the very thing we have been resisting for so long with all our strength. We labeled it the worst sin of all. We had years of dogmatic fear and shame telling us that just sticking our toe in the water of arousal would drown us in sexual depravity (notice the extreme thinking). With this kind of pleasure-phobia present in the most innocent of our sexual desires, it's nearly impossible to imagine gathering any pleasure from a sexual experience.

Third, when the only thing many ex-gays hear about the "homosexual lifestyle" is that it is horrible and degrading, how else are they going to behave when they finally "fail" at being straight and have to leave their cloistered bubble? It is self-fulfilling prophecy, as ex-gay survivor Darin Squire has reflected:

Because the ex-gay teachings told me there was no such thing as a healthy gay lifestyle and that all homosexuals were perverts, prostitutes or sluts, the year that followed was filled with self destruction, anonymous sex and dysfunctional relationships.[13]

As if this is not challenging enough, our upbringing and abusive backgrounds probably gave us very little instruction on how to negotiate sex and make wise decisions. What is the best course of action to learn to enjoy sex? What choices maximize pleasure and minimize risk? As adults, we are faced with making decisions and being responsible for our own outcomes — especially decisions that shape our sex lives — and many have very little idea of how to approach it.

I found the answer in integration. I have experienced this balance not just with spirituality and sexuality, but also with moderation and experimentation (although none of these are necessarily opposites). When it comes to life experience, specifically my sexual experiences, I have recognized moderation as the times when I am not going anywhere beyond my sexual comfort zone. It's living safely within my caution signs. Don't let this sound like I'm in a confined, suffocating space. I think moderate living is a lot larger area than we imagine "bland" or "tame" living to be. Ex-gay and religious-abuse survivors have often been told that everything enjoyable "in the world" is carnal, that even the most simplest of activities can seem like living "la vida loca." The truth is that many millions of wonderful experiences (sexual or otherwise) feel great, and they are absolutely good, with very little risk of negative consequences involved.

The tricky thing about moderation is that it, too, can mean a lot of things to a lot of people. For example, some of us are comfortable with a certain degree of vulnerability. We love to talk every little thing out and beat the dead horse whenever possible. There are others who are more private. Neither characteristic needs to be stigmatized, and both characteristics fit comfortably within a wide moderate ground. Moderation can be tricky also because it seems to vary over time. There might have been a time I felt that I wanted to take very little risk in my life and stay very safe within my boundaries — that was my prerogative. Then there were other times that I wanted to be doing anything but "sitting around," and I didn't want to miss out on one moment of the action. Finding the balance — that middle ground — even as it changes, is what moderation is about to me. Don't get me wrong, I'm not suggesting that everyone "should" live moderately. I am suggesting that we probably have our own sense of centeredness where we feel safe and very little fear of ill fortune can reach us there.

Determining the parameters of my sexual safety zone was an important step for me to begin to understand the outlying areas of my sexual pleasure. How did I determine my moderate zone and sexual edges? I experimented. As we develop from childhood to adulthood, we begin to have a natural curiosity about our bodies as well as the bodies of others. That curiosity doesn't necessarily stop at a certain age. It can grow and grow. Unfortunately, that curiosity can get easily squelched when others oppressively enforce their sex-negative and even sexually abusive ways on us. Many people have never given themselves permission to even look at the human body naked, let alone have the beautiful opportunity to touch one.

So what happens in a laboratory when a scientist experiments? The scientist designs a set of circumstances that she/he thinks will have a particular outcome, then initiates the circumstances and records the outcome. The experience can then be repeated or modified to determine if the outcome changes or remains the same. This is a loose description of the scientific method that my business partner, Mark Hollenstein, uses in his coaching practice. Mark, too, is a religious abuse survivor. He is a former fundamentalist Christian pastor, and now a certified Life Coach. In our workshops, I have watched him facilitate participants' growth by using this process. He will say, "Did the experiment give the desired outcome? Maybe yes. Maybe no. But that's what the experiment is for — to find out if whatever it is you are doing works for you. Learn from it and you move onto the next experiment." You can read all the books you want, and take the wisest guide's word for it, but you can't really know the value or the pleasure of many activities in life — especially of a sexual nature — unless you experience them for yourself. You might find that a particular activity isn't for you, and now you have informed yourself about some of your sexual parameters. Next, you can change your edges and move on to the next experience. Not only is this a great way to educate yourself; it's a whole lot of fun, too. Isn't that what life experience is about?

Imagine, this dance of moderation and experimentation can be the key for you to gradually create the sex life you have always dreamed of — whether it is by yourself or with a partner. When I have worked with "gay virgins" (homosexual men who have not yet had sex with another man) who want to take their first steps toward enjoying gay sex, this experiential balance has been enormously helpful, and it has brought about some wonderfully pleasurable first-time experiences for them. Whatever your past experiences, you have the opportunity from now on to design your sexual pleasure in a manner that specifically caters to you.

That said, I have a few tips specifically for the ex-gay and religious-abuse survivor. The first tip is this: sometimes we can have such specific expectations of how an experiment is going to turn out (What, ex-gays having high expectations?) that we can set ourselves up for disappointment. Of course, when it comes to sexual experimentation, it's a foregone conclusion that we all hope for a positive experience. Here's how Mark puts it:

> *One of the beautiful benefits of experimenting is that it helps the mind slow down and let go of limiting, long-held beliefs. When I run an experiment, I give myself full permission to notice everything with as little judgment as possible. I notice where the experiment is taking my thoughts. I notice physical sensations. I notice my emotions, pleasure, pain or indifference. I notice if my reactions ring true to my authentic self, or I notice the voices of others' beliefs and imposing opinions. The art of noticing lets me off the hook in the moment from drawing any immediate conclusions. For example, just because I notice I feel uncomfortable for a few seconds or minutes during an experiment does not automatically mean I don't like the experience. It is in this moment that I simply take note of my discomfort but keep going. Often times, I discover that the unpleasant feeling gives way to euphoria, and I am glad I kept going. Sometimes the discomfort persists, and I adjust accordingly. Still, everything I notice is data that helps me make more informed decisions for the abundant life I want.*
> — *Mark Hollenstein, Certified Life Coach.* [14]

The second tip is that experimentation is not a tidy process. Experimenting will tell you what you want to do, and what you don't want to do. Mishaps are going to happen. Try to design the experiment so that it does not blow up in your face and the faces of others. Some people embrace radical change by taking leaps and bounds into the unknown. Without a doubt, the risks are high, and they may rapidly learn that one misstep can spell devastation. I admire this type of person's tenacity. However, for the ex-gay and religious-abuse survivor, I suggest taking small steps, at least at first. Risking too much all at once has led some people straight back into the closet. Why risk so much? Create a solid and safe place for you to feel secure (moderation). Then test the waters gently, with as much risk as you are comfortable allowing. I have edged my way out there with as much awareness as possible, minimizing the possibility of "injury." I've learned a lot very quickly, one small step at a time. I've gotten in over my head a time or two, but I have no regrets. In fact, many small steps, wisely taken, have led to an exceedingly abundant life.

Above all, I committed myself to the process of discovering my sexuality. I finally began to be free of the fear of failing. I knew I would make mistakes, but that my process would eventually lead me to the right place.
— *Ron Poindexter, Ex-gay Survivor.* [15]

The third tip is this: I meet a lot of folks who, when I explain the dance of moderation and experimentation, are very quick to dismiss the experimentation part and hunker down, safe and sound within the sexual lines that have already been drawn for them. Where you draw your line is your business, but if you are simply defaulting behind the line that has been drawn in the sand for you, chances are you will end up wanting. Isn't that part of why the ex-gay experience didn't work for you in the first place? How do you know for sure unless you risk? Are there still experiences you want to have? Are you completely content with your life as it is? I think the only lines we can draw with any certainty are the ones we draw for ourselves out of personal experimentation and experiences. Otherwise, how will we really know?

Besides, the lines that were drawn for me kept moving. The lines were drawn, I followed their rules, and it was not enough. It was as if the line was moved to higher ground. I would toil and struggle up the walls and jump the hoops that were given me. Once I crossed that line, I heard: "Nope. Still not enough." When I stopped running to keep up with the lines others were drawing for me, I finally started living. I will draw my own lines now, thank you very much.

I like to use the analogy of seeing a movie. A good friend might say, "That was the greatest film I have ever seen!" Does this mean I skip seeing the film and I decide it's the greatest just because he said so? I could. But the only way I can truly relate to what my friend is saying is for me to see the film for myself. You can take the words of others for anything you choose, but they cannot live your life. Besides, who's to say that the experience that is condemned by others won't be the very experience that changes your life and could possibly transform the whole world? That's what experimentation is for.

I have met all too many ex-gay and religious-abuse survivors who wrestle with regret because they waited too long to step outside of their imposed "comfort zone." Ex-gay survivor David Christie speaks of his ex-gay experience:

Every day I feel the burdens of regret and grief. I grieve for my own years of anguish, but also for the confusion and pain I caused my wife, my family, and my friends. And sure, I spent a lot of money in this process, but what I want back more than anything is the time and energy I put into it. At school, my peers are a decade younger than me, and hardly a day goes by that I don't wonder: Where would I be now if not for my ex-gay detour? Where would I be professionally? How much more financially stable would I be? How much more confident? How much closer to self-actualization? I realize such questions could poison my progress, but nonetheless, they arise naturally, and I must wrestle with them. [16]

I think David is a great example of grieving and mourning the loss of the past, and at the same time he is able to use it to propel himself forward. The acceptance of his past helps him value the present and future. Sadly, there are others who have let the majority of their life pass them by. I don't want anyone to wallow in regret. Right now, you have the opportunity to never regret another moment. The clock is ticking. Step to it, baby!

You may have realized by now that this integrative approach can be applied not just to one's sexuality, but to many different aspects of life. I have a saying that goes like this: "I can change without growing, but I can't grow without changing." This emphasizes to me that I can take all kinds of risks and not learn from them. But it also means I have to risk something to grow. I'm pretty sure there's no way around it. Moderation is my safe core. Experimentation is the adventure of finding my edges. Integration is the umbrella under which this all resides.

Back when my music career was making the transition from conservative churches to LGBT- affirming venues, one Sunday evening I performed a concert in a Southern Baptist church about 40 minutes from San Francisco. I gave the performance my all, bid the audience goodnight and proceeded back across the Bay Bridge into the "Emerald City." I felt "on." I had energy to spare. So I went to a favorite hangout in the Haight Ashbury District, called the I Beam. On Sunday nights they had a tea dance that rocked my world (dancing once again!). I could go and lose myself in the music. I would dance the stress and sweat out of my system. I dared myself to get up on stage and stake out a spot for everyone to see. I actually was given a compliment on my steps for the song, "Taking a ride with my best friends," by Depeche Mode. I was on fi-yah!

At some point that night I asked myself, "Can I really go from a Southern Baptist church to a gay dance club in one night?" My answer was, "Yes. Hell yes!" It felt a little schizophrenic. I couldn't do it now because I am so open about my sexuality that Baptists don't invite me to their churches. But was it my path on that particular night of my integration process? Absolutely. And did I learn something from that experiment? Yes. I am not schizophrenic, but wonderfully diverse from my past to my present and to the future. All that I experience is a part of me. This body, mind, and spirit being has the capacity to comprehend it all in one, with all my gifts and all my facets. I am capable of loving and being loved. With little to no regret, I embrace all of my life with gratitude.

Intuition

One of the tools that has been refreshingly handy in my recovery process is intuition. I have been fascinated to find that in my interviews with ex-gay survivors the overall answer to the inquiries about using intuition is almost always, "What's that?" Indeed, when my own therapist suggested that I use my intuition to discern if a guy I was dating would make a good life partner, my answer was the same, "Huh, whazat?"

Intuition has been defined as, "Direct perception of truth, fact, etc., independent of any reasoning process. A keen, quick insight. The quality or ability of having direct perception or quick insight."[17] Even reading these simple definitions urges a skeptical voice inside me to say, "How can you trust such a nebulous thing as intuition?" I recognize this voice as the same one that long ago enforced "God first, others second, me last." It seemed that any kind of trust in myself, as with intuition, was completely undermined in the ex-gay environment. I believe that one of the reasons it is possible for some to live such dichotomous lives — leaving common sense, let's say, in the church while they go out and take foolish risks — is a result of having their intuition constantly invalidated. It is as though their own personal (God-given) compass was traded in for someone else's sense of stability, but it cost them subservience to the abusive system, and sometimes it costs them their lives.

If this makes particular sense to you, I suggest sitting down with someone who knows you (perhaps a close friend or a therapist) and go over some of your experiences where your intuition was telling you the best course of action. You'll be surprised. I would wager your intuition is wiser than you give it credit and a lot more trustworthy than ex-gay ministers believed it to be. When it comes to sexuality and finding your way, your intuition can be a great asset to take care of yourself and to maneuver challenges adeptly.

Relationships and Trust

Within the ex-gay programs, friendships are closely monitored by those in charge. After all, if two guys get too close they may fall into "sexual sin" with one another. The leadership's eyes are felt by the participants. I can only imagine the degree of tug-of-war that must go on in this environment every minute of the day. My mind would be constantly going, "I'm so glad to be here supported by these other people struggling with the same unwanted feelings. I want to support them, but I shouldn't get too close to anyone, because I may be tempted and jump their bones. How close is too close? What if someone comes on to me and I can't resist? I want to pray for my brother, but I have such a deep desire to cuddle with him, which is wrong...." The 24/7 struggle sounds like some kind of cruel torture. Of course, this kind of rampant fear and distrust extended to people in the outside world, is in this example from Peterson Toscano:

> *During my time in the program, I received a letter from my favorite cousin. He was like an older brother to me. The letter affirmed his love for me as he let me know he had been thinking of me in the program. He then added a gentle remark that indicated he would accept and love me no matter if I were gay or straight. Receiving this letter from the outside, I felt threatened. It seemed the very thing that staff warned us about. I interpreted his remarks as a way of tempting me to accept my attractions for other men. I shared the letter with the staff, who reinforced my fears with the belief that although my cousin probably meant well, he unwittingly operated as a force against me and my Ex-gay life. I never responded to the letter and cut off all communications. For this action I received affirmation and praise from program leaders and fellow participants.*[18]

Making matters worse, to keep participants in line some ex-gay leaders have further pathologized any connection they deemed too close by labeling it with particular psychological terms, like "enmeshment" and "relational dependency." Some ex-gay literature went so far as calling lesbian and gay relationships "monster enmeshment," "emotional cannibalism," and "sexual vampirism."[19] Leaders would warn participants not to get too close to others for fear of becoming "enmeshed" or "emotionally dependent." Enmeshment is a specific term coined by psychotherapist Virginia Satir, used in conjoint family therapy to describe dependent family members (like a father and daughter) who are so overly involved with each other that all sense of individuality is repressed.[20]

Although there are dysfunctional familial relationships that fit the description of these clinical theories, I have never seen or heard of one developing in the ex-gay world. Unfortunately, though, their tactic worked. Participants became so afraid of possibly being "dependent" or "enmeshed" that they didn't dare get close to anyone. In fact, it worked so well that the long-term effect on a number of ex-gay survivors I have met, is that they are unable to trust anyone. They are so trained to keep their emotional distance that they feel too paralyzed to draw near to loved ones, even though their ex-gay experience is now ancient history.

> *The biggest problem I still face is fear of close relationships with others — especially women. Fear of "emotional dependency" or "enmeshment." Fear of needing someone. Fear of... I don't know. Just fear, and now [I have] just a consistent inability to wholly participate in friendships with others. I know that it's not true — that while some relationships can be unhealthy, most are not. Closeness and yes, even at times emotional dependency should not be demonized. There are times when we all need others, and to be shamed for relationships that we had while ex-gay, those that others deemed unhealthy; relationships that may have been getting us through some of the tougher moments in our ex-gay process... it is a great harm and a great disservice to us at a time when we were the most vulnerable, and the most laid bare, needing others around us. I am 36 years old and beginning a new life. I am still trying to put some pieces together, and still trying to figure out relationships. Still trying to untie myself when it comes to closeness with others; needing others; being able to receive from others.*
> — *Christine Bakke, Artist and Ex-gay Survivor.* [21]

As I emphasized in the section on discovering what sexuality means to you, a healthy relationship often blossoms from the coming together of healthy individuals. I am happy to report that as I have put into practice the steps included in this chapter about sexuality, my ability to trust has strengthened. As I have taken little steps toward connecting with others and, at the same time, increased the acceptance and trust of myself, I have learned to draw close and hold dear a variety of connections in my life.

Here, in this section on relationships is where I must again bring up the reoccurring theme of dancing. It appears in the form of both a confession and a sex tip rolled into one. I found that one of the most wonderful ways of connecting with a romantic partner is slow dancing — really! I'll put on some sultry, groovy lounge music. I'll stand in the middle of the room and take the hand of... I'll call him Stefan, and pull him close to my chest. Our movement to the music distracts my brain from over-thinking the experience. I take in his aroma. His hands spread out over the surface of my skin. We gaze into the color of our eyes up close. It doesn't matter whether we're in time with the music or steps are not aligned. Somehow, holding our full bodies so closely, I am affirmed in our connection, in my masculinity and sexuality. Whether it is an occasion to lose our clothes one item at a time, or not, it is our very own collaborative moment of heaven, and I could do it for hours. This is indeed the activity to where Baptists are afraid love making will lead. It is also an activity that I highly recommend to all the couples who come to see me for ways to improve their sex life. Try it. I promise, you'll like it.

Learning to Receive

How well do you take a compliment? Chances are, if you are an ex-gay and religious-abuse survivor, you're not very good at receiving one at all. What's worse is that you probably don't believe a word of the verbal blessing bestowed upon you, regardless of how factual it might be. I think the only reason I got use to receiving compliments was all the years of performing. Nightly, people would thank me and compliment me on my ministry and music concerts. I wasn't going to invalidate their desire to contribute their heartfelt reaction to my music. I would literally grit my teeth and say, "Thank you, that's very kind," while on the inside I was raking myself over the coals for missing a certain note, or flubbing a lyric. Over time, having to respond respectfully this way to audiences softened me. I realized that compliments are ways of connecting to others and I began to accept that they couldn't all be off-base with their praises. Maybe there was some truth in their words and I could let myself off the hook.

Clients who have a hard time enjoying their sexuality sometimes have a hard time receiving compliments. I even help them practice receiving a compliment "properly." I might say, "Gosh, George, that is a beautiful dress you have on." And this particular client might say back, "Oh, this old thing. I think it makes me look fat." My response humorously is, "So are you calling me a liar?" We have a chuckle and I explain that not only is deflecting compliments a way to invalidate a person's sincere positive feelings about you; it's also a way you tell yourself that you are unworthy of receiving good things in your life. So I approach it again, "Wow, that's a great frock you're wearing today." Usually, it takes them two or three times to stop deflecting and just say a simple "Thank you." Sometimes it takes all their will power, and I have to say it with them, "You can do it, thaaaank yoooou."

Can you see the connection between an inability to receive compliments and the inability to receive pleasure in general (much less sexual pleasure)? Ex-gay and religious-abuse survivors have ended up feeling so undeserving of love — so unworthy in God's eyes — that it's nearly impossible to believe that we deserve anything good in our lives. If we can't learn to receive anything in general, we surely won't have it easy learning to receive sexual pleasure. In fact, some sexologists contend that the ability to simply receive is fundamental to enjoying sexual pleasure. It's my experience that most people mentally comprehend the logic of this but find it hard putting it into practice — getting our mouths to actually say the words, "Thank you," and really soak up the compliment in our heart. Receiving is the challenge. We just don't have enough opportunity to learn to receive in general, let alone learn to receive sexual pleasure.

I learned to receive by way of an amazing, and unexpected, experience. In relaying it to you, I hope you can "receive" some of it into your heart, too. Maybe you can soak up some of the flood of unconditional love that was heaped on me by way of an amazing man. In the late 90's, a friend raved about a masseur named David who could only work on medium to smaller men because he was up in years. His lack of stamina did not allow him to do a decent job on bigger physiques. Yet he enjoyed and received so much from giving touch, he charged next to nothing. Curious, I had to check him out. At our first meeting, he reviewed his credentials and listed the many styles he had been trained in, including tantric and prostate massage. He also made it clear that he would, of course, respect wherever I set my boundaries. The massage was outstanding, and it set into motion a close friendship for the next seven years.

We would meet every couple of weeks, and we became so comfortable with each other that I could ask for any variety of techniques. He would show them to me using my own body as the guinea pig. Consequently, my boundaries of what should and should not be touched gradually and naturally fell away. Be sure to visualize this picture clearly. It was not as if whenever we got together he was ready to pounce down my shorts. Quite the opposite. Whenever we got together, with all the gifts, talents and techniques at his fingertips, he was ready to make me feel incredibly relaxed and blissful right down to the micro-fibers of each and every one of my muscles.

Yes. There were occasions I was relaxed and horny, and he could lead me into erotic exercises which would energize me and produce one of those mind-blowing (as is so popularly labeled in the massage world) "releases." But just as valid were the occasions that he would primarily massage sore areas in my hands, when I could talk him through exactly where the pain was and he would selflessly follow my coaching to the letter, for what seemed to be an eternity. So when I walked through his door, I knew without a doubt that he was there for my well being — whatever my needs were. In fact, the first few years I really struggled inside with guilt that I should somehow be returning his blessings in kind, since it seemed I was benefiting far more than he was. Then, it gradually began to dawn on me that this sense of obligation was really a waste of time. What genuinely gave him the most joy was helping me be relaxed and at peace — body and soul. Why was I wasting energy worrying about it, when I could simply soak it up?

This connection began to touch me on an even deeper level. As I trusted him more, I became aware that I was consequently able to receive more from him — even more than from anyone else in my life. With family, with friends, and even intimate companions, I always had a certain awareness of their needs, and rightly so. I wanted there to be a balance between their needs and my own. While I cared deeply for David, his needs were not the focal point of our session — mine were. With David it didn't matter what his needs were, or what his day was like, or what he looked like. It didn't matter that I wasn't attracted to him. I could abandon any need for approval. During our times together, my need to keep up appearances completely left my mind. I trusted him thoroughly enough that I could be completely selfish. He enjoyed it when I was able to be completely selfish with his touch — he reveled in it. Do you know how rare it is to have a connection like that? Do you know how blessed I was to have a friend such as David? I could truly and completely abandon all my concerns about anyone and anything, and he would stand with me vigilantly, holding my hand, touching my wounds, healing my body.

This connection created an opportunity to release not just physical tension, but stored up emotions as well. It was through the safety of David's hands that I experienced an unanticipated sobbing release. He innocently mentioned something while he was touching me, and the sadness started to flow. It felt as though I had years of tears to drain, and it certainly ranked up there with the top ten tear-dumps of my life. When I finally emptied out, I realized he had stopped massaging me and was simply embracing me. It was enormously healing.

About five years into our friendship, David was diagnosed with throat cancer, and he died a brief two years later. I have yet to find, and I probably won't ever find, another friend like him — much less a masseur. Yet the strange thing is, no one can ever take his love away from me. I know, without a doubt, from years of experiencing his touch and attention, that David loved me unconditionally. Gay men are more often than not rejected by the "male world." To have an older man to look up to and really know that this mentor wanted me to receive pleasure by way of his loving touch was very rare indeed!

Furthermore, to have a mentor not only accept a man's sexuality, but also encourage and educate another man's sexuality in such a tangible way, is something that not even the best of parents can do. That is the gift David gave to me, and it is like no other I have received in my life. When I am at peace with myself in every way, when I take pleasure in touch, and when I am satisfied sexually in the deepest possible perception, I know that this is what David wanted for me. I imagine David laughing from the heavens, saying, "Yes, you deserve every bit of it!" I like to think he's saying that to all of us.

Pleasure Is Reason Enough

What better experience can we have to learn to receive than pleasure? If all the pages about sexuality haven't sent you over the top yet, hold onto your britches. We're going to address, specifically, the wonders of pleasure. Could it get any more fleshly? You bet! Pleasure has a lot of names, like happiness, contentment, vitality, joy, fulfillment, positiveness, health, laughter, and others. Of course, all these words refer to slightly different aspects and experiences, and many of them overlap to the degree that any number of them can be felt simultaneously. To simplify the idea, I like to think pleasure is what we feel in our body when we are stimulated positively, wherever direction it comes from physically, mentally, spiritually, or/and emotionally.

Most people associate pleasure with reward, like cause and effect: when he works hard at his job, he'll save up enough money to go on a trip to Hawai'i. If I can lose ten pounds, I can buy that swimsuit I've wanted. When a child obeys her parents, she gets an allowance. Indeed, research has shown that positive reinforcement far exceeds punishment-based, negative reinforcement when it comes to learning new behaviors. This is true in humans as well as in animals. Generating pleasure can be a good thing for everyone.[22]

Yet, as a sexologist, I am not surprised that some of my clients who find little satisfaction in sex are the ones who find very little use for pleasure in general. It's as if they have such an uncontrollable work ethic that even the reward of diligence has lost its value The saying, "the prize isn't worth it unless you work for it," certainly holds some truth. Sure, we need a degree of security, the ability to survive, and basic human rights, but pleasure is far more than just a reward.

I think people tend to believe that the only way to deserve pleasure is through work or through suffering. Ex-gay and religious-abuse survivors have subjected themselves to such an unrealistic work ethic that they set themselves up for failure, and thus they end up believing they do not deserve any kind of pleasure. Dr. Stella Resnick's first words in her book, *The Pleasure Zone*, are these: "We're not as happy as we might be — not in our everyday lives, not in our love lives. And it's not because our lives or our loves are lacking. Rather, it's because most of us have lost the ability to fully take pleasure in what we have."[23] We have trained ourselves to actively reject pleasure because deep down we believe we don't deserve it. But this narrow view of "pleasure as reward" does not encompass the wide variety of benefits that pleasure offers to our health and wholeness.

The ability to give ourselves pleasure is important, just as touch is, but we don't need money, or piles of stuff, or Prince(ss) Charming to do it. Some of the most joyful people I have ever met live in poverty. Pleasure doesn't have to be put on hold until after we make a million dollars, or after years of therapy, for that matter. We can have access to it any time we want it. You have the capacity to generate pleasure with your own two hands, and it is important to do so. When an infant in the womb finds his genitals and begins to stimulate them, is he thinking, "I've been a good boy today so I get to receive pleasure?" [24] Of course not. Pleasure is a natural part of being human — even in the womb. Although it can be used to motivate us to do this or that, pleasure is an accessible positive energy that we can experience for no other reason than that we are capable of feeling it. Isn't that one amazing gift to celebrate?

Let's consider just a few of the benefits. Research shows stress to be a leading cause of heart disease as well as decay of the immune system. [25] It has also been proven that a constant suppression of feelings and emotions can have strong negative effects on the body and the mind. [26] Guess what research is finding builds up the immune system and even creates longevity? Pleasure. [27] Take, for example, one of the most accessible and natural experiences of pleasure, which has become so therapeutic to a person's health that it now has a field of study all its own: gelotology. This is the research and understanding of laughter and its effects on the human body. Having a hearty and regular laugh can strengthen the immune system. [28] It helps lower blood pressure. [29] So helpful is this simple pleasure, that there are several types of therapeutic programs just to get people healthy by laughing, such as, humor therapy, clown therapy, laughter therapy, laughter meditation, and laughter yoga. [30] On a emotionally blue day, I can pop one of my favorite comedies or stand up routines into the DVD player and within minutes my giggles have got me up and going again. Is this a pleasure I must earn? Of course not. Is it valuable? "When it comes to enjoying a long and healthy life, those who laugh, last." [31]

One of the most basic ways to give yourself love and acceptance is to give yourself pleasure. We can look at this in the broad sense. You can buy yourself something special or take yourself out for a nice dinner, maybe to a movie, but the real act of showing your affection is taking yourself home and making love — yes, to yourself. If it's good enough for a boyfriend or girlfriend, then why is it not good enough for you? There have been times in life that the stress was so bad, I was so broke, and I felt so depressed that literally the only act I could think of that was just for me and for no one else, was giving myself sexual pleasure. Just as standing naked in front of a mirror is a kind of self-acceptance, loving masturbation is putting that self-acceptance into action. The natural ability to give sexual self-pleasure is also a powerful activity for healthy well-being. It heightens the senses, exercises the body, celebrates life, strengthens self-esteem, and just feels damn good. Our bodies knew how good pleasure felt before we were born. We have been taught, after the fact, to feel shame about it with words like, "Don't touch your nasty down there."

Now I am going to go out on a limb and guess that the topic of pleasure has most readers cringing and confused. I'll bet there is a mental dialogue going on where one voice is rushing to the extreme, "Yes, but what if my pleasure becomes an addiction? How will I know when the pleasure becomes an obsession?" Since there's a good chance that this mental discussion has already started, especially in the heads of ex-gay and religious-abuse survivors, let me join in. First, I want to point out that this line of thinking is, once again, going to the obsessively negative extreme, as we all have been taught. I doubt that many of you thought, "Isn't it wonderful that Jallen is affirming my God-given skill of making myself feel deep, satisfying sexual pleasure!" Unfortunately, many were thinking, "What? You're suggesting I give myself a break and enjoy life a little? Ack! What if I abuse it for the rest of my life, and Satan deceives me? What if I become addicted to pleasure? What if I'm frolicking down the highway to hell, blah, blah, blah...." Still, it's a valid question, and certainly a real fear for many survivors. How do we know when pleasure turns to obsession?

I'm happy to suggest that the answer to this concern is in the body experiencing pleasure itself. What is one of the common characteristics of a real addiction? The addict no longer finds pleasure in it. In fact, addicts often need more and more to even come close to the high they once experienced. They feel controlled by their addiction. Compulsive behavior or addiction is a way to numb the body and to avoid what a person is really experiencing. Does this sound pleasurable to you? Yes, an alcoholic might profess that they, for example, love their liquor, that liquor is their only friend and they couldn't live without it. But very few would feel that it gives them the deep satisfaction in their bodies that they once felt, if they ever felt it at all. And is liquor bringing more and more pleasure and satisfaction to the body? On the contrary, an alcoholic's body is being poisoned, and I can guarantee that the body is screaming about anything but pleasure during a hangover the morning after. That's not enjoying pleasure for pleasure's sake. That's using "pleasure" to avoid the realities of life — unpleasant or otherwise.

In many ways, pleasure can be the defining characteristic of whether an activity is obsessive or not, and our body naturally reflects it. Let's say I gain pleasure from lightly caressing the top of my hand. If I do this long enough, my body gets used to it, even to the degree that my body will numb itself to the repetitive sensation. Am I receiving pleasure if I go numb? Not anymore. I can't feel it. Yet, in our society, we believe the extreme that to get more pleasure we must do more of the same. "More is better." So should I rub harder? Maybe, but that will eventually increase the numbness. Why not recognize the numbness, listen for the pleasure and find another spot that feels good? This analogy shows the real motive of obsessiveness: it's not about savoring pleasure, it's about numbing oneself to reality. Pleasure and obsessiveness are two different things, and if you're present to your pleasure, I don't think it's easy to cross over into the habitual numbness that comes with compulsive dependency. That is, unless you want to. It has been my experience that when I am present in my body and the above points are put into action — understanding what sexuality means to me, identifying my sex-negative messages and turning the volume down on them by being informed, communication, etc. — the possibility of going overboard is slim to none.

Truth is, I work with a lot more people who are afraid of being sexually compulsive than I work with people who are truly clinically sexually compulsive. That is not to say that sexually compulsive people don't exist. What I am suggesting is that all of our society's sex-negative and fear-based messages keep us so afraid of our sexual pleasure that even the most innocent of sexual desires get bathed in the hysteria that all sexuality is "sexual addiction." We can trust our bodies. We can trust the factual information about sexuality. We can trust our own experiences and intuition. We can trust and enjoy pleasure. All of these are great indicators for knowing whether or not an activity is obsessive. An excessive fear of sex in general is not necessarily an indicator that an activity is obsessive or compulsive.

At the very least, even if you are skeptical about all this pleasure stuff, I suggest that when circumstances go awry, you try not to be so hard on yourself. When bad things come your way, instead of choosing self-criticism, instead of being critical, try to choose self-kindness. Just ease up on those reins because this, too, can be a way of giving yourself pleasure — little steps.

All of this to say that pleasure is not a frivolous reward for years of harsh struggling. It is not an enemy of the spirit. It is a very good force in the world with amazing benefits. The idea that pleasure can be too much of a good thing has yet to be tested to its fullest capacity. As I like to say, "Wouldn't the world be a better place if everyone had a happy and healthy sex life?" Would we really have all the war and hate if everyone was being sexually satisfied? It surely would cut down a lot of evil in the world, and that couldn't hurt. Indeed, sexual pleasure is not only good; it can be a source of healing.

Sexual Healing

When I was on the road performing music in GLBT venues, I was invited by a particular group to sing at one of their retreats. This was a cluster of churches that was made up of predominantly gays and lesbians; however, everything about them reflected a conservative Pentecostal denomination — with all the pro's and con's. In fact, they took every opportunity to point out that they were Christian first and gay/lesbian second. As their guest, I began to wonder why they had to bring this up again and again. Why was there a need to create a hierarchy about it in the first place? It seemed that several of them were all but saying, "Gee whiz, if I could get rid of this gay stuff, I would, but I can't so I just want everyone to know I love God better." It didn't strike me as the way I would talk about a wonderful, amazing gift from God that I had come to embrace as I have my sexuality.

When I drove into this wooded retreat location, it clearly stated on the entrance sign that the property was owned and managed by some branch of the Baptist denomination (and you could fill a forest with all the different branches of the Baptist denomination). I thought, "Wow! How progressive that a Baptist retreat center would be open enough to welcome a bunch of LGBT Pentecostals!" As the weekend progressed, however, I found out that the Pentecostal leadership had conveniently failed to mention that they were actually gays and lesbians, too. But that shouldn't matter anyway, right? After all, they were Christians first.

As their integrity began to wear thin on me, their organizational skills, or lack thereof, ate away at the schedule's stability. Of course, on a weekend like this — especially with Pentecostals — services can go on for a very long time. People can be anointed by the Spirit and preach and preach and preach and preach. I somewhat expected it. But my invitation to perform kept being put off and off and off, until I almost had the sense that they didn't want to hear what I could contribute. It felt as though they were trying to win me over to their "holy roller" experience. As much as I wanted to be flexible, I began to get fed up.

Also attending was a handsome gay man doing an article for some gay rag about this LGBT Pentecostal denomination. I'll call him John. He had a religious background, so he knew what he was getting into, but somewhere on the second or third day I could tell John was getting a belly full of the Spirit as well — the kind of belly full that made him nauseous. We started to hang with each other, sharing insights, and making subtle jokes. These folks in their long services could get so intense. We began to feel like the bad boys in the back pew, though I don't think anyone saw us this way.

The last night of the retreat, the service was once again going into overtime — way into overtime — and John and I stepped outside to get some air. We gradually drifted away from the service. Soon the sounds of crickets and frogs were in competition with the voices of worshippers. The whole camp stood empty except for the lights from our group. There were plenty more cabins scattered around the property than we had people to fill. It was a warm night. The stars peeked through the trees. We both were being cocky and flirty. Pretty soon we were holding hands. I think I made some reference to not having any privacy in the cabins and, therefore, I was horny. This confession was all we needed to start making out in the dark.

Within no time, our hands were all over each other, and we wondered which cabin would be safe enough to sneak into for some real privacy. We randomly picked one and stepped inside. We gasped. There in the dim light, we could make out a set of wooden pews, and at the far end an altar and podium. It was not for sleeping. From the outside it looked like any of the other cabins. On the inside it was a little chapel. I thought, "Ugh. Wooden pews are not comfortable for sex." Everything in the room was wooden, from the floors to the podium. But then it occurred to me, "All right, if it's all wood, where's the best place to honor and appreciate this gift that we get to share?"

(This paragraph is to be spoken aloud with a booming voice:) And behold: Thusly did the sons of God bow upon the altar, sharing the sanctity of their bodies in servitude and loving kindness one to another. Woe to the people of God who, fearing the condemnation of others, only performed certain spiritual gifts — prophesy, prayer, and words of wisdom. But, behold, brothers in Christ, Jonathan and Jallen exercised their wondrous gifts where others fear to tread, by passionate laying on of hands, and speaking in tongues, and receiving liberating freedom that only comes from the healing ointment of life. Amen. (King James Version, of course)

Although I truly am not trying to be disrespectful, I share this story, albeit somewhat tongue-in-cheek, to demonstrate a point. While John and I shared that intimate time, which included humor, joy, sexiness, sacredness and ecstasy — it felt healing, as well. The crazy juxtaposing of a couple of gay boys going at it in a "sanctuary," on property owned by Baptists, under the auspices of and within ear-shot of a group of semi-closeted queer Pentecostals, somehow added up to the collective universe shouting out one big medicinal, "Yes!"

No, I can't tell you what ailment was actually being healed. I can only tell you what I sensed was going on inside of me, even though, to this day, I don't mentally comprehend exactly what was going on inside. It felt like a safe mending or a tight knitting internally of items that had been torn apart. It was a warmth and a glow of my heart being made whole, and I have felt it often in the most ecstatic, euphoric, spiritual and even sexual moments of my life. I had felt that very same vibrational healing when prayed over in my own charismatic church, years earlier. I had felt it while joined, hand-in-hand, with my Faerie brothers and sisters. Miraculous healing goes on all the time, and no one can explain it. Why can't healing go on unexplained in our sexual moments as well? Ex-gay and religious-abuse survivors have spent much of their "spiritual life" being taken advantage of, being lied to, wounded and, most of the time, not realizing it. Is it then so far fetched that some of the healing can occur in genuinely pleasurable and freeing moments, without putting a litany of specific intellectual descriptors to it? I say, "Amen and Amen!"

A Good Example

I have been warned by friends and fellow survivors that this chapter on sexuality is going to be hard for some of the more conservative ex-gay survivors to swallow. This does not surprise me since I've been studying sexuality for years now. Discussing it is like falling off a log for me, but most people have never given sexuality this kind of going over. If this has been too ambitious for where you are in your recovery process, that's all right. To close this chapter, consider one of the best examples of sexual and spiritual integration I have ever known: Jesus Christ.

When Jesus healed, he almost always touched the sick, something that was against the law not only because of the possibility of contamination, but also because it was viewed as being religiously "unclean." In one story, Jesus embraced children and freely enjoyed their affection at a time when children were treated not as people but as property. As an act of love for his followers, Jesus washed their feet, an act typically left to servants.

Once, on an even more erotic level, Jesus allowed a woman — perhaps even a prostitute — to pour expensive oil on his feet. She then used her own hair to wipe up the oil and clean his feet. Is that sexy, or what? Another story of intimate affection is when the disciple that "Jesus loved," probably John, laid his head in Jesus' lap while relaxing after the Last Supper.

Regardless of the social standards, it seemed that Jesus enjoyed his body, connecting through touch with his friends and his own sense of sexuality. There are many stories of Jesus' activities that allowed for his sexuality to come out even when going against the laws of the day. This is especially seen in the books that were not included in the Bible as we know it today.

Incarnation is another way in which Jesus is an ideal example of integration. Rather than being half human and half God, he was both fully human and fully God at the same time. That's integration. If Jesus could allow himself to be completely human, I wonder if we can allow ourselves the same humanity (and perhaps the same divinity as well)?

Applying the examples of Jesus to our contemporary setting, we needn't allow the religious laws of our day to tell us how we should experience our sexuality or spirituality. It's not my intention to indoctrinate the masses about sex and religion. I just don't think we should go on believing that the Religious Right has the final say on morality, especially concerning spirituality and sexuality. And yet, all too often, the LGBT community takes its marching orders from outdated and unrealistic beliefs about sexuality and spirituality. But no more! True, some of those beliefs are rock-solid good ones, but all too many of them are unquestioned and unconsciously followed with dreadful consequences.

Ultimately, if the Religious Right has firmly convinced itself that the spirit is from heaven and sex is from hell, this only emphasizes the need to celebrate diversity all the more. After all, they continue to be resolutely wrong about homosexuality. Why in the world should we agree with them about sexuality and spirituality? For no other reason than to piss off the Religious Right, I will continue to find the sacred between my legs. I will strive for ecstatic transcendence in every sex act and I will see the divine eyes of God or the Goddess in the eyes of those around me. I'm not going to let the Religious Right tell me where I find my enlightenment or my pleasure. And don't you let them keep you from yours, either!

Some time ago, my parents sold and moved out of the house I grew up in. Although my first few years of life had a couple of different locations, this house my parents were selling had been and will always be to me the home of my youth. So it felt both sad and affirming of my adulthood to close the door on a space that held so many memories. On the very last day I took a walk down by the river next to our house, and I knew the spot I wanted to find. There, in a shady grove of secluded oak trees, was the site where I had showed God so many years before, my seriousness about never masturbating. This time, I knelt with all gratitude to the God whose love, patience and delight flooded every part of me at that moment. I honored that kid who wanted so desperately to be the embodiment of Christ. I imagined that boy — still in my heart — playing forever in that river forest like some naked, wild Peter Pan. I celebrated all the wonders of my body, mind and spirit by orgasming and spilling my seed on foliage that now grew over the hole where once a stake pierced the ground.

CHAPTER 10

Embracing Adulthood

More Steps in My Recovery Process

A YEAR AFTER HIGH SCHOOL I attended a friend's graduation party thrown by his parents. At some point in the party he mentioned driving to the lake the next day for fun in the sun and water. Suddenly, his mom popped up and said, "Now I want to know when you're going, when you're coming back, who you're going with, and what you'll be doing!" There was a pause because her enthusiasm seemed so over the top, especially on the day my friend was celebrating. But just then she burst into laughter saying, "Oh. I'm so glad I don't have to do that anymore. You're an adult now and you are responsible for yourself." I think her second statement stunned me more than her joke. "You mean to tell me there are parents who actually affirm their child's adulthood?" I thought. Let me say that when I graduated from high school, my parents curbed a number of house rules to show they respected my privacy... a little more. Whether I was just plain scared of being an adult or whether my parents didn't know any better, I don't remember being... I don't know... slapped on the back and told, "Well, son, you're an adult now. You go out there and win the world and we'll be proud of you." I think there were some words like that when I went to college, but all I remember is the awkwardness of saying goodbye.

I don't fault my parents for this, because with the prevalent glorification of youth, our society creates incentives to remain a child. Why become an adult? Sociologists observe that the category of "teenager" came into existence in the mid-1900's with the advertising awareness that parents spend their money on what? Their kids.[1] Therefore, put the attention on the "innocence of childhood." Prolong this period as long as possible and just imagine all the money that can be made. I get the sense that capitalism would even say, "Why spend money on someone who's on their way out? There's no financial future in that." This is a societal phenomenon unique in history. In contrast, the vast majority of cultures throughout history placed their attention on and had great respect for those who have lived the longest.

Furthermore, many societies had rites of passage into adulthood. The child got to a certain age, usually around puberty, and a ritual acknowledged that he (usually male) was no longer a child but an adult, with all the rights and responsibilities of that role. One such ritual we still see today is the Bar Mitzvah in Judaism. What kind of ritual does our society have in general? Maybe high school graduation. Maybe a college degree. Marriage is certainly a ritual aspiring to adulthood, but what about all the people who do not get married, or can't get married? What's more, a lot of parents have no idea how to let go, when to let go, or if they even need to ever let go, so their children have to create a negative, if not divisive, experience just to get out the door.

The truth is, with the glorification of youth and the lack of affirming transitions into adulthood, many people perceive themselves as anything but adults, even though they could be in their 20's, 30's or 40's. This is the whole idea behind Dan Kiley's classic book, *The Peter Pan Syndrome.*[2] Quite frankly, in this society, why would anyone want anything but childhood? A child is not responsible for his actions. A child always has the parents to get her out of trouble. It's a lot easier than growing up and addressing the realities of one's life. Indeed, resistance to embracing our adulthood is yet another way to avoid dealing with the realities of our lives. Ultimately, though, whether we think we are adults or not, we are responsible for ourselves. And being an adult who behaves like an irresponsible child is probably not the best way of dealing with our lives, though I suppose a lot of people try.

People with this general unawareness of adulthood are perfect candidates for ex-gay and other religiously-abusive environments. There is enormous emphasis on God as a father and all true Christians as God's "children." There is image after image in scripture and in sermons of the Father holding helpless little ol' me in his strong arms. God is the shepherd, and we're the stupid little lambs that wander aimlessly till God brings us back to the fold (and even breaks our legs to keep us there; yes, I was actually told God was like that). All too often this kind of subjugation is the only teaching we receive. Entire lives have been devoted to being the child in the shadow of God. Rarely was there a hint of the parts of the Bible that portray us as the bride or partner of Christ. Never was there any emphasis on being a sibling of Christ or being a co-creator with Christ, bringing the loving and just Reign of God into our world.

As all of this began to dawn on me, not only did I find myself feeling anger about how screwed up our society is (once again), but I also sincerely asked the question, "How do I embrace adulthood for myself?" This is where my perception of God evolving into a healthy parent was helpful (as outlined in the chapter on spirituality). Yet, no matter what kind of parent I might have, I had to take my own steps toward adulthood.

One way that I embraced my adulthood was just by taking responsibility for myself. I know that sounds obvious, but for ex-gay and religious-abuse survivors, it can be a tall order. I have already addressed this topic in a number of different ways — acknowledging denial, deciding what I believe spiritually, exploring what sexuality means to me, and so on. I think it also means "stepping up to the plate" regarding my life. If my dreams are to come true, I am the one that must put the wheels in motion. No waiting for someone else, namely God, to magically do it for me. When I make mistakes, I take them on the chin and learn from them. I had to figure out how to get from point A to point Z, and how to have a good time in the process.

In fact, creating adulthood was one such goal. I couldn't simply wait for some mentor to come along and bless me with his wisdom and affirm my adulthood. I had to create adulthood and rituals to affirm myself. That was part of why I joined the Radical Faeries — to create rituals that had real meaning for me. I read the book, *Iron John*, by the father of the men's movement, Robert Bly. It was an amazing read about becoming a man, gay or straight. The book named many myths, cultures and life experiences that affirmed my adulthood. I embraced it with all my heart. I saw the valuable lessons, wisdom and gifts that only a true adult could attain.

I was blessed with youthful looks, which frustrated me sometimes because a lot of people wouldn't take me seriously. Now in my 40's, although I have great gratitude for my young features, a simple way that I committed myself to adulthood was by not hiding my grey hair. It is coming in by force, or so it seems. It might be a silly thing, but I try to wear my silver with pride. I feel as though I've earned it, and I'd like to think it's a sign of wisdom.

Another way that some cultures delineate different stages in an individual's life is by changing the person's name. Jews sometimes changed an ill person's name to help them heal; the new name represented a new, healthy life.[3] I think the point at which a person begins to chart their own course and feels that they are their own person is an excellent time to select a new name that is particularly self-descriptive. Although it's somewhat rare in our society to change a name, while I was purposefully embracing adulthood I felt the need to change my name. For a long time, the nickname Jallen had been tossed around as a condensation of my first and middle names, Jeff Allen. Because the name is unusual, it seems to describe the creative energy that is uniquely me. Although some friends and family were challenged by the change (I think Mom and Dad felt slighted), I've stuck with it.

If you begin to look for symbols, rituals, and even people, that can affirm your adulthood, you will find them. This was true for me as my awareness of the need grew. One of my most profound experiences was in the form of a movie: 1989's Academy Award winner for Best Foreign Language Film, *Cinema Paradiso*, directed by Giuseppe Tornatore. This film rocked my world. It's a story about a boy, Salvatore, who bonds with an old guy, Alfredo, who runs the local movie theater in a tiny Italian village. The story follows the boy as he grows up and learns the craft of movie-making from Alfredo. In turn, the boy helps his mentor around the theater, helps him get a high school diploma, and even saves the old man from a fire. I don't have room to explain all the beautiful visuals, humorous dialogue and engaging storytelling that make up this masterpiece, but there was a pivotal moment for me that most people probably don't even catch yet brought me to my knees. After the youth does his time in the military, he returns to his hometown to find it changed, or maybe he has changed. He has become a young man. He makes plans to leave and find his way in the world. When he musters the courage to finally say goodbye to Alfredo, who is now blind as a result of the fire, the old man suddenly grabs onto Salvatore's neck, and I was expecting him to cry, "Don't leave!" Instead, the old man almost harshly says, "I don't want to hear from you. I want to hear about you." Although these words might have been brash, they were all about love to me. This old man was kicking the bird out of the nest while, at the same time, visualizing the highest hopes and dreams for his young friend. When that old guy said that, it stung my eyes wet. It felt like a slap in the face, yet everything in me was feeling overwhelming gratitude. This was the kind of loving kick-in-the-pants that I was looking for. I sobbed and nearly doubled over for the rest of the film and out into the parking lot. My boyfriend at the time, Stuart, was so supportive: "Are you all right?" Through my tears I said, "Yes, I'm fine. I feel like a man."

Letting Go

It seems that one of the elements that was essential for me in embracing adulthood is often referred to as one of the keys to growing old gracefully: learning to let go. Ex-gay and religious-abuse survivors have a lot of letting go to do. Some survivors aren't able to happily let go of aspects of their ex-gay life. Their lives seem to be ripped from their souls by the organizations that rejected them. Being honest about one's sexuality, leaving an ex-gay or religiously abusive environment, has cost everything for so many people. Therefore it's not surprising that "letting go" is not one of our favorite things. I can be touchy about letting go of aspects of control in my life. I try to keep a loose grip, nonetheless. Letting go seems to have an element of being willing to be out of control, and that is very scary for most people. In fact, for some, the option of letting go of control is... well, not an option at all. I have seen too many great organizations and wonderful ministries die in the clutches of their creator's or founder's hands because he or she could not let go of control enough to let their "child" grow beyond their grip. When the time is right, I believe it is the highest calling of a true parent to let go and let their child become an adult.

I feel so fortunate to have a perspective that helps me see the bigger picture. As a composer, I find that writing a piece of music is like raising a child. I nurture it, give it room to grow, and eventually send it out into the world. Whether I perform it or someone else performs it, the piece of music gets its "message" across even if I'm no where to be found. Learning to let go now is basically practice for the day when, in death, I will have to let go of everything. Will this be done gracefully? I might as well practice now. Below are a number of things I have had to release, in my recovery process.

Of course there are the obvious aspects. I have had to let go of all the dreams and fantasies of what a good Christian man should look like. I've had to let go of the fantasy of having a wife, the kids, the white picket fence, and my family's pride in what an ideal "man of God" would look like. I have had to let go of what I was going to do for God, and how I was going to be The Example of a "kewl" contemporary Christian. As the joke goes, "Jesus may love you, but I was going to be His favorite!" This may sound silly, but after years and decades of living within that kind of belief system, to just let it all slip through my fingers was no easy task.

Speaking of favorites, I have had to let go of an enormous amount of judgment and condemnation. No matter how much I think I have become non-judgmental, there always seem to be more ways I am critical — of myself and of others. The degree to which I judge seems to be on an ever-deepening continuum. There have been plenty of times that I have thought, "Hey, I'm not as tight-assed as I use to be, or as judgmental as a lot of fundamentalists are," only to realize just how arrogant that statement can be. I hear it in the words of a lot conservative Christians who earnestly think they are without judgment but, because they have never had to look outside their bubble, can't see just how exclusionary they are.

To this day, I have to continually let go of perfectionism — the judgment of self. I learned these unrealistic standards from the church, and this kind of letting go felt like a sign of weakness. It felt as though I couldn't cut it for God. When I first graduated from college and was self-employed, making it as a full-time singer/ songwriter, I took a course on how to schedule my time, how to set goals and achieve them step-by-step. I literally had every hour of my week planned out. At the end of each day, the hardest thing for me to do was accept that I hadn't completed every single task I had planned. I had to let myself off the hook. I had to learn to love myself. The standards I hold myself to — comparing myself to others — are sometimes ridiculously unrealistic. And I have to keep letting my expectations go.

I have tried to let go of the word "should," because it always seems to be about judgments. The word doesn't seem to deal in the present tense. It's always about what I am not, or what someone else is lacking, or what I "should" be some day. I just don't need it, whether applied to myself or to others.

I have let go of what religion and church once meant to me. I have seen LGBT people come out, be rejected by their congregations and denominations, and then start their own church. Nothing is wrong with this — in fact, it can be very important to claim your spirituality for yourself in this manner. However, too often these "new" churches have all the structure, ritual, traditions, trappings, judgments, drama, negativity, etc., of their former church. It certainly smacks of religious compulsion. It's not my sense that these folks are nurturing their faith so much as they are trying to recreate the past. Let it go.

I am amazed at the number of ex-gay survivors who have gone through hell and yet, when asked to share their experience, clam up: "I am not comfortable talking about my past ex-gay leaders because they meant well and I don't want to speak badly of them." Even after the leaders have utterly ex-communicated them, taken away everything they loved, and sometimes tossed them out with no place to go, the survivor's sense of loyalty still hangs on. And their pattern of silence still keeps them trapped. Their sense of obligation to protect others is stronger than their desire to speak the truth. Just as a battered wife will defend her abusing husband, ex-gay and religious-abuse survivors can remain loyal because that's what feels most comfortable. Let go of loyalty to those who oppressed you. They have not earned it. Your silence could very well be allowing your abuser to continue unabated. Let it go and speak up.

This is not easy work. I had whole seasons of letting go and, in turn, whole seasons of feeling deep loss, mourning and grief. I also had an overwhelming sense of being lost, because I had let go of so many things I used to manage my life. When I let those things go, I had to find different ways of motivating myself. One of the hardest things I had to let go of was the desire to control and suppress my emotions. Actually, I began to realize that I probably never had any control over them in the first place. Loosening my grip on what emotions had been to me deserves a section all its own.

"Controlling" Emotions

I had done a great job of teaching myself not to feel. I was terrified of
my emotions — especially my attraction to other men. But in shutting
down those feelings, I shut myself off to most other emotions as well.
— Ron Poindexter, Ex-gay Survivor.[4]

In my ex-gay group we joked about one person whom we called the Zombie for Jesus, because he seemed to have such a shaky hold on his emotions. I can't say I was much different. Just because I kept a tight lid on my emotions and desires didn't keep them from building up. Not at all. The emotions just kept coming. I would just keep stuffing. Keeping up my patterns of denial and suppression was exhausting. Even after I came out and was in the process of accepting myself, I was at a complete loss as to what to do with this stockpile of emotions.

Finally, I got a clue. I realized it took a lot more energy to resist my emotions than it did to feel them. Holy constipation, did that ever make a lot of sense! I felt as though my emotional history was a giant ice cube that was no longer surrounded by its original mold and was just starting to thaw. Quite frankly, I was afraid, as many of us are, that if I began to feel all the years of repressed feelings, the melting process would never stop and it would overwhelmingly flood every part of my life. I was truly afraid of drowning in a lifetime of suppressed emotions. Perhaps this is the simplest definition of a nervous breakdown: stuffing everything for so long that finally something snaps the dam that held it all back and the flood of emotion just won't stop.

I sat many an hour in therapy feeling positively miserable about past experiences, knowing I wanted to express it — cry it out, just get it out of me. Yet I would ask my therapist, "Why can't I cry? (Fix me. Fix me!)" He would gently suggest that maybe it wasn't that I couldn't cry, but that I was deeply, habitually afraid of crying — so deeply that I couldn't even recognize it as fear. True to form, I would get to talking, forget my "control" of the conversation to the point that sadness might slosh out a bit through my tear ducts, and I would panic. It was a paralyzing panic: "What if I lose control, and never stop crying?" Some unseen giant clamp would bear down and seal me tightly shut, and I would sit again in silence.

But I kept working at it over a long period of time. As with sexuality, I experimented with my emotions to try and loosen them up. I sometimes use the tried and true "watch a sad movie" trick. I would "practice" by watching a movie that I knew in the past had made me cry. My top favorites were *Ordinary People*, *The Shawshank Redemption* and, as I've already mentioned, *Cinema Paradiso*. To this day, when I occasionally feel emotionally constipated, I put on a tear-jerker and it really helps. My latest favorites have been *Finding Neverland* and *Lars and the Real Girl*. They get me every time.

As with other processes mentioned in this book, flexing my emotional muscles was slow going. But sticking with years of therapy paid off in ways that going just for a short time could never have achieved. Gradually I would shed a tear or two more. I would laugh a little harder and more freely. I could be present without getting overwhelmed. I began to see that no one emotion stayed too long. I can honestly say that when I started to cry, I was able to stop. The fear of looking like a blubbering fool left me when I was in an environment of safety, with close friends or my therapist. The reality about emotions was actually the opposite of what I believed. Keeping a tight lid on them was the behavior that could make me explode, lose control, and break down. Feeling my emotions in the moment and letting them flow was the very act that made them manageable.

If your experience is similar to mine, consider all the years you may have submitted yourself to emotionally-phobic environments. For those of you who have a lot more years of anguish to get out, don't let this be overwhelming to you. Let it be your justified time to get unfinished business out of you. After all, what are the alternatives — heart disease, ulcers, losing your temper?

Still today (is the work ever done?) I'll have a stray memory come to the surface with a potent emotion that needs releasing, and the oddest things will trigger them — a scene in a movie, something a friend says, a dream. Now, when mine arise, I simply feel them. I let them pass through my body. Maybe I tell someone about them, and I release the energetic charge, like releasing a bubble to the wind. Now it feels as though I have emotional space in which to stretch out. I have found that there are many memories, rich and varied, strong and heartbreaking. I can survey them all and not go into a tailspin. I like having that freedom, and it's all because I have allowed my emotions to integrate with my mind, body and spirit.

The other surprise I have gained from all this letting go is strength. I think it comes with freedom. As I let all those feelings out, I was not reduced to a blubbering, whining wreck. Quite the opposite. I am clear, free, and strong.

Retreading Old Patterns

I'm sitting in therapy, and we're going to play the word association game. As we begin, my therapist says, "Just say the first thing that comes to mind." Immediately I feel that I'm fighting a losing battle because, more often than not, my first thoughts on any given subject are what I believe God would want me to say rather than what I, the authentic person, would say. Now it can be argued that the thoughts that I think God would want me to say are still my own thoughts. Yes, it may be the first thought that comes to mind, but it does not mean that it is who I am, and here's why: I've got "God first, others second, and me last" so ingrained in my mind that my very identity is formed around it, like ivy covering a fence. I truly don't know if it is possible to remove the ivy without destroying the fence.

If these self-neglecting ideas have been pretty much set from childhood, is there anything that can be done? For one thing, I have chosen not to play word-association games. Although I may have little success on the spur of the moment in resisting those ideas and patterns set in childhood, I do better when I give myself some time. I have learned some methods of compensating, but that has taken years of practice, therapy, and self-love.

The best way I can explain this is by equating my "God responses" with a knee-jerk reaction, which can be defined as "an immediate unthinking emotional reaction produced by an event or statement to which the reacting person is highly sensitive."[5] There was a time when, if someone said something, my knee-jerk reaction was to speak godly things in response. Was it a question? Could I quote scripture? What could I say to bring the love of Jesus into their hearts? That's just the way I had been programmed. Yes, it really smacks of brainwashing, but I was not as concerned about labeling it as much as I was needing a solution. As I began to work on it, like learning to identify my parent's voices in my head, I learned to hear my "god talk" — my knee-jerk reaction. Sometimes I would have a reaction and it would take days, if not weeks, to identify it and get beyond it to find my own opinion. Gradually, I could reduce the time between the knee-jerk and my authentic response. These days, after years of practice, the knee-jerk, for the most part, can be just a blink of my eye. I pause, find my voice, express it, and I can rest in it.

Still, on occasions when I am really under a lot of pressure or stress, my ability to make decisions can grind to a crawl because it is so hard to find my own voice — especially when working within groups or when deadlines are bearing down. It is as if all of the old voices in my head are talking at the same time. I can get lost in it all, I get very quiet, and I shut down. Sometimes, decisions take more time than others, and that's just got to be okay.

Creative Expression

In the religiously abusive environment, participants often feel at the mercy of God's "will," as preached by the leadership. I remember having a constant fear that God was going to "call me" to go to some distant country to be a missionary, as if that would have been the worst thing that could happen to me. There was often this feeling that God was going to ask me to do the very thing I hated the most, just to test my loyalty, as when God asked Abraham to sacrifice his son.

Many an ex-gay and religious-abuse survivor put dreams and careers on hold while they went through an ex-gay program. David Christie, when he decided to join a residential ex-gay ministry, said this:

> *I had to move. I had to change churches. I had to change friends. I dropped out of a promising graduate school career and took on a dead-end office job in order to minimize conflicts with my ceaseless schedule of therapy, support groups, and related events. Hoping to truly purge myself of homosexuality, I threw out old letters and photographs, books, and music — things I loved, but which I had come to believe were negative influences.* [6]

Another problem was that many of our more colorful talents and creative gifts, like costume-making, dancing, and hair styling, for example, fell far outside what was deemed acceptable to certain gender stereotypes. Therefore, many of our imaginative dreams, talents, and creative energies were choked out. Talk about being stripped of the very gifts God had given us!

I like to think of creativity as being like sea anemones. When the ocean tide is out and I explore the pools among the rocks and sand on the California Coast, I often can identify the sea anemones. Granted, they just look like blobs of greenish jelly lying in the crevasses above the water line. If I give one a poke, it recoils and recedes even more into the rock, while it squirts out water along with a kind of venom that is harmless to me but keeps fish from biting them. A sea anemone doesn't look like much. In fact it looks completely helpless, but that's because it's in the wrong element. If it stayed above the water line for too long, it would dry up and die. However, within a few hours, the tide turns and submerges the rocks and all that requires this particular creature to thrive. When those sea anemones are surrounded by the right element — the salty sea — they bloom and stretch. They dance and flourish with every color imaginable.

For too long, many an ex-gay and religious-abuse survivor has been in the wrong element — a place where they were helpless, lifeless, and starving. They were poked and prodded only to suppress, spit venom, and recoil further. But now they have left that environment, and they can surround themselves with elements that nurture their gifts. I have worked with ex-gay survivors who are quite literally picking up where they left off before they subjected themselves to the ex-gay world.

Of course, creative energy is not limited to the traditional arts. It's using your energy to be creative in whatever field, vocation, or set of gifts you have. I know a number of survivors who have used their creative energy to reflect and express their experiences of abuse and dependency. In doing so, they have produced beautiful art, penned moving stories, and shared their souls. Most wonderfully, it has been this kind of energy and expression that have been enormously healing not only for the creators, but for all who experience their works, as well. Here's what one artist, Christine Bakke, has done:

> *I have been able to process my ex-gay experiences most powerfully through my art. It's been useful for me and other survivors to explore big emotions that we don't always have words to express.*
>
> *For one art piece, I did collages on playing cards. The collages visually represent my ex-gay years. Included were all my hopes and dreams, then the failures, the destroyed dreams and finally, the beginning of healing. I called it "My House of Cards" since it exposed the unstable house of cards I'd built for myself over the years.*
>
> *In another piece, I took a mirror and smashed it so that it splintered in pieces. It reminded me of the years that I saw myself as broken because of the ex-gay teachings that said I could not be whole and healthy as a lesbian. I glued the pieces together and wrote on the frame, "If you see a broken image, examine the mirror." Not only did this allow me to express the pain of seeing myself as broken all of those years (and it's cathartic fun to smash things), but it served as a powerful reminder that it was only the ex-gay thinking that was broken, and not me.*
>
> *The art-making process is therapeutic for me, but I believe that other survivors are often moved on a deeper level by viewing all kinds of art than they are by hearing words. It reaches someplace deep where the stored emotions are but where words don't always live.*[7]

Innocence

It seems our society groups the ideas of pre-pubescence, naïveté and innocence under one category. In doing so, it is often believed that all of these slip through our grasp somewhere around the age of thirteen, never to be experienced again. Maybe that's accurate for pre-pubescence, but as I looked at the definition of "innocent" a phrase took me by surprise. See if your eyes catch it as well: "Innocent. One free from, or unacquainted with, guilt or sin."[8] With the idea of "innocence lost" upstaging my thoughts, I had forgotten that innocence is the state of being guiltless.

To a certain degree, I believe guilt is a healthy emotion that is a natural response when a person's behavior runs contrary to personal values and beliefs. If a person murders someone, I hope they feel some degree of guilt. I think the reason the definition felt so refreshing to me was that I realized "innocence" meant free from shame, as well. Much of what I experienced in the ex-gay and religiously-abusive environment was not guilt but shame, even "toxic shame" as John Bradshaw described in his book, *Healing the Shame that Binds You.*[9] This shame is not about what you do (as guilt is), but about who you are. Bradshaw writes:

> *When shame has been completely internalized, nothing about you is okay. You feel flawed and inferior; you have the sense of being a failure. There is no way you can share your inner self because you are an object of contempt to yourself.... This internal critical observation is excruciating. It generates a tormenting self-consciousness.... The condition of inner alienation and isolation is also pervaded by a low grade chronic depression. This has to do with losing one's authentic self. Perhaps the deepest and most devastating aspect of neurotic shame is the rejection of the self by the self.* [10]

No longer was I condemned. No more did my very skin and heart feel dirty and sinful. I was not the problem. I could see that shame no longer had a place in my life. As an adult, I was, in fact, innocent as a child — shame free. I felt that I was seeing all of life with a new and fresh perspective.

Maturity

I wrote earlier that "I can change without growing, but I can't grow without changing." This saying came from my ex-gay experiences. I was so obsessed with changing my sexuality — to conforming to what was imposed upon me — that it stunted any real growth. I was changing without growing. This is where some ex-gays are to this day, caught in the loop but not going much of anywhere. For me, embracing my adulthood meant that my overall goal was to mature, and hopefully become wiser because of it. I realized that what this journey was teaching me was not limited to a few years of learning in a classroom. Growth is something I get to enjoy — with all gratitude — until the day I die, and maybe even beyond.

CHAPTER 11

All I've Learned Comes Home

Keeping Love the Focus with My Family

IF I WERE TO SPEAK of my recovery process with just a few words (if that's possible) it would be "learning to love without conditions." Cliché though this may be, no other experience has evidenced this process more than my relationship with my parents as, over more than 20 years, I have tried to be authentically myself before them.

I know some people come out to their families and the only real option for them is to nip a lot of the drama in the bud. Let's say a lesbian daughter says to her parents, "Unless you accept me and my girlfriend just like you'd accept me with a boyfriend, we have nothing else to say to each other," and with that she's out the door and so ends that chapter of her story. This was not the route for me. One reason I knew I was not in a place to cut them out all together was that during those periods of silence (after I came out) I started having nightmares, usually involving my parents horribly dying and me finding out after the fact, or dreaming that their deaths were my fault. It was not in me to stop communication so resolutely.

I guess my authenticity was growing pretty tenacious because I was not going to give my parents the sadistic "pleasure" of being a kind of parental victim: "Oh, woe is me. Our son has been seduced by the dark side, please feel compassion and pray for us." This has actually been my greatest motivator to avoid contracting HIV. I will not fulfill my parents' or the fundamentalist church's negative stereotype of what a "poor, lonely, sex-crazed, disease-ridden homosexual" is supposed to be, because that isn't me and it is not the LGBT community.

Furthermore, the idea of cutting them out of my life because they would not accept me did not sit quite right with me. Wouldn't that be simply acting out the same rejection they might use on me? Although I couldn't articulate it at that point, the hunch that I needed to behave in contrast to my parent's reaction kept me from closing the door entirely. But that neither meant I knew what I was doing, nor that my strategy for staying connected with them was sound.

On the contrary, my first stance was that I would be the one to educate them. After all, I was the only (out) gay person they knew, so I took it upon myself to enlighten them on the subject. They asked me to see a Christian counselor. They were aggressive to fix me. But I was close behind and I tried to work every situation in my favor to educate them. If they wanted me to see a counselor, I would agree, with a couple of conditions. First, the counselor had to be a fully licensed psychotherapist, and second, the three of us would see the counselor together. I wasn't going to put my ass on the line unless they were, too. Furthermore, I figured it would do us good to have a referee in the room. If I remember correctly, I made the two-hour drive to my parents' town only a time or two before the sessions ended. Mom and Dad lived so thoroughly in the assumption that I needed to change that they genuinely didn't know why they were there. I made it clear that I already had a therapist, that I had tired, to no avail, to change my sexuality and that I was happy with it. So the counselor really didn't have much to work with aside from maybe generating a few communication skills.

The Family Reacts

Around the time I came out, I was closer to my grandmother than at any other time in my life. She was up in years and there were aspects to her that didn't seem to keep up with quickly changing times. She did not know how to drive or even how to write a check. So, although we were close, I figured that talking about my sexuality was pretty much beyond her sphere of comprehension. But this did not bother me. We both knew we loved each other and that was enough. Right after the coming-out-concert-cancellation debacle, Mom told me not to tell grandma because it would just upset her. I wasn't so sure how much it would upset her. I had an inkling that the possibility of Grandma simply not understanding was what would be most upsetting — to my mother. But I had no plans to say anything.

A couple of months after this conversation, I caught word through the grapevine that Mom had told Grandma that I was a homosexual. I was livid. Somehow it was okay for Mom to upset Grandma? When I confronted my mother, I let her have it: "What gave you the right to tell Grandmother about my sexuality after you told me not to?"

"Well," she said, "Grandmas have great praying power, so we thought she should know." Essentially, Mom was using my grandmother to get more leverage with God about my sexuality. Soon after, I received a letter from my grandmother in my mom's handwriting. It was the longest, most detailed letter I ever received from Grandma. Mind you, I'm sure Grandma helped my mother write the letter. I'm sure Grandma was present in the room, but the letter said a few things that I never heard from my grandmother's lips. I laughed audibly at it but I was saddened by my mother's intrepidness. Looking back on this incident, I realize that my parents are not the kind of people to think up these "spiritual guerrilla warfare" tactics, but they were motivated to do everything they could to "turn me from sin." This was most likely on some advice from their church or Christian radio (which they avidly listen to), and it was an abusive use of religion, and of my grandmother, for that matter.

The next time I visited Grandma our interaction was the same as always. She would fix me a big meal and I would let her. That seemed to give her a sense of maternal usefulness during her long, lonely days. Over a greasy pork chop I updated her on my life, telling her I shared an apartment with a friend. To test the waters, I also said that I was seeing a nice Christian guy, but she did not respond. I wasn't even sure she understood what I said since her hearing was going and often I'd have to shout to communicate. I debated about offering to answer any questions that she might have after finding out about my sexuality. Finally, all I mustered was, "So I heard Mom told you that I'm gay." Grandma wasn't beaming when she said, "Well, yes." She seemed more uncomfortable than angry, and after a long silence she asked, "Well, do you do the cooking?"

I couldn't help but chuckle under my breath, "Oh, sometimes I do, but I also eat out a lot." I assume that in her mind the only concept she had of homosexuality was that I would take on some of the "female roles" in a living situation, which included cooking. This was the complete and total sum of our conversation about my sexuality. God love her!

As word got around my mom's side of the family that I was gay, responses were mixed but mostly silent. One of my favorite cousins was quick to send me a note, which included the following:

> I just finished reading your informative newsletter. As I read it I found myself agreeing with you on the aspect of love and respect as a priority. I feel saddened for you in that you don't "fit into" the little mold our family thinks we all should fit into. I'm sad that some people think you are demonized. How dare they. You stated that you want to be known for your love and not hate. Well, I just want you to know I love you very much, cousin. I want you to know that there are those in our family that do love and accept you just the way you are. May God continue to bless you.[1]

This is the kind of family member that makes me tearfully beam with pride, for this kind of love I have felt since my birth. Over time, there were others who came forward to offer their support. However, at the other extreme, there was one uncle who was harshly opposed and outspoken about my sexuality. I suppose this would be an appropriate time to say, "There's one in every family." But I suppose this could be said about me, as well.

I will give my uncle this much, he is a Southern Baptist minister and he previously had me sing at his church. I assume there was some camaraderie he felt with me, both of us being in the ministry. I believe he had even used some of my music and lyrics in his preaching and writing. So when he found out about my sexuality I think he felt betrayed. He wrote me a long letter or two which included some of the same ol' outdated and misused research material I'd seen time and again in the ex-gay world. I don't think I had the time or energy to have much discourse with him, and I felt it couldn't have helped matters anyway. I had heard through the grapevine that he was being pretty vocal in the family about me, so when the day came that I was actually going to see him, I didn't know what to expect.

My grandmother had gotten to the point that she could no longer live on her own. Several aunts and uncles (my parents included) got together to help her go through and condense her possessions, many of which would be distributed among family members. I was available to help so I joined them. Much to my surprise, this uncle said nothing. In fact, I realized right away that he was going to attempt the "act as if he doesn't exist" treatment. After all, there are so many times in the Bible when Jesus would treat people that way, that I figured he was just trying to imitate Christ's love, but I'm not bitter (wink, wink!). Even his wife, my mom's sister, seemed to be under strict orders to do the same, because she did not say anything to me until she was well out of earshot of my uncle.

I wasn't about to let him get away with such blatant and rude hypocrisy. When the end of the day came, I walked right over to him and placed my open hand directly in his path for him to shake: "It was really good to see you, Uncle. I'm glad you're here to help with Grandma's stuff." There was a long pause as everyone in the room became silent, and he finally, barely shook my hand. I think he did it only because he was on the spot and didn't know what else to do. Granted, I said it with a big ol' shit-eatin' grin on my face. I was proud of the fact that I got to be the one to offer hospitality and civility, since he was treating me worse than he would any stranger. This empowered me. It confirmed to me that the outcast is the one to set the example.

Tit for Tat

For about seven years, my parents and I constantly attempted to change each other — they wanting me to be "healed" of homosexuality, and I wanting them to accept me as I was. It seemed no visit or phone conversation was exempt from our educational tactics. It's hard to say if the reason I was trying so hard was to counter their aggressiveness, or vice versa. I just know that pretty quickly a need for balance emerged. I would tell myself that if they wanted me to read some book about becoming straight, then it was only fair that they would read a book of my choosing. I remember asking my mom if she had read a particular book I had given her. She replied, "I tried, but it just hurts me to read it." I didn't care if reading a book made hair sprout out of her eyeballs. I was reading what they gave me, so the least they could do was to read what I gave them.

I received a letter from my father in which he invited me to go to the Promise Keepers Conference — the evangelical version of the men's movement in the early nineties. As you can guess, with the Promise Keepers straight masculinity was next to godliness. Here is a portion of what I wrote back:

> *Dear Dad,*
> *Thank you for including me in what makes you excited. I have thoroughly looked over the stuff you sent me and I can see that there are lots of things that you would enjoy and want to share with me. I, on the other hand, am very reticent to hear several of the speakers. Several of them are very outspoken against gays and lesbians like me. I quite frankly would get pretty angry hearing them. I am also cautious to be pressured into any kind of altar call or commitment time because I fear it would only disappoint you. I have a feeling the time would be tense for both of us because I am gay and am not ashamed of it.*
>
> *However, I do want to make my dad happy. And I do think that circumstances exist that would allow me to come with you. In a sense we could strike a bargain. I would be willing to go to your conference if you would be willing to go to a conference of mine. This conference is called Evangelicals Concerned ConnECtion. Both you and mom would be welcome. It is the highlight of my year and God has created much healing in my life because of it. I am willing to find out what makes my dad happy, as long you're willing to find out about what make me happy. Please know that I love you and have given much thought and prayer over this matter.*

I knew that striking this balance would simply mean neither of us would go to each other's conference. I knew that this balancing act was my justification to educate them, but it was also my first attempts to take care of, and stand up for, myself in the presence of my parents. If I had simply taken everything they had thrown at me without ever trying to make some kind of response, I would have felt all the more frustrated with my voice completely squelched. Yet imbalanced our connection stayed, and this was most apparent in the way we spent time together. After I came out, Mom and Dad shied away from visiting me. It wasn't from lack of opportunity since many of my relatives lived within an hour or two of my home and my parents would visit them often. Almost all of our time together was when I visited them. I don't want to sound like a whiner, but at the time it just increased my frustration.

Another complication was that soon after I came out I began my serious relationship with Stuart. We moved in together and even had a commitment ceremony a year to the day after meeting each other. Mom and Dad made it clear that they could never set foot in a house where I lived with another man and that Stuart was not welcome in their house. Initially, out of respect, I would reluctantly visit them alone since I'm an independent person, and I have no problem spending vacations apart from a partner. What made these visits nearly intolerable was that, without Stuart, my family continued to imagine that I was actually single and that I would possibly get married to a woman someday. I would try to bring Stuart up in conversations but all reference to him was ignored.

After two years I couldn't play the game any more. Our annual camping trip was coming up and all my aunts, uncles, and cousins would be there. I wanted to introduce them to Stuart. Over the previous years they had heard about him and a few wanted to meet him. Others, of course, did not. But I had been patient — for years, to make a point of it — and it was time for Stuart (who was strong, loving and courageous throughout) to meet the family. I was still very proud of my family and I wanted Stuart to get to know them a little.

As camp drew closer, Mom and Dad went into nothing short of a temper tantrum, crying and sobbing during phone conversations. They would voice their pain as if a violent act were being inflicted by their ungrateful son, but it was clear what was actually forming their nightmares: my bringing Stuart meant they could no longer deny that I was straight or single. I think this also translated in my parents minds as meaning that everyone would view my gayness as a parental flaw. What would the relatives think? Oh, the shame they were exhibiting. If they could have stomped their feet, fallen on the ground, and pounded their fists in the dirt, they would have — if they had thought it would get me to change my mind. Over and over I tried to stay calm and firm, which tended to infuriate them more. "Mom and Dad, I've respected your wishes for over two years and kept Stuart away. Now it's time for Stuart to meet the family." During one conversation, Mom said, in her best martyr's voice, "Well, if you bring Stuart, I guess we'll just have to stay home." This only revealed further what this showdown was all about — their shame. I stayed firm, if not coy: "I hate for you to miss out on family camp, but if that's what you think you should do, I can't stop you."

I knew better. Mom and Dad would not miss family camp, and they didn't. It is true that they were not comfortable while Stuart and I were there. In fact, most of the time, when we would come around and, for example, take a seat at the campfire, Mom would excuse herself. Then there was dealing with that particular uncle who had his grown daughters trained and ready to take a stand. These were two women I had known literally all their lives yet when I saw them, said hello and gave them hugs, you would have thought we were complete strangers. Well, no, actually they would have treated strangers a lot better than they treated me. They were stiff as boards. I was so surprised that I thought it was some kind of joke and, "Don't you want a hug?" slipped out of my mouth before I had a chance to think otherwise. One of them said disappointedly, "No, no, we don't." I also began to realize that whenever I was around, this uncle's family would herd my cousin's children quickly away from me. Some of this was out of plain old fear and ignorance. I understood that some of their rude behavior was simply passive-aggressive (I guess not so passive) responses to "the pain you are causing your parents." I guess there have been other occasions when family drama was this severe, but I can't recall it, and I sure was never the "cause" of it all. Other relatives treated Stuart and me with civility and loving hospitality. I think they even surprised themselves about it. I knew that if I were to ask them what they thought about homosexuality we wouldn't see eye-to-eye, but these relatives chose to make their love for me more important. These relatives will forever be the example of Jesus in my family, and believe me, this is not a statement I make lightly.

While we were there I kept my guard up and a smile on my face. I was trying to show them that homosexuals were not evil people. Although I didn't flinch before them, I heard their declaration of exclusion loud and clear. It's too bad that some of them turned their backs to my face — their own blood. It was only well down the road from the campground that the shock really sank in, and I felt devastated. As I deeply felt the sadness of acknowledging just how unwelcome we were made to feel, however, I finally sobered up about a few things.

My desire to be fair in this education process was not their desire. They plain didn't care about being fair, as far as I could tell. It felt as though they didn't want to read or do anything much to understand me. All that this striving for balance did was infuriate me, because I was the only one striving for it. Heed these words: One person working on a relationship does not a relationship make.

Not even our theological arguing was balanced because, quite frankly, religion is not based on logic. It's supposed to be based on faith. Yet, in the religiously abusive system, religion is based on whoever manages to be "God's voice." I confronted my parents about whether they thought I was going to hell or not. I knew some of the teaching they were receiving pushed strongly that homosexuals went to hell, yet Baptists firmly believe that once a person is born again they are saved forever from hell. So they were in a theological double-bind. My mom's response was, "Well, you'll go to heaven but there won't be as many jewels in your crown." Somewhere a flock of angels was on laughing gas that day. There were even times, having been well educated about what the Bible said (and didn't say) about homosexuality, that I could run theological circles around them. Yet, when I could soundly prove my point and all their religious artillery was emptied out, it was as if a record skipped a groove in their minds and they would just start over again.

It felt as though my parents were saying they loved their theology more than they loved me. I realize now that it's not quite so "either/or," but at the end of the day, whom did they believe? Not me. They sided with their theology, and I sure felt unsupported. To feel as though my parents could not stand with me was such an isolating experience that it felt like a constant, aching virus that stayed in my body poisoning me for years. If I couldn't trust my own flesh and blood to believe me when times were tough, I had little hope that anyone else would find me trustworthy.

To be sure, I can be an intimidating debater, and I was aggressive about educating my parents, but that enthusiasm runs in our family and all too often our "discussions" would devolve into emotionally charged, tear-stained arguments where neither side was listening. In fact, this emotional drama was so consistent on the phone and when I visited, that after the camping trip I started to dread our times together. I would visit and the arguing was so difficult that I no longer felt safe or comfortable in their house. I literally felt trapped and over-exposed. A time or two, I packed my bags and left prematurely. That was a big step for me because I was well aware that leaving would in some ways ruin the weekend they had planned to spend with me. I'm sure there was some passive aggressiveness on my part, walking out like that, but truly, it just did not feel safe after having such vehement arguing with no resolution in sight. Driving away from my parents' home (prematurely or not) became a devastating experience. Most of the time, Mom would shed tears as I drove off. I was racked with the guilt of being the black sheep, convinced of all the pain I was causing them. Should I have said more? Should I have said less? Should I have spent more time? I felt like such a failure and disappointment to them. Our connection felt so strained that I could hardly see the road through the tears and sobbing.

On one particular premature drive-away I began work on a set of lyrics that evolved over several trips. It gave me something to focus all the sad energy on. I often work creatively as a ritual to help me figure out some of life's most puzzling scenarios. How could people like us profess that the reason we fight and argue is that we love each other, when the sound and the feelings in those arguments seemed to have so little love and respect in them? Our verbal combat was so severe that it felt as though love had been long ago forgotten. As a result, I wrote one of my favorite set of lyrics.

Following orders, behind enemy lines
Severing conscience, severing ties
Catching the opponent by surprise
I raise my gun, his face in sight
I see the fear in his mud stained eyes
He starts to cry and it shakes me to the core
What was it we were fighting for?
 Stuck in traffic, running late
 Horns are blaring, cars jam lanes
 I raise the finger, and yell in hate
 Then down the road I see the crash
 The pool of oil, the broken glass
 A white sheet covers up the corpse
 What was we were fighting for?
Broken vows, discarded rings
Divorce is a lesson in apathy
People get used in jealously
This ship is sinking and I can't stop her
Losing ballast, bailing out water
Just when were the kids thrown overboard?
What was it we were fighting for?
 Ever eager to show how big I can be
 No one ever really dies in shoot 'em up movies
 The drama, the glory, bombs bursting in air
 It's so easy to forget how to care
 Comfort is what we are striving for
 Living is what we are killing for
 Truth is what we are lying for

Compliance is what...
Denial is what...
Is love is what we are fighting for?
Words and phrases, symbols and signs
Body language, small white lies
Sincerity seems always in disguise
Before I start keeping score
Before I pick up the weapons of war
I think I'll listen carefully once more
What was it we were fighting for? [2]

Moratorium

One thing the attempt at balance did for me was heighten my awareness of listening carefully. I can tell pretty quickly when a debate breaks down into an argument because the balance between listening and speaking tips — on both sides — toward speaking. All it takes is one person in a discussion to tip that balance and the debate grinds to a halt and will go nowhere. Time and again my parents and I would start in on a conversation. We'd start getting impatient. We'd start interrupting each other. We had such an enormous need to talk, so desperately wanting to be heard, and yet we weren't able to listen.

The time I spent contemplating the situation began to change focus. Rather than just trying to educate them, I started to consider how to bring our love to the surface without invalidating our respective perspectives. In one letter, I wrote an attempted solution:

> *One thing that [I] think would help me to keep proper perspective about our relationship is that I am, for a while, not going to talk about "the subject" at all with you. I just will not talk about it. I will however, debate with you till I'm blue in the face by letter. I suggest you do the same. That keeps our homes safe and welcome places instead of, sometimes, war zones. I don't want to be scared to come to your house, and you have nothing to fear coming to mine. Keeping our debates in letter-form will only help us say things better and help enhance our love in person.*

This guideline of silence became the next chapter of our interaction, or I guess I could say non-interaction. I think everyone involved was, on some level, relieved.

Whew! After several years of pulling against each other in this no-win tug of war, what a relief to simply stop.

As months turned into years, I think the enforced silence became, if anything, an opportunity for reflection. Mom and Dad grew accustomed to the silence partly because in general their generation is more accustomed to being silent in uncomfortableness, and partly because they didn't want to know the details of my life. In this silence they learned to ask no questions whose answers had the potential to create tension between us. This was both a blessing and a curse. A blessing because the arguing stopped. A curse because over time they knew less and less about me, how I was growing and what was important to me. Our connection was whittled down to the shallowest of interactions compared to the level of closeness I maintained with friends.

It devastated me to realize that in some ways my parents really didn't believe that "honesty was the best policy." I remember several conversations when I would confront them about it and I could see them struggling between their commitment to the truth, and their discomfort with who I was. They actually would rather be blissfully ignorant than really get to know me, for fear of what they would learn about me. Because of this, the rejection I felt from them seemed to cut deeper and deeper. I know they have some desire to know their son through and through, but when they found things they did not agree with (and they didn't have to look far beyond their narrow perspective), it was too much for them unless they could try to do something about it. So we were silent. At the time, this only felt like rejection to me, even though the moratorium on the topic was my idea in the first place. Over time, though, I continued to change. And perhaps they did, too.

Letting Go of Expectations

One significant experience was visiting my brother, a Southern Baptist minister, and my sister-in-law. My brother (nine years my elder) and I had not been close. So I had gone out of my way to stop by, see their new house and try to visit with them a while. I showed up, we chatted about a few family topics, and minimal questions were asked of me. I think we had some dessert. But within 45 minutes we were sitting in front of the television in silence.

I couldn't believe it. It seemed like record time for running out of things to say to each other. I dismissed myself and got back on the road. Once again, as I drove away, tears rolled down my cheeks. Yes, partly I cried because they really didn't seem to have any interest about me and my life — at least there seemed to be more uncomfortableness than there was interest. Perhaps my bother felt I had caused so much pain to my parents that indifference was a way to punish me. Mostly, though, I cried because in many ways this is how my family behaves. I was expecting them to have as much passion for talking, communicating and self-disclosure as I had. But it's not who they are. And I began to see that it was possible to accept and love them without expecting them to be like me.

I was gradually taking another step in my recovery, and perhaps it's just part of growing up. Although it was perfectly natural for a son to want the acceptance of his family, as I grew stronger, I knew that it was not a requirement for me. There were times in the past when all my energy was focused on figuring out a way to be acceptable to my family. Then there were these more recent years of trying to educate my loved ones so they could accept me. Sounds redundant, doesn't it? At last I was learning to the best of my ability to let go and simply accept them as they are, and myself as I am. It was not easy. It took a long time and a lot of self-examination. Eventually I came to understand the difference between expectation and hope. I no longer expect my family to accept me, but I can hope for it, and I will always leave my door open to them.

Smudge on the Family Photo

My therapist in one particular session challenged me about the kind of "pain" I was inflicting on my parents — how I was, in their words, "hurting them by choosing to be gay." I did the typical dissecting: "Well, they call it pain and it's not like I'm cutting them, but I'm their son, so they care about me when they think I'm going the wrong way, blah, blah, blah!" Again, my therapist asked if I believed I was a pain to them, and I chimed right in using words like, "black sheep, the youngest, artistic, queer." Of course I was stressful for them. In addition, with all the obsessive focus they had had on fixing me over the past few years, of course they would feel I was "high maintenance."

My therapist asked me again, "So you are a real setback to your family?" On some level I really believed they saw me as a detriment rather than an asset. What was I to think from all their condemnation? This was before I knew what religious abuse was, so of course it was easy to believe that I deserved a kind of rejection for simply not being in line. This was worse than my sister dying, remember?

A fourth time my therapist cut through my psycho-babble and in so many words said, "So you really are the smudge on the family portrait?" His repetitive questioning finally pushed me to connect the dots on my own. Another extreme thought: Would they have been better off if I never existed? I don't think anyone was suggesting that. Wait a minute here…

Was it true? Regardless of what my parents thought, was I such a horrible son? It began to dawn on me that, after all that we had gone through, I had actually started to believe that being gay was the pain in the side of my family. This was a kind of internalized homophobia and self-hate. Did I ask to be gay? Was it a choice? Of course not. Then why was I taking on the responsibility of "ruining" the family when I wasn't able to choose my sexuality in the first place? Further, was there something my parents had done to set themselves up for disappointment? It began to dawn on me that I had to let myself off the hook for "creating" all this so-called trouble in the family. Damn it! Here I was dealing with yet another version of struggling to accept myself.

I sat in therapy with tears flowing again because I felt the heavy burden lift off my back from taking responsibility for all of my family's pain. Somewhere inside I had felt responsible not just for their pain, but for their happiness as well. If they weren't perfectly content, then I must have been a bad son. It was classic co-dependence. I was believing that if I could achieve my parent's approval by the way I behaved, I would keep my family from feeling pain altogether. But in reality, I was making myself miserable by suppressing my honest feelings, and at the same time hampering their ability to directly face realities about their son. I cried because I was beginning to realize I wasn't such a bad son after all.

As these revelations began to sink in over the weeks that followed. My back straightened, so to speak, as I let go of taking responsibility for my family's happiness. This gave me more energy to take better care of myself. As my perspective broadened and strengthened, even if my family still harbored ill will, I was okay with that because I knew that I had done everything in my power to accommodate them.

Ultimately, we're all adults who are quite capable of taking care of ourselves. So if they have some dire offense that still needs to be resolved, they can take their own steps to address me about it. After all, I am not a mind-reader. Even if they still experience "pain" from my being gay, well then, so be it. All I can do is live as authentically as I can before them. I can't be anything else and, if that causes my parents sorrow, they can to take it up with "The Parent upstairs."

A New Level of Authenticity

This new-found liberation and strength helped me keep the time with my family focused on the love we had for each other, which in the past when we argued felt so elusive. I often reminded myself that for me to give and love authentically, I had to take care of myself mentally, spiritually, and physically. I had to give healthy love from a healthy foundation. One way that I learned to do this was by limiting the length of my visits. Experience has taught me that I have about 48 hours — three nights maximum — with my family before I start getting cranky or too caught up in unimportant irritations. Quite honestly, I get cranky when I'm around anyone non-stop for more than 48 hours. My batteries seem to get recharged mostly in solitude, and I learned to respect that in terms of my time with family.

Another step for me to be authentic and keep the focus on love was to stop censoring myself about my own life, although there was still an unspoken moratorium on the debate about homosexuality (and it can stay there, for all I care). In my desire to be loving and not rock the boat I would over-think options, like walking on eggshells. After a while my desire to accept them began to feel more like suppressing myself. So, if we were talking about a subject and my thoughts involved my boyfriend, I would say it, even if they were visibly uncomfortable about it. I wasn't going to rub anyone's face in it, but I couldn't let them go on believing something that was not true about me. My parents can believe whatever they want about God, about heaven and hell, but when it comes to who I am, and if I am to stay involved in their lives, it's important for me to at least try to give them accurate information about myself. I have no control over what they do with it, and I think a lot of times they simply don't get me, and that's okay. I just do what I can to lay factual information before them and to keep my door open for them to see who I really am.

One way I did this was to consciously speak of Leo (my former partner of 12 years) and myself as a unit. So when it came to the holidays and Dad would invite me home for Christmas but not Leo, there would no longer be a big argument about it. He would say, "Son, we'd really like you to come home for Christmas." I would simply say, "Dad, we'd love to come for Christmas!" Of course, they were not comfortable with Leo being there, so then I'd say, "All right, but I'm spending the holidays with my spouse." This strategy worked well for me because it placed the burden of inhospitality on their shoulders. No more guilt about this "predicament" I put the family in, when in this situation the only predicament was that my parents were being rudely exclusive about who came for Christmas at their home. It was silly, too, because for years I'd bring college buddies home for different holidays. It was not my problem. It was theirs.

Missing from the Family Photo

There were still challenges, though. The worst it ever got was the Christmas when Mom wanted a family portrait taken — my parents, myself, my brother, his wife their kids, and the great-grandkids. Leo, of course, was not invited to be in the photo. I knew how important it was to my parents, but I could not in good conscience stand in that photo without Leo. I addressed it and gave my answer in a letter:

After giving thought and prayer to holiday plans, I think I will be home with Leonard [Leo] for Christmas, but I would like to come visit you sometime the beginning of December. I seriously considered being present for the family picture. I know that it holds importance to you. However, I'm having a tough time surmounting my level of discomfort with the photo session.

I choose to gloss over our differences because I desire to stay in touch and keep our love a priority. I see beyond you excluding Leonard because it is important to spend time with you on your terms. These are things I do because that's how I can maintain a relationship with you, my parents. Going to a photo session where I would either have to fake being single or be honest by having Leo there and throwing the session into potential conflict, is more than I can handle. Do we really want a picture of that? There's also something inauthentic about a family who would rather not have their son home for Christmas because of who he holds dear but would like him home for a family portrait... "What's wrong with this picture?" I am willing to compromise even with the family picture, but if you do not have the grace to even allow someone who is important to me into your house, I have very little pride in being in my family's portrait.

Don't get me wrong. It pains me greatly that we find ourselves in this predicament. It seems over the past years "silence as a rule" has helped us stay focused on what's important. But I for one have to speak up and say years are passing by and I am regularly saddened that my blood related family keeps such a distance from me because of our differences.

I know this is not easy. I desire to talk about it all you want and reach a better understanding. I don't discount the efforts you have made to visit the new house and interact with Leonard when he has been present. Indeed, those moments have been highlights for me. Thanks for taking the time to read this letter.

Your son, with love.

So, believe it or not, my family had the photo taken without me and it hung in my parents' house for several years. I thought of it as a testament to the fact that it was more important to my family to not include me than it was to include the person

I have chosen to live my life with. How did that make Leo feel? Despite the way they treated him, he did his best not to give them much credence, though it bothered him. How does it make anyone feel to be ignored and excluded?

I'm not saying it was easy for my family. Evidently it's quite a challenge for many Christians to keep love a priority in the light of LGBT concerns. Yet I wondered sometimes what my relatives were thinking when they refused to hug me or even shake my hand, or refused to let my partner into their house. If this was the love of Jesus, no wonder so many people are disillusioned by contemporary Christianity — even hate it for its members' hypocritical claims of loving inclusion. I know there are big chunks of Christianity that truly strive to show Jesus' love in everything they do, but — sorry, folks — James Dobson's and Pat Robertson's political agendas are drowning you out. I'll tell you this much: Leo did not come to a better understanding of God by way of my family.

A Slow, Subtle Turn in the Tide

Over the course of about 10 to 15 years I grew tremendously in trying to keep the lines of communication going. I can't speak for my parents, but it seemed they grew, too. The process started with finally being honest with my parents about my sexuality. We dove into several years of trying to change each other until we shut down in exhaustion. Out of that silence I tried to refocus my perspective on loving them as best I could, realizing that I can't change them anymore than they can change me. I let go of my expectations of them but kept hope alive as well as keeping my door open to them. Taking better care of myself, I tried to focus on our love without censoring who I am in front of them.

Occasionally, I would search my heart for any further expectations that might set me up for disappointment. The expectations have been minimal. However, I found one hope that stands out. Over time, I hoped my parent's fear of what it means to be a homosexual would dissipate. I hoped that at the very least they would feel at ease when I am, or other LGBT people are, in the room. I hoped they would eventually realize that there is nothing to fear about spending time with their son, as always. I'm not suggesting they change their convictions. I just wished they could feel less uptight and tense around me and the subject of my relationship or sexuality. I didn't expect this change, but I hoped for it, knowing it would ease their stress (which, of course, helps ease mine, too).

Lo and behold — gradually, oh so gradually, it began to happen. My parents seemed less mortified when I mentioned my boyfriend. They seemed calmer and not so resentful at the mention of his name. Leo and I had bought a house and I think fixing it up gave my parents a common subject for us to talk about (they built their house from scratch). Conversations about yard work and plumbing seemed to "normalize" us.

Another reason I credit for this change is that when my parents sold the house I grew up in and built their dream home in the country, they changed churches. Their new church was much larger than the one my siblings and I grew up in and it seemed more healthy, too. Consequently, Mom and Dad got to know a lot more people, some of whom, I can only guess, know or are related to homosexual people, too. I think they simply feel less alone in their relationship to me, and I think that's great.

It is immensely important to let it be known that my mother has deeply regretted the "worse than my sister's death" statement and on more than one occasion has tearfully and sincerely asked my forgiveness for ever saying it. Also, remember the cousins who refused to hug me on that camping trip? I was surprised to be pulled aside by one of them at a family function. She proceeded to apologize for her unkind behavior, as well.

Stepping Across the Threshold

I think the following experience shows the progress my parents and I have made. I have always loved Cirque Du Soleil. My own artistic sensibility revels in the ability to take art that we all know and transform it into a completely new interpretation and this, I feel, is what Cirque Du Soleil has done for the circus, so I wanted to share that experience with my parents. However, I really didn't know how to coordinate it in such a way as to get us all together. On a visit to their house my dad asked if I had ever seen a movie about Cirque Du Soleil. "Seen a movie? Dad, I've seen the real thing!" and with that I knew my foot was in the door.

Thus began talks with my parents urging them to come to San Francisco for an afternoon and see a matinee of Cirque's latest show. I knew I had to remove all the obstacles to get them there — make it so there was no reason for them not to come. So I bought their tickets as a Christmas gift that year. I also wanted to make them as comfortable as possible, so the two of them weren't just coming into the big scary city all alone to go to some crazy show with their homosexual son. Therefore, I invited two of my mom's brothers and their wives, my very cool aunts and uncles to join us. They jumped at the opportunity. My relatives would have a stabilizing effect on my parents and this was really shaping up to be something big!

A dream I really had no expectation of ever becoming reality was actually going to take place. Not only that, but since they were going to be coming a several-hour distance, we set it up to have everyone first join Leo and I at our house for lunch and then all go to the show together. To my utter shock, everyone agreed. Holy family reunion! My parents and relatives were actually coming to my house!

Yes, there was a wild wisp in me that wanted to rub my parent's nose in it: "I thought you said you'd never enter our house!" But that voice was shut right up and put in its place by the overwhelming admiration and respect I had for my parents in taking this enormous step. Mind you, I did not think for a minute that Mom and Dad had changed their religious beliefs. I didn't care about what they believed. Stepping into my house was no commentary on what they believed, except that they loved their son and they wanted to see where he lives. I know every one of them was curious to see our 120-year-old Victorian in San Francisco, and this was their opportunity. I was thrilled to welcome them into my home.

With six of them coming and only two of us, I also invited my closest friend, Michael, since he knew me so well, came from the same religious background and was exceedingly capable of generating genuine conversation. Besides, I really needed all the support I could muster and it was so helpful to have him there.

When the day came I was beside myself with excitement. It was a beautiful clear day in the city so we mingled on the deck with sandwiches. Leo manned the kitchen. Michael talked baseball with my uncles (I didn't even know he knew about sports) and I showed the ladies around the house. We eventually ended up in the living room around the piano. It was a family tradition at reunions that everyone played music on various instruments or sang something. This time was no different. Someone said to me, "Play something for us." Michael sat down and played a piece at the piano. Then I sat down and sang and played. And when they realized that what I had performed was on the last album, they wanted to hear that, too, which felt great because Michael and I produced it together. It couldn't have been a better song to play. I had originally written it for the wedding of my close friends, Jay and Ron, and I explained this as I introduced it. Here are the lyrics:

With all the world of choice and all my loves to see
How will I decide upon the one for me?
But your words spoke the truth
And when you flashed that smile and eyes of blue
From your touch I knew
I would choose you
    When my voice like a stone convinces me I'll fail
    When visions weigh me down, self-judgment tips the scale
    I could choose this stress
    Or I could choose the strength you say I possess
    Let all my plans fall through
    I'll believe you

You create the magic. You and I create this magic that we feel
God's own passion flows through any two
Who would risk their hearts and choose
Tell me true or false could I change my mind?
Pick from A to Z. Who else could I find?
I can ace the quiz
Without a doubt I know what my answer is
What else can I do?
I would choose you[3]

We all packed into a couple of cars and went to the circus. We had great seats with an aisle in front of us for plenty of leg space. A female clown at one point spotted my dad's bald head, polished it off and gave it a big red lipstick kiss. She then turned around to another bald man in the row in front of us and did the same thing. Throughout the show this bald man had his arm lovingly around another man and my family must have noticed. Not that it meant anything, but lightning didn't strike anyone dead, either.

After the show, everybody went home and the pleasure of it all got the better of me. I sobbed tears of joy for I don't know how long and I glowed for a week. It was no less than one of the happiest days of my life. No expectations, just enjoying the people I love, doing wonderful things together. It took on an even greater meaning when, soon after, one of the uncles who had visited, died. It was one of the last events my mom and her brothers shared together.

My Father's Honesty

On another occasion, Dad and I were driving somewhere and he began to tell me a story about his church buddies on one of their RV camping excursions that, truth be told, I was only mildly paying attention to. He said something like, "We were playing cards one evening. There were, oh, five or six of us and one of them began to talk about those evil homosexuals in San Francisco who are trying to destroy the church and family in America…." Whoa! The shock of those words filled my system with adrenaline that made my heart jump, and my attention instantly was wide awake. Dad paused while my mind raced. I could tell that what that guy had said truly hurt my dad's feelings, and telling me about it was difficult. I hardly drew breath because of the lump in my throat, but I managed a hushed, "Ah, dad, what did you do?"

"Well, it got real quiet around the card table because several of them know you," he said, referring to some of his friends I had met in the past. I already had tears down my cheeks and Dad's eyes were getting glassy as he said, "I finally spoke up and said that my son is one of those homosexuals in San Francisco and I'd really appreciate it if you'd pray for him." I was in shock. Though he might have couched it in the form of a prayer request (I don't mind, I welcome all the prayer I can get), my father had just told me that he came out about my sexuality to his manly Christian friends. He ended the story with: "The guy really apologized and the card game sure stayed quiet for a while."

As the power of what my dad had the courage to do sank in, I carefully mustered my appreciation, "Dad, I know we don't see eye-to-eye about the whole sexuality thing, but I want you to know that it really means so much to me that you would be honest with your friends about me so they would know that I'm not some evil stereotype." That was all I dared to say in addressing it for fear of ruining the moment. I think he said something about agreeing with me that we didn't see eye-to-eye about it, but I didn't care. He wanted to tell me what had happened even if he didn't altogether comprehend why. It had certainly landed him in my shoes unexpectedly. It definitely brought us closer together, and that was worth it all. In this instance, despite our differences, love was preeminent.

What Matters Most

Another amazing experience depicting the progress of love between my parents and me was in the final devastating months of my 12-year relationship with Leo. Mom and Dad could see that I was suffering and I had briefly told them times were bad, but I had not given them any details. One reason was that if they couldn't be present with me in the good times of my relationship, there was no way I — pardon how arrogant this sounds — there was no way I was going to give them the privilege or opportunity to listen to my relational grievances, especially when it could leave them an open door to go preachy on me. However, when I knew the relationship was at an end, I made plans to tell them. On a particular visit, I took the plunge, but I realized I had to set some ground rules for what I was about to say. It went something like this:

"Mom and Dad, I want to tell you about what's been happening between Leo and me, but I really need you to simply listen to me. I'm going to tell you the story of what's happened and it would not be helpful if you were to respond with scripture or preaching. I'm just going to relay the circumstances that have unfolded as best I can."

As I explained the crumbling connection with the man I loved, tears streamed down my face and, as any mother would, mine cried, too. I knew there was a particular reason that made it difficult to tell them my relationship was failing. Yet this difficulty became the very vehicle of explanation. "…It's hard to tell you about what's happened because, quite frankly, I've felt like a failure in front of you. I know we don't see eye-to-eye about most of my love life, but one thing that I have admired in your relationship is that you two have stuck it out all these years (55 plus years), and that was at least one thing I felt I could, and wanted to, imitate in my relationship." More crying. "So please believe me when I say that I have done everything in my power — everything I can possibly think of to make this relationship work. But I've had to come to grips with the reality that one person working on a relationship does not a relationship make."

After a long pause that indicated I was done, my mother said, "Well, you know we have always thought that it would be a lot easier on you if you married a woman." This might seem somewhat cruel but I could hear that at least they weren't barking Bible verses at me. They were actually considering my well-being, but then she stopped, changed her thought and said, "But you know what, we love you anyway and that's what matters."

I was so shocked at what she said that I wasn't able to absorb the genuine love that she was giving. Whether she had rehearsed those words or they fell naturally from her lips, she had finally got it right. It was like some kind of 20-year-old quiz that at long last she had found the correct answer for. I responded in tears, "Thank you. That's exactly what I needed to hear."

Since then I have replayed that scene in my mind many times, and I have let their love sink in — whatever they are able to give, I am willing to receive it. Quite honestly, it was more than I had even hoped for. Since, for the most part, I had let go of my expectations of them, this experience ranked in the stratosphere as far as I was concerned. I'm happy to report that I've now had several opportunities with my parents to talk honestly and casually about our differences and love has stayed the focus. Recently, when I expressed my fear that we might fall into one of those old arguments, my dad's response was, "I think those kinds of conversations are a part of our distant past." Wow! These days, after a visit with my family, I drive away with a smile on my face — really! It astonishes me, too.

I have come to realize that I am very blessed to have parents who really strive to put love in the forefront of everything. They might attribute that love to Jesus, but the love is coming through nonetheless. Despite the religious abuse, despite the misuse of scripture, despite the sexual ignorance, despite all the false hope, love has been stronger. So many families completely reject their child when it is discovered that he or she is a homosexual. So many families might acknowledge the "gay thing" once and then never talk about it again. I am now in a rare and lucky percentage of families that, despite the challenges, have used our differences to ultimately reinforce our love for each other. Although they have always loved me, I can now feel it more than ever, and I hope they can feel it from me, too. I think they can. I try to keep my door always open. They are my parents, after all, and I am their son.

Small and afraid
I felt on my first day
When this little boy was scared to go to school
With a kiss and a hug
And an oh, so gentle shove
Mom waved goodbye but in her heart she cried
And when the apron strings were pulled
Despite the pain she kept her cool
I took for granted all the while
How a mother loves her child
    Now as a man
    I will never understand
    How it feels to give birth from the womb
    But I have loved as a spouse
    And I think I've figured out
    How to conceive and give birth from my heart
    And the way I'll grow old gracefully
    Is letting those I love grow free
    Like the Lord let go the beloved One
    So a mother loves her son
And I may not ever fully know
How to love and then let go
But I think I get it more than some
How a mother...and a father...love their son
Because my parents love their sons [4]

An Invitation

My Hope for the Future

WHILE ON THE ROAD in the Midwest some time ago, I was asked to sit on one side of a "debate" arguing against an ex-gay minister. It came to no overt reward. I presented my experience and had supporters in the audience. The "opponent" wasn't interested in listening. He spoke his rhetoric and had his supporters in the audience. I wasn't interested in listening. I could only hope that there were people there who could hear the authenticity in my voice. Most people were there for a fight, and after all the years with my parents I knew that arguing without listening did not produce acceptance, but mostly division. Although I know I have the strength to go toe-to-toe with the leading ex-gay "experts," I usually don't find the benefit in it. I've pretty much decided to not participate in such debates unless there is a clear understanding of what we can accomplish together. I wish the goal of debating could be not just about winning an argument, but about striving for common ground in the light of respecting our differences.

I constantly struggle with showing compassion and respect to people I strongly disagree with. By respect I mean that I want to affirm the life choices of any person, trusting in the humanity and freedom that we all have to make responsible decisions for ourselves. Live and let live. I believe it is part of a democracy as much as loving others as myself (not to mention part of Christianity).

I think we live in a society which doesn't always value respect. We have so few examples that show us how to live with our differences. I have rarely experienced any public discourse — in the media, in politics, or in academia — where the participants could genuinely, respectfully disagree in a civil manner. It seems that we believe so strongly that our differences are intolerable that this is brought into reality, like a self-fulfilling prophecy. What part of Jesus' all-encompassing love is found in that belief?

I am impressed by organizations like the Gay Christian Network,[1] that truly work to create peace and understanding among all the people who find themselves part of this spiritual and sexual debate. Some people do not want to generate mutual respect, however. No matter what is done, they insist on their rightness and righteousness in the light of considerable evidence to the contrary. And so the silence falls deep and wide (if we're lucky enough to avoid arguing). There is a sad void of inability to connect. For myself, that empty space is enough for me to search for commonality and allow respect to bridge the gap. I can only show up and build half of the bridge.

As a person who often sits outside the box of mainstream society, I have the benefit of seeing the world from a different perspective, much as the LGBT community sits outside the mainstream straight world. As the outsiders, historically and iconically, we get to be the people who teach the majority how we want to be treated. I wish it could be otherwise. I wish the majority (the straight, white, male-dominated, mainly religious population, in this case) could see the harm exclusion is doing and reach out with compassion and justice. It rarely happens that way in reality, though. As with my parents, if I want them to accept me as I am, more often than not I have to lead by example. In doing so, I learn I don't need their acceptance, but to make the world livable for all of us I want to believe I could be a "good neighbor" and have mutual respect for our different approaches to life. Love can grow where we least expect, if we let it.

> *The time has come to choose, will you walk in my shoes?*
> *Can you surpass the limits that you have*
> *And take a walk in my shoes?*
> *On this hope relies, if you see with my eyes*
> *Justice is a light that burns out all the time*
> *If you see with my eyes*
> *I swim or sink. A boxing ring*
> *What makes you think I've got it easy?*
> *Don't turn your back. Don't just react*
> *What vision lacks will be made up by truth*
> *When you walk in my shoes*
> > *Feel the knife dig in if you feel with my skin*
> > *Beating to the brain know the shock of pain*
> > *If you feel with my skin*
> > *Forced underground, thrown out of town*
> > *Hate is the sound of someone's ignorance*
> > *It's just routine for one like me*
> > *No cruelty is worse than not to see*

Then you call my ruse, and ask me to walk in your shoes
As the table turns I am asked to learn
Can I walk in your shoes?
Sweet comfort keeps our minds asleep
And we just heap sand in our vision
The pain of change — too high a price
Can we catch sight that we may both lose?
Gotta walk in your shoes [2]

I'm not saying this is for everyone. I'm not even sure I'm right or good at it. As I wrote above, this is what I struggled with. I want to do my damnedest to understand all sides of an argument. I want to encourage everyone to succeed, to be healthy and happy. If even Dr. Nicolosi, today's most outspoken conversion therapy guru, firmly believes that the path he is on is exactly where he is supposed to be, I will give him the benefit of the doubt and respect that he is on his journey of life, and accept that he's right where he's supposed to be. I also truly hope he is an authentic and integrated man inside and out. Even for people who feel that they need to go through conversion therapies to find their happiness, although the experience was damaging to me, I respect the choices and paths they take, as one adult human being to another. I am not consciously invested in judging them.

Determining Effectiveness

However, there is a distinct difference between putting myself in a place of judgment over others (which I strive not to do) and, as a sexologist, determining the effectiveness of a treatment that is potentially doing harm to people. For more than 30 years, the ex-gay flag has flown in the face of a slew of questions that deserve answers, if not for any other reason than to ensure the health and well-being of its participants. Where are all the genuine success stories? What is the "effective treatment method" that changes a gay person to straight? How do ex-gay supporters account for all the people who did not find change but felt they were mostly damaged by the experience? Why aren't these "professionals" honestly looking at all the evidence and taking responsibility for it? Why might ex-gays be unhappy about their sexual feelings in the first place? Why are homosexuals required to change to be included in today's general perception of Christianity? What does this have to do with the unconditional love of Jesus Christ?

The truth of the matter is that the ex-gay's fundamental belief that homosexuality is a sin has now created a kind of industry. Their benign-sounding call, "We just want to help all the sad people with unwanted homosexual desires," is like a fast-food restaurant putting out the call, "We just want to help all the sad, obese people." Yet they insist that the only way to get thin is to eat their fatty, sugar-laden menu. They fail to acknowledge that the ex-gay movement perpetuates the very problem it claims to solve. Sadly, as long as they preach the dogma that homosexuality is wrong, there will be people who believe they should be changed.

> *The very existence of Change of Orientation programs perpetuates the idea that homosexuality is bad, and this is one of the reasons I've been against these programs being available. They send the message to people that "This is change-worthy, and we strongly urge this to be changed. In fact, we may insist on it being changed and if you were a good person you would want it changed."*
> — Dr. Gerald Davison, Professor of Psychology,
> University of Southern California[3]

What of religion in general? Clearly, the ex-gay movement is, at the very least, an outgrowth of the out-of-control power abuse in large parts of the church. The manipulation is so strong that huge ministries and denominations can move political forces to instigate acts of war and exclusion, while any sign of compassion is lost. Indeed, the church's reputation in many areas of our society is that of paranoia, half truths, and hypocrisy. I ask you, "What would Jesus do?"

Celebrating Diversity

I can't speak with complete sureness about what Jesus would do in this situation, but I can tell you what I am doing in hopes that it will inspire and energize others to support the healing and recovery of those damaged by the ex-gay movement and religious abuse. I want to actively support survivors and others to free themselves from the enslavement of conformity and to live more authentically. It might sound idealistic to hope for everyone to be so self-actualized. I could paint a pristine utopia where everyone gets along and everyone agrees about mutual respect and equality, but in actuality, I don't see the world's future becoming that.

Many people believe that for everyone to get along, everyone must agree. When I have heard other people describe the ideal world, they often include that eventually it will homogenize into one big culture — that our ethnicity will be singular as well as our beliefs. I don't think that view of the world is utopia. I think it's more like clone-topia. In fact, I find it rather dehumanizing to assume that we will all agree someday. I also believe that it would be a horrible loss to our cultural richness and diversity to have all the traditions and idiosyncrasies of a given society lost because we have all become one race. What a loss that would be. Furthermore, getting everyone to agree and act the same way is not necessarily a recipe for a full and wonderful life, any more than having the "right" theology makes a person a good Christian. I have a hunch it misses the point.

A helpful perspective, I believe, is agreeing to disagree. Yet the fact of the matter is that we already function this way. We all live on this quickly-shrinking world with crowds of people that don't agree on anything, it seems. And we manage to survive and enjoy life, for the most part. True, impoverished, third-world countries might beg to differ on that point, but as a gross over-simplification, the human race is going stronger than ever before, for better or for worse. Instead of simply putting up with our differences, keeping the status quo, or insisting that the population conform to only a specific and narrow kind of family structure (which most of us do not fit into anyway), I suggest we turn the view about our differences on its head.

Diversity suffers from the same obsessive negativity as sexuality. Whenever I can, I try to flip that negativity to positivity. Persecution of what's different is the behavior of infantile bullies, gotten so out of hand that it has somehow become socially acceptable. Oddly enough, most everyone has felt the negative sting of being different at some point in life, probably at a young age. Some visual feature made you stand out and someone called you a name and it struck at the very core of your self-worth. Was it true? Did your big nose, or small size, or big feet, or strange name, or skin color give any reflection of the worthwhileness of your whole being? Of course not. Unfortunately, when I write that it has gotten out of hand, I can point to any number of horrific genocides that continue to happen all because, "they are different from us."

What would happen if we attempted to make our differences — such as the birthmark — the very signposts that point to our self-worth? I remember hearing a story in my youth that had a lasting impression on me. It was of a girl who was born with a rather prominent birthmark on her face. When she got to the age of realizing that she was different because of it, her father insisted that the mark was an angel's kiss and that she was lucky because of it. The kiss, he said, would enable him to distinguish her from everyone else. Sappy? Yes. But the moral of the story is that the girl's self-esteem did not suffer, because what made her different was viewed positively rather than negatively.

What would be so horrible about applying that to all our differences? We've got all kinds of days, months, and even years dedicated to opportunities to learn and celebrate — President's Day, Independence Day, Martin Luther King Day, Black History Month, Parents' Days, the Year of the Dog, etc. You have something that is neglected or overlooked? Let's celebrate it! Yes, even religions. Let's have a Methodist Day and learn and celebrate what's great about Methodists. This is not an opportunity for Methodists to put down all the other religions and puff themselves up, hypothetically speaking. It's a day to focus on what's great about Methodists. Most of all, these are opportunities to generate respect and mutual understanding among our widely diverse population that numbers in the billions and is still growing.

Even the genetics of nature reflect the importance of diversity when an endangered species gets so few in number that it interbreeds. Mating and giving birth within such a small number of family members can spell further disaster destroying what few numbers there are left.

It's not enough just to agree that we disagree. We have to go a step further and affirm each other in our differences. We have believed for too long the lie that to hear another person's differing opinion automatically invalidates our own. It does not. In fact, often, hearing a different opinion creates greater strength in our own. So let the gender traditionalists be at peace with the gender-non-conformists. My understanding and experience of marriage does not obliterate your understanding and experience of marriage. Let's treat each other with equality and inclusion. There's nothing to be afraid of.

Celebrating our differences helps turn down the volume on the rhetoric and stigma of viewing people as "less than," as well. The LGBT community had a long "debate" with Los Angeles Shock Jock radio host, Dr. Laura Schlessinger, about her view that homosexuality is a human "flaw," like, say, blindness. I suppose some people take offense when being gay is corralled with a disability. I take offense that anyone is marginalized as "flawed." What value is in that? Who could possibly benefit from being labeled "flawed?" Sure, if a blind person had the opportunity to receive sight, it would be silly not to take full advantage of it. Yet, who's to say that blind people aren't the best people they can be just as they are? How short-sighted are we not to experience people in all their different beauty, just as they are? To think anything less is a kind of blindness that goes far deeper than what our eyes can see. We are all human. We are different. We all have our set of challenges. Life is too short and too wonderful to waste time creating inaccurate hierarchies.

Of course, simply celebrating our differences does not solve all of our challenges. Although I strive to respect ex-gay believers as human beings, I will not be silent about the harm they continue to inflict.

Telling Our Story: Talking About It

I can not shy away from talking frankly and authentically about my spiritual and sexual journey (hence this book). To do this, it takes two things: authenticity and communication. It's that simple. First, I want to address communication — specifically, talking about sexuality. For all intents and purposes, the world is experiencing a sexual revolution like never before, in the privacy of our homes and on our computers. I contend that this "privacy" may work against us since it might perpetuate a sex-negative obsessiveness. It seems that the general public is in denial of just how sexual we all are because it's hidden away behind closed doors. How do we bridge that gap from all those computer monitors to stopping restrictive amendments to our constitution, stopping the Religious Right's sexual hysteria, getting sexuality education to those who need it, celebrating everyone's diversity, and establishing equality (sexual or otherwise) for all? We have got to talk about it, sing about it, write about it and shout about it! Simple? Yes, but oh, so challenging.

I know this might sound intimidating for many people. Most of us go through our day feeling ill-equipped to be vocal about important issues, afraid of how people will react. But it is easier than you think. You don't have to be an expert. Simply be yourself. When people ask me what I say to reparative therapists and their supporters, I tell them that I am, most of all, honest about my own experience. Ultimately, that's all anyone can do. I was taught by none other than Evangelical Baptists who said that no one can refute what has happened to you. We can debate the Bible, we can debate psychological theory, but we can't debate someone's own experience. If you are your authentic self, you can express yourself eloquently every time.

It's still challenging to know what to say sometimes. Are you the kind of person that thinks of the perfect response about five minutes after a conversation has ended? I am, and I wish sometimes I had a time machine to jump back just a few minutes so that I can deliver a clever and informative statement. Guess what? I've included in the Appendix a sort of "time machine" called "Steps to Telling Your Story," so that you can be ready to respond authentically any time.

Whether this story-telling process is helpful for you or not, I still encourage you to talk about your spiritual and sexual journey. Only by bringing our experiences into the light of day will our society further defuse its fear around that which is "different" and begin to see that we are already living happily together in a wonderful, diverse world. As a sexologist, I have found that most people welcome a frank discussion about sexuality. People can be so eager. I get tired of answering the question, "What do you do?" at parties, because suddenly everyone thinks it's okay to tell me all their sexual concerns. People are chomping at the bit to talk about sex. I know it's not like this everywhere in the world, and repercussions can sometimes be severe. But I'm pretty sure the only way for it to get better is to talk about it.

Telling Our Story: Rigorous Authenticity

Somewhere in my early teens I happened to buy a comic book at the local grocery store. Little did I know that this particular comic would end up being one of the most pivotal editions in the last half of the 20th century, *Giant-Sized X-men #1*. This comic would set in motion the still-growing popularity of a number of key figures in the Marvel Comics world, including none other than Wolverine (though my favorite hero of this group is the swashbuckling Nightcrawler). What intrigued me most was the unusually inclusive premise of the super-group itself (although their name is gender-specific). Here were a number of young women and men whose super powers usually appeared genetically around the time of puberty. Evolution had begun to create the next generation in human development. Some of the characters' mutations were truly challenging, like not being able to touch another person without absorbing all of that person's memories and personality. Other mutations gave people amazing gifts, such as the ability to fly, or the ability to rapidly heal any physical wound. Unfortunately, in the story, the rest of humanity was so intimidated by these natural advances that they began to fear and persecute mutants. As a result, these gifted people had to go into hiding, even though their abilities were sometimes the very keys to humanity's survival. Are you seeing the parallel? The whole mutant and X-mythology is a great analogy to the LGBT community, although it was not until I was in my adult years that I was able to recognize the parallels.

Just as I was beginning to experience the hormonal "heat" of my gay sexuality, I found a safe place (even though it was the fictitious hideout of the X-men, "The 'X'avier Institute for Gifted Youngsters") where my uniqueness not only was accepted but also could be nurtured and honed. Mine could potentially be the very gift that "saved humanity." A number of these iconic characters became mentors who taught me truly important life lessons, and, above all, gave me hope that there could be a world where people could revel in their uniqueness. Furthermore, over the years (I am now a card-carrying comic geek), the path of many of these super heroes has led them to be so confident in themselves that they no longer need to hide their identities. They are thoroughly themselves wherever they go. It was within this world that a hero named Northstar became one of the first openly gay Marvel heroes. He is an altogether different kind of "X" gay!

This is celebrating diversity at its finest, although it takes you and me developing our authenticity with the diligence of a super hero. Of course, with my Evangelical background ("We're gonna save the world for Jesus!") and with these superheroes as my role models ("Up, up and away!"), it probably sounds like I have a savior complex. To a degree it's true that I sometimes have to "turn the volume down" on my desire to help people. But I no more think that my gifts can help make the world a better place than I think everyone's gifts can help make the world a better place.

Authentically sharing your unique gifts has potential and power that is stronger and more far-reaching than most people realize. Your gifts can range from who you are to what you do, what you learn, whom you love, what you dream. The gifts that LGBT people have to offer affect every aspect of life. As the classic example goes, if all the gays and lesbians decided to stop working on a given day, the world would slow to a crawl, and plenty of churches would be disabled, as well. Just think of all the choir members, music directors, organists, teachers, priests and organizers that would be noticeably missing if LGBT people stopped what we were doing. We are everywhere and we contribute irreplaceable gifts. We don't have to settle for simply being accepted by our society. We can show our stuff in such a way that the population realizes there's nothing to be afraid of — that we have always been an integral part of any society.

Furthermore, there are contributions that the LGBT community makes that no other community can claim. As I mentioned, we are poised at a very important time in history. As a sexologist, I can attest to the fact that a lot of LGBT people tend to be ahead of the curve when it comes to understanding sexuality, simply because we've had to take the time to figure out why we didn't fit in. We sometimes had to play the part of a straight person just to survive. We had to ask the hard questions that don't even cross the minds of most straight people. We have educated ourselves and, in doing so, we are teaching others as well.

The LGBT community has the opportunity to end the persecution and oppression against sexual and gender minorities. Hundreds of years from now, history will show that it was our LGBT community that put its foot down, drew the line against injustice and inequality, and made the world forever better for all that followed. By embracing our authentic sexuality, we are creating a climate of inclusivity that allows everyone to be more authentic, and not only in their sexuality. The easiest way to increase authenticity in the world is by putting our gifts, talents, and authentic selves out there for all to see and enjoy! We are what I call, "steadfast outcasts." It is the outcasts, the weird ones, the mutants and the freaks in most communities that force the majority to question their assumptions and see life in a new way. To me, this is what Jesus Christ was all about.

Once upon a time a princess left her condominium
And through the urban sprawl she wandered
When she grew tired and returned to her live-work space
She found that her palace doors were locked
> *They spoke to her through the key hole*
> *Her princess status was up for debate*
> *And even though she felt lonely*
> *She had all the time to wait*
So she's washing in the fountain
And sleeping in the tree
For she knows she belongs there
And she's content to wait in peace
She's a steadfast outcast and her exclusion is unjust
She's a steadfast outcast, she knows that they'll adjust
> *And when the neighbors threw a party*
> *She saw others were condemned*
> *Like the wrinkled troll, the one-eyed giant*
> *And that strange talking foreigner never did quite fit in*
So they're washing in the fountain
And sleeping in the trees
They saw the party through the windows
But they were kept from the feast
They're steadfast outcasts and they will not go away
They're steadfast outcasts, they demand respect just the same
> *Over the years the princess grew wise and street smart*
> *She didn't need the castle anymore*
> *For any palace is a prison*
> *If we all too quickly lock our doors*
Now they're dancing in the fountain
And they're swinging from the trees
Though they never had the penthouse
Their own souls gave them prestige
They're steadfast outcasts, and the party is now outside
They're steadfast outcasts, to the envy of those inside
> *We are steadfast outcasts, let the doors swing open wide*
> *We are steadfast outcasts, there's no need for us to hide*
> *We are steadfast outcasts, let our differences take pride*
> *We are steadfast outcasts, let your patience be your guide* [4]

Let Me Embrace You

While writing this book, I spent months going over the years of struggle, the difficult experiences, and the arguments that raged inside me. It felt as though I was often debating (in my mind) with ex-gay and abusive religious leaders from my past, all over again. I was reminded that for a long time I had felt that I was in a constant state of damage control as a result of my ex-gay experience and religious abuse. Eventually, though, I reached a period in my life when I began to feel that I had gotten "over the hump" in my recovery process. I felt I was on a downhill slope and was, for the most part, moving on with my life. I didn't have to duke it out anymore. I didn't have to engage survival mechanisms that no longer served me. I didn't even have to stand poised in the face of skeptical opposition, ready to defend my recovery process and where it led me. Not only did my ex-gay and religious abuse experience find a peaceful place in the past, but I realized that I could use the past and take it a step further: I could be proactive.

So in closing, this is an invitation to all who have struggled under the weight of the constant need to change, and for whom the constant strain to grasp that fleeting goal is never achieved. The best definition I have ever heard for insanity is doing the same thing over and over again, expecting different results.[5] God doesn't want you burdened with that kind of craziness. I don't want you burdened. You don't want to be burdened, and there are many others who rejoice in the opportunity to genuinely help you lift that burden off your back. You can stand tall, free, and fully accepted. There is a large and strong network of support whose door is open and accepting. You simply have to step through it.

I affirm your responsible adulthood, and your God-given strength of will to make wise and fulfilling choices in your life. This may mean that you follow an ex-gay path to find out for yourself if you can be authentically happy in such a life-long commitment with so little actual change in sight. I have the joy of telling you that the alternate path of unconditional self-acceptance, although challenging at times, has been wonderfully fulfilling, abundant and fun. I have found joy far beyond anything I could imagine. Whatever you choose to explore, you are the one fully responsible for your body and its pleasure. It's the only body you get, and it doesn't work forever, so enjoy it accordingly.

It is not your calling to be divided and paralyzed by the constant raging war that you have been told to wage against yourself. You have the opportunity to feel whole, to receive unconditional love that can be felt in every part of your being. In fact, you deserve this wholeness and love just as you are. You have the power to make peace, end the war, and feel the tangible contentment that comes from truly following the example of God's unconditional love. Embrace your sexuality and experience a depth of gratification, possibly like never before. Learn to hear your true inner voice and know what it says clearly without the crosstalk of everyone pressuring you to become something you are not.

To those in leadership whose sexuality must be locked down in order to put food on the table, to keep relationships intact, or to maintain your wall of reputation, I pray you are truly happy. I hope you feel deeply content. Right now, just between you and this book, you can exhale. You get to consider the possibility of being fully known and fully accepted. Before your emotions scramble away, before your arms go up in defense and you say, "No, no, no," consider what it would feel like to let your guard down forever and receive the love that comes from unconditional acceptance. You know the choices are out there to adjust your connections to family and loved ones so that you can care for them, while at the same time being fully authentic and leaving the facades and secrets behind. You can live your life without the constant fear of regret or rejection in the back of your mind.

Although life is always full of challenges and I'm still learning to let go and receive, I now can go days, weeks, and whole seasons feeling great about myself, with little shame in sight. You, too, can experience life and the world without a single shred of fear that you will not measure up. Out here, it is not a circular rut where trying to change from one thing to another is repeated over and over again. Out here, my goal and fulfillment are not just change, but growth. When change occurs it is a deepening and enrichment of who I have been all along. The many-faceted elements that make you unique are not flaws, but gifts, and they are preciously valued. You can fully, rigorously, and without reservation enjoy all the gifts God has given you, sexuality included! My door, and the door of many others, is open to you without requirements. You can step through that door. If you are afraid, reach out to that someone who will walk through it with you. You know who they are. This much I can tell you: It's quite glorious on this side.

There is a road where my life grows
This path I dance, no map proposed
Although the earth might bruise my feet
This is the course that feels complete
      And what will come on winds unseen
      What will upturn our staid routines
      Though conflicts still refuse relief
      Our visions are beyond belief
I will not douse this flame inside
To sense your touch, all shame aside
To risk and trust, I reap and sow
But with no veil my passion glows
      Life's joys are like a waterfall
      So many gifts both great and small
      So if I drown, of this I know
      I plunge the depths, where pure love flows
Where byways cross and meadows merge
My loved ones meet, our paths converge
With mind at peace and heart exposed
I share this road where my life grows [6]

Acknowledgments

MANY PEOPLE contributed their time, energy and support to the creation of this book. My first debt goes to my mentor, Jack Pantaleo, who read this manuscript multiple times in different incarnations. Thank you for all the time, humor, and perspective you invested in me, Jack. I also thank you for your precious friendship and guidance over the years.

My humble gratitude goes to the close friends who took the time to read over the preliminary drafts: David P., Cat, Ron, Jay, Peterson, Christine, and Dirk. As always your stability, input and friendship are some of the most cherished gifts in my life.

Mark Hollenstein, my business partner and friend, has supported me from the inception of this book. You've listened to me cry, read passages, and work through my process. You are the best Life Coach anyone could ever want.

I am completely indebted to Findhorn Press for getting this very book in your hands. Thank you Thierry for taking such a risk on a first-time author. You have made this experience truly enjoyable. I would not have met these fine publishers if it was not for the generous introduction by author, Darren John Main.

This work is more complete because of the resourceful research assistance of Thomas Remble Ph.D. (c).

To my therapists over the years, Dr. Ed Wimberly, Dr. Michael Baum, and most recently (for the past decade now), Dr. Arnold Friedlander: For all the quality listening, for all the hours of sitting with me in my stubborn silence, for not fixing me, for all the sober reflections, you have been consummate professionals and close friends. Thank you.

Many ex-gay and religious-abuse survivors took the risk and contributed their stories and quotes. Thank you for being vulnerable in this very public way. People will, indeed, be helped by the courage of your words.

For your love and continued support, I thank my parents, the Brock Clan, the Ricks Clan, the Yes Please Clan, Mikey, David K., Leo, iii, Spanky, Stefan, Bradley, Stevee, and Gecko.

I find moments every day when my heart genuinely feels some sense of deep gratitude for all the people who have added to the mix that makes up "me." Each of you has made my survival possible and worthwhile, and you continue to fill my life with colorful, crazy abundance. Thank you all.

Steps to Telling Your Story

YOU MAY NOT BE ABLE to go back in time. But this little mechanism, if put into practice, will always help you — "the next time." This is another tool I learned years ago from Evangelicals Concerned, at one of their conferences where Dr. Anna Spradlin and Beverly Taylor created and explained this process.

First, pick out the top 10 pivotal experiences in your life. You might only have five. You might have up to fifteen. But any more than that is going to probably be too much to manage in a verbal story. If you can't narrow them down, you might pick the most important in light of a specific topic, like your coming out process, or what spirituality means to you. They can be negative experiences, too, like a relationship ending or losing a job. They can be anything you want as long as they stand out as the most important moments of your life. These are your stepping stones that have gotten you to where you are today. List these events chronologically with just a word or two for each event, such as: 1. I realized I was gay. 2. I went to a Christian college, etc.

Second, give yourself the time to write about each stepping stone, one at a time. Write all you like. This might be the first time you really explore in detail what happened to you in, for example, an abusive relationship. You might want to share the story — maybe even read it — to a loved one or therapist. (Did I say this process was going to easy?) The important thing at this point is to give yourself the space and time to write out anything and everything you want.

Third, now condense down all you have written into one paragraph for each stepping stone. Therefore, if you had seven stepping stones, you'll have seven paragraphs.

Fourth, you will condense each paragraph down to one sentence. I know this is challenging, but remember, the goal is to be ready to talk about your story — or just a part of it — on the spur of the moment. Imagine, if someone confided in you about their fear of coming out and you were to respond with a three-page litany about how hard it was for you to come out! That would probably not have the desired effect. However, responding with just one sentence of authentic empathy could be just the thing that person needs to hear.

This Stepping Stones Process, as I call it, is a great way to familiarize yourself with what's important in your life and how to express it in writing or verbally. To those of you who have experienced the damaging effects of ex-gay and religious abuse, this process can be very helpful and healing, whether or not you ever share it with anyone else. I have been able to get proficient enough with my different stepping stones that even in front of an audience I can tell my whole story in ten sentences if I need to. Or, with another audience, I can give a sentence or two about this part of my life and give a paragraph or two about that part of my life. Finally, I can go into detail about just one part of my life that has a particular connection with the people or person I am talking to. The Stepping Stone Process has even been important in writing this book, and I have Anna and Bev to thank!

Bibliography

Abramson PR, Pinkerton SD. *With Pleasure: Thoughts on the nature of human sexuality.* Oxford, UK: Oxford University Press, 2002.

Aquinas, Thomas. *Summa Theologica.* Notre Dame, IN: Ave Maria Press, 1948.

Bawer, B. *A Place at the Table: The Gay Individual in American Society.* Simon & Schuster; 1st Touchstone edition (1994)

Bawer, B. *Stealing Jesus: How Fundamentalism Betrays Christianity*, Crown Publishers (1997)

Besen, Wayne. *Anything but Straight.* Stroud, UK: Hawthorne Press, Inc., 2003.

Bieber I, Dain HJ, Dince PR, Drellich MG, Grand HG, Gundlach RH, Kremer MW, Rifkin AH, Wilbur CB, Bieber TB. *Homosexuality: A psychoanalytic study.* New York: Basic Books, 1962.

Booth, Leo. *When God Becomes a Drug.* Los Angeles: Jeremy P. Tarcher, Inc., 1991.

Bradshaw, JE. *Healing the Shame that Binds You.* Deerfield Beach, FL: Health Communications, 1988.

Brown, Rita Mae. *Sudden Death.* New York: Bantam Books, 1983.

Bullough, Vern. *Sexual Variance in Society and History.* Chicago: University of Chicago Press, 1980.

Bullough V, Bullough B. *Sin, Sickness and Sanity.* New Haven: Meridian Books, 1977.

Chandola T, Britton A, Brunner E, Hemingway H, Malik M, Kumari M, Badrick E, Kivimaki M, Marmot M. Work Stress and Coronary Heart Disease: What are the mechanisms? *European Heart Journal* online (2008): http://eurheartj.oxfordjournals.org/cgi/content/full/ehm584v1.

Chaya MS, Kataria M, Nagendra R, et al. The Effects of Hearty Extended Unconditional (HEU) Laughter Using Laughter Yoga Techniques on Physiological, Psychological, and Immunological Parameters in the Workplace: A randomized control trial. *American Society of Hypertension 2008 Annual Meeting*, 2008, online. http://www.abstracts2view.com/ash/.

Cho, Margaret. *Revolution*. Video. Cho Taussic Production, 2004.

Cooper, David. *God Is a Verb*. New York: Riverhead Books, 1997.

Countryman, L.W. *Dirt Greed & Sex: Sexual Ethics in the New Testament and their Implications for Today*. Philadelphia, Fortress Press. 1988

Dillard, Annie. *Teaching a Stone to Talk*. New York: Harper & Row, 1982.

Dillon KM, Minchoff B, Baker KH. Positive Emotional States and Enhancement of the Immune System. *International Journal of Psychiatry in Medicine*. Vol. 15 (1985-86).

Easton D, Liszt C. *The Ethical Slut*. Emeryville, CA: Greenery Press, 1997.

Erzen, Tanya. *Straight to Jesus*. Berkeley: University of California Press, 2006.

Ford, JG. Healing Homosexuals: A psychologist's journey through the ex-gay movement and the pseudo-science of reparative therapy. *Journal of Gay & Lesbian Psychotherapy*. Vol. 5, No. 3/4 (2001).

Gagnon J, Simon W. *Sexual Conduct*. Piscataway, NJ: Aldine Transaction, 2005.

Gardella, Peter. *Innocent Ecstasy*. Oxford, UK: Oxford University Press, 1985.

Green, RJ. When Therapists Do Not Want Their Clients to Be Homosexual: A response to Rosik's article. *Journal of Marital and Family Therapy*. Vol. 29, No. 1 (January 2003).

Heath, RG. Pleasure Response of Human Subjects to Direct Stimulation of the Brain: Physiologic and psychodynamic considerations, in *The Role of Pleasure in Human Behavior*. New York: Hoeber, 1964.

Helminiak, D. *What the Bible Really Says About Homosexuality*. Alamo Square Distributors (2000)

Hooker, Evelyn. Parental Relations and Male Homosexuality in Patient and Nonpatient Samples. *Journal of Consulting and Clinical Psychology*. Vol 33(2) (Apr 1969).

Johnson D, VanVonderen J. *The Subtle Power of Spiritual Abuse*. Minneapolis: Bethany House Publishers, 1991.

Karslake, Daniel. *For the Bible Tells Me So*. Documentary video. First Run Features, 2007.

Kellogg, JH. *Plain Facts for Old and Young*. Burlington, VT: I.F. Segner, 1882.

Kiley, Dan. *The Peter Pan Syndrome: Men who never want to grow up*. New York: Dodd Mead, 1983.

Kinsey AC, Pomeroy WB, Martin CE. *Sexual Behavior in the Human Male*. Philadelphia: W.B. Saunders, 1948.

Klein, Marty. *America's War on Sex*. Westport, CT, Praeger Publishers, 2006

Manuaci T, Reznick F. *One Nation under God*. Documentary film. firstrunfilms. com, 1993.

Marks, Jeremy. *Exchanging the Truth of God for a Lie*. RoperPenberthy, 2008

MacDonald, C. "A Chuckle a Day Keeps the Doctor Away: Therapeutic humor and laughter. *Journal of Psychosocial Nursing and Mental Health Services*. Vol. 42:3 (2004).

Meivner, I. Sonographic Observation of in utero Fetal Masturbation'. *Journal of Ultrasound in Medicine*. Vol. 6:2 (February 1, 1987).

Montagu, Ashley. *Touching*. New York: Harper Paperbacks, 1986.

Murray, Tom. *Fish Can't Fly*. Documentary video. TJoe Murray Videos, 2005.

Palladino, Grace. *Teenagers: An American history*. New York: Basic Books, 1996.

Pantaleo, Jack. *Spirituality and Sexuality: An invitation to wholeness*. San Francisco: RixArtz, 1994.

Peck, M. Scott. *The Road Less Traveled*. New York: Simon & Schuster, 1979.

Poindexter, Ron. *Love One Out Conference*. thECable Newsletter, Autumn 2005.

Resnick, Stella. *The Pleasure Zone*. Newburyport, MA: Conari Press, 1997.

Rogers, J. *Jesus, the Bible, and Homosexuality: Explode the Myths, Heal the Church*. Westminster John Knox Press (2009)

Rosik, C. Motivational, Ethical, and Epistemological Foundations in the Treatment of Unwanted Homoerotic Attraction. *Journal of Marital and Family Therapy*. Vol. 29, No. 1 (January 2003).

Satir V, Gomori M, Banmen J, Gerber JS. *The Satir Model: Family therapy and beyond*. Palo Alto, CA: Science and Behavior Books, 1991.

Savage, Jon. Teenage: *The Creation of Youth Culture*. Viking Adult. 2007

Scanzoni, L. Mollenkott, V. *Is the Homosexual My Neighbor?* Harper One (1994)

Scroggs, R. *The New Testament and Homosexuality.* Augsburg Fortress Publishers (1983)

Serovich J, Craft S, Toviessi P, Gangamma R, McDowell T, Grafsky E. A Systematic Review of the Research Base on Sexual Reorientation Therapies. *Journal of Marital and Family Therapy.* Vol. 34, No. 2 (April 2008).

Shidlo A, Schroeder M, Drescher J. What Needs Fixing? An introduction. *Journal of Gay & Lesbian Psychotherapy.* Vol. 5, No. 3/4 (2001).

Stafford, Tim. An Older, Wiser Ex-gay Movement, *Christianity Today.* Vol. 51, No. 10 (October 2007).

Tannahill, Ray. *Sex in History.* Chelsea, MI: Scarborough House, 1982.

Tousey, Ben. *My Egypt.* Bloomington IN. Yhabbut Publishing, 2006.

Wade C, Tavris C. *Psychology.* 6th Ed. Upper Saddle River, NJ: Prentice Hall, 2000.

Wade, Jenny. *Transcendent Sex: When lovemaking opens the veil.* New York: Pocket Books, 2004.

William, Robin. *Live on Broadway.* TV video. Home Box Office, 2002.

Wink, W. (editor) *Homosexuality and Christian Faith: Questions of Conscience for the Churches.* Augsburg Fortress Publishers (1999)

Ziegler J. Immune System May Benefit from the Ability to Laugh. *Journal of the National Cancer Institute.* Vol. 87:5 (1995).

Endnotes

INTRODUCTION

1 APA Task Force on Appropriate Therapeutic Responses to Sexual Orientation, *Report of the Task Force on Appropriate Therapeutic Responses to Sexual Orientation* (Washington, DC: American Psychological Association, 2009).
2 http://www.iashs.edu/history.html

CHAPTER 1

1 Matthew 6:1-9
2 Bieber I, Dain HJ, Dince PR, Drellich MG, Grand HG, Gundlach RH, Kremer MW, Rifkin AH, Wilbur CB, Bieber TB: *Homosexuality: A psychoanalytic study* (New York: Basic Books, 1962)
3 Hooker, Evelyn: Parental relations and male homosexuality in patient and nonpatient samples, *Journal of Consulting and Clinical Psychology*, Vol 33:2 (Apr 1969), 140-142
4 "Song of the Outsider," © Jallen Rix, 1989

CHAPTER 2

1 The best overall history I have read is in Tanya Erzen's book, *Straight to Jesus* (Berkeley: University of California Press, 2006)
2 Keynote address at the Anti-heterosexism Conference, West Palm Beach Florida, November 2009
3 Manuaci T, Reznick F: *One Nation under God* (documentary, firstrunfilms. com, 1993)
4 Ibid.
5 http://www.exodus-international.org/

6   Manuaci T, Reznick F: *One Nation under God* (documentary, firstrunfilms. com, 1993)

7   Erzen, Tanya: *Straight to Jesus: Sexual and Christian conversions in the ex-gay movement* (Berkeley: University of California Press, 2006), 35

8   Manuaci T, Reznick F: *One Nation under God* (documentary, firstrunfilms. com, 1993).

9   http://web.mac.com/chicagolarry/ChicagoLarry/Sad_Lives_of_Colin_Cook. html

10 Manuaci T, Reznick F: *One Nation under God* (documentary, firstrunfilms. com, 1993)

11 Hooker, Evelyn: Parental relations and male homosexuality in patient and nonpatient samples, *Journal of Consulting and Clinical Psychology*. Vol 33:2 (Apr 1969), 140-142

12 Shidlo A, Schroeder M and Drescher J: What Needs Fixing? An introduction, *Journal of Gay and Lesbian Psychotherapy*, Vol. 5, No. 3/4 (2001), 1

13 Manuaci T, Reznick F, *One Nation under God* (documentary, firstrunfilms. com, 1993)

14 Erzen, Tanya: *Straight to Jesus: Sexual and Christian conversions in the ex-gay movement* (Berkeley: University of California Press, 2006), 147

15 Ford JG: Healing Homosexuals: A Psychologist's Journey through the Ex-gay Movement and the Pseudo-Science of Reparative Therapy, *Journal of Gay and Lesbian Psychotherapy*, Vol. 5, No. 3/4, (2001), 81

16 Ford, JG: Healing Homosexuals: A Psychologist's Journey through the Ex-gay Movement and the Pseudo-Science of Reparative Therapy, *Journal of Gay and Lesbian Psychotherapy*, Vol. 5, No. 3/4 (2001), 69

17 Besen, Wayne: *Anything but Straight* (Stroud, UK: Hawthorne Press, Inc. 2003), 151

18 Poindexter, Ron: *Love Won Out Conference*, thECable (Autumn 2005), 6

19 http://www.apa.org/pi/lgbc/publications/justthefacts.pdf

20 Personal correspondence, 1998

21 http://www.beyondexgay.com/Narratives/David

22 Erzen, Tanya: *Straight to Jesus: Sexual and Christian conversions in the ex-gay movement* (Berkeley: University of California Press, 2006), 93

23 Personal correspondence, September, 2008

24 Erzen, Tanya: *Straight to Jesus: Sexual and Christian conversions in the ex-gay movement* (Berkeley, University of California Press, 2006), 98

25 Ex-gay Survivors Tell Their Stories at the Anti-Heterosexism Conference, West Palm Beach Florida, November 2009

26 Erzen, Tanya: *Straight to Jesus: Sexual and Christian conversions in the ex-gay movement* (Berkeley: University California Press, 2006),163, 173, 174

27 Ford, JG: Healing Homosexuals: A psychologist's journey through the ex-gay movement and the pseudo-science of reparative therapy, *Journal of Gay and Lesbian Psychotherapy*, Vol. 5, No. 3/4 (2001), 85

28 Besen, Wayne: *Anything but Straight* (Stroud, UK: Hawthorne Press, Inc. 2003), 3

29 http://www.beyondexgay.com/Narratives/Darlene

30 http://www.beyondexgay.com/Narratives/RandyB

31 Rosik C: Motivational, Ethical, and Epistemological Foundations in the Treatment of Unwanted Homoerotic Attraction, *Journal of Marital and Family Therapy*, Vol. 29, No. 1 (January 2003), 13 - 28

32 Green, RJ: When Therapists Do Not Want Their Clients to Be Homosexual: A response to Rosik's article, *Journal of Marital and Family Therapy*, Vol. 29, No. 1 (January 2003), 30

33 Serovich J, Craft S, Toviessi P, Gangamma R, McDowell T, Grafsky E: A Systematic Review of the Research Base on Sexual Reorientation Therapies, *Journal of Marital and Family Therapy*, Vol. 34:2 (April 2008), 227-238

34 Personal correspondence, June 2009

35 Personal correspondence, September 2008

36 Manuaci T, Reznick F: *One Nation under God* (documentary, firstrunfilms. com 1993)

CHAPTER 3

1 Johnson D, VanVonderen J: *The Subtle Power of Spiritual Abuse*, (Minneapolis: Bethany House Publishing, 1991), 20

2 Booth, Leo: *When God Becomes a Drug* (Los Angeles: Jeremy P. Tarcher, Inc., 1991), 2

3 Personal correspondence, September 2008

4 Personal correspondence, 1998

5 Manuaci T, Reznick F: *One Nation under God* (documentary, firstrunfilms. com, 1993)

6 Personal correspondence, September 2008

7 Personal correspondence, June 2009

8 http://www.courage.org.uk/articles/article.asp?id=65

9 Ford JG, Healing Homosexuals: A Psychologist's Journey through the Ex-gay Movement and the Pseudo-Science of Reparative Therapy, *Journal of Gay and*

Lesbian Psychotherapy, Vol. 5, No. 3/4 (2001), 71

10 Personal correspondence, September 2008

11 Personal correspondence, July 2008

12 Johnson D, VanVonderen J: *The Subtle Power of Spiritual Abuse* (Minneapolis: Bethany House Publishing, 1991), 49

13 Johnson D, VanVonderen J: *The Subtle Power of Spiritual Abuse* (Minneapolis: Bethany House Publishing, 1991), 31

14 Manuaci T, Reznick F: *One Nation under God* (documentary, firstrunfilms. com, 1993)

15 Personal correspondence, September 2008

16 Manuaci T, Reznick F: *One Nation under God* (documentary, firstrunfilms. com, 1993)

17 Manuaci T, Reznick F: *One Nation under God* (documentary, firstrunfilms. com, 1993)

18 http://www.beyondexgay.com/article/busseeapology

19 Presidential Address, September 22, 2001,

20 Personal correspondence, March 2009

21 http://www.courage.org.uk/articles/article.asp?id=65

22 Booth, Leo: *When God Becomes a Drug* (Los Angeles: Jeremy P. Tarcher, Inc., 1991), viii

23 Rix, Jallen: *Gentle and Honest, Time on a Chain* CD, Eighthnote Records, 2000

CHAPTER 4

1 *The American Heritage® Dictionary of the English Language, 4th Ed.* (New York: Houghton Mifflin Company, 2009) change font

2 http://www.beyondexgay.com/article/bogleapology

3 Stafford, Tim: An Older, Wiser Ex-gay Movement, *Christianity Today*, Vol. 51, No. 10 (October 2007)

4 http://www.exgaywatch.com/wp/2007/11/a-critique-of-jones-and-yarhouses-Ex-gays-part-1/

5 http://www.boxturtlebulletin.com/tag/jones-yarhouse-study

6 Wade C, Tavris C, *Psychology, 6th Ed.* (Upper Saddle River, NJ: Prentice Hall, 2000)

7 Tousey, Ben: *My Egypt* (Bloomington, IN: Yhabbut Publishing, 2006), 53

8 Personal correspondence, 1998

9 Personal correspondence, August 2009

10 Karslake, Daniel: *For the Bible Tells Me So*, documentary, First Run Features, 2007

CHAPTER 5

1 Keynote address at the Anti-Heterosexism Conference, West Palm Beach Florida, November 2009

CHAPTER 6

1 Murray, Tom: *Fish Can't Fly*, documentary, TJoe Murray Videos, 2005
2 Karslake, Daniel: *For the Bible Tells Me So*, documentary First Run Features, 2007)
3 Romans 8:38-39
4 http://www.beyondexgay.com/Narratives/David

CHAPTER 7

1 Karslake, Daniel: *For the Bible Tells Me So*, documentary, First Run Features, 2007
2 Genesis 18-19
3 Ezekiel 16:48-50
4 Leviticus 18:22
5 I Corinthians 6: 9-10 and I Timothy 1:10
6 Manuaci T, Reznick F: *One Nation under God*, documentary, firstrunfilms. com, 1993
7 Deuteronomy 21:18-21
8 Karslake, Daniel: *For the Bible Tells Me So*, documentary, First Run Features, 2007
9 "Love Letter," © Jallen Rix, August 1990
10 Romans 1:20
11 Genesis 2:20
12 "God Is God," © Jallen Rix, 1988
13 Dillard, Annie: *Teaching a Stone to Talk* (New York: Harper & Row, 1982), 15-16

CHAPTER 8

1 Tannahill, Ray: *Sex in History* (Chelsea, MI: Scarborough House, 1982), 142.
2 Tannahill, Ray: *Sex in History* (Chelsea, MI: Scarborough House, 1982), 146.
3 Aquinas, Thomas: *Summa Theologica*, Vol. II-II (Notre Dame, IN: Ave Maria Press, 1948), 10-11
4 Tannahill, Ray: *Sex in History* (Chelsea, MI: Scarborough House, 1982), 279
5 William, Robin: *Live on Broadway*, video, Home Box Office, 2002
6 Pantaleo, Jack: *Spirituality and Sexuality: An invitation to wholeness* (San Francisco, RixArtz, 1994), 14
7 Bullough, Vern: *Sexual Variance in Society and History* (Chicago: University of Chicago Press, 1980), 542-543
8 Bullough, Vern: *Sexual Variance in Society and History* (Chicago: University of Chicago Press, 1980), 544
9 Gardella, Peter: *Innocent Ecstasy* (Oxford, UK: Oxford University Press, 1985), 44
10 Bullough V, Bullough B: *Sin, Sickness and Sanity* (New Haven: Meridian Books, 1977), 60
11 Kellogg H.: *Plain Facts for Old and Young* (Burlington, VT I.F. Segner, 1882)
12 Tannahill, Ray: *Sex in History* (Chelsea, MI: Scarborough House, 1982), 145
13 Deuteronomy 5:7
14 Acts 8:26-40
15 Personal correspondence, June 1998
16 Personal correspondence, June 2009

CHAPTER 9

1 Gagnon J, Simon W.: *Sexual Conduct* (Piscataway, NJ: Aldine Transaction, 2005)
2 Easton D, Liszt C: *The Ethical Slut* (Emeryville, CA: Greenery Press, 1997)
3 Kinsey AC, Pomeroy WB, Martin CE: *Sexual Behavior in the Human Male* (Philadelphia: W.B. Saunders Publishing, 1948)
4 Abramson PR, Pinkerton SD: *With Pleasure: Thoughts on the nature of human sexuality* (Oxford, UK: Oxford University Press, 2002)
5 Personal correspondence, 1998
5 Pantaleo, Jack: *Spirituality and Sexuality: An invitation to wholeness* (San Francisco, RixArtz, 1994), 3
6 Wade, Jenny: *Transcendent Sex: When lovemaking opens the veil* (New York:

Pocket Books, 2004)

7 "Jesus Down at Stonewall," © Jallen Rix, 1993

8 http://www.homonomo.com/

9 "When you Touch Me I Know," © Jallen Rix, 1992

10 Personal correspondence, 1998

11 Montagu, Ashley, Touching (New York: Harper Paperbacks, 1986)

12 Personal correspondence, July 2008

13 Conversation with Mark, March 2009

15 Personal correspondence, 1998

16 http://www.beyondexgay.com/Narratives/David

17 The Random House Unabridged Dictionary (New York: Random House, 2005)

18 Personal correspondence, September 2008

19 Erzen, Tanya: *Straight to Jesus: Sexual and Christian conversions in the ex-gay movement* (Berkeley: University of California Press, 2006), 151-152, 170

20 Satir V, Gomori M, Banmen J, Gerber JS: *The Satir Model: Family therapy and beyond* (Palo Alto, CA: Science and Behavior Books, 1991)

21 Personal correspondence, March 2009

22 Heath RG: *Pleasure Response of Human Subjects to Direct Stimulation of the Brain: Physiologic and psychodynamic considerations, The Role of Pleasure in Human Behavior* (New York: Hoeber, 1964), 219-243

23 Resnick, Stella: *The Pleasure Zone* (Newburyport, MA: Conari Press, 1997), 1

24 Meivner I: Sonographic Observation of in utero Fetal Masturbation', *Journal of Ultrasound in Medicine*, Vol. 6:2 (February 1, 1987), 111

25 Chandola T, Britton A, Brunner E, Hemingway H, Malik M, Kumari M, Badrick E, Kivimaki M, Marmot M: Work Stress and Coronary Heart Disease: What are the mechanisms? *European Heart Journal* online (2008), http://eurheartj.oxfordjournals.org/cgi/content/full/ehm584v1

26 Wegner DM, Schneider DJ, Carter SR, White TL: Paradoxical Effects of Thought Suppression, *Journal of Personality and Social Psychology*. Vol. 53:1 (1987), 5-13.

27 Dillon KM, Minchoff B, Baker KH: Positive Emotional States and Enhancement of the Immune System, *International Journal of Psychiatry in Medicine*, Vol. 15 (1985-86), 13-17

28 Ziegler J: Immune System May Benefit from the Ability to Laugh, *Journal of the National Cancer Institute* (1995), 342-343

29 Chaya MS, Kataria M, Nagendra R, et al: The Effects of Hearty Extended Unconditional (HEU) Laughter Using Laughter Yoga Techniques on Physi-

ological, Psychological, and immunological parameters in the workplace: A randomized control trial, *American Society of Hypertension 2008 Annual Meeting* (2008)

30 MacDonald C: "A Chuckle a Day Keeps the Doctor Away: Therapeutic humor & laughter," *Journal of Psychosocial Nursing and Mental Health Services*, Vol. 42:3 (2004), 18-25

31 Resnick, Stella: *The Pleasure Zone* (Newburyport, MA: Conari Press, 1997), 126

CHAPTER 10

1 Palladino, Grace: *Teenagers: An American history* (New York: Basic Books, 1996), 136

2 Kiley, Dan: *The Peter Pan Syndrome: Men who never want to grow up* (New York: Dodd Mead, 1983)

3 Cooper, David. *God Is a Verb.* (New York: Riverhead Books, 1997)

4 Personal correspondence, 1998

5 *The American Heritage® Dictionary of the English Language, 4th Ed.* (New York: Houghton Mifflin Company, 2009)

6 http://www.beyondexgay.com/Narratives/David

7 Personal correspondence, March 2009

8 *Webster's Revised Unabridged Dictionary* (MICRA, Inc., 1998)

9 Bradshaw JE: *Healing the Shame that Binds You.* (Deerfield Beach, FL: Health Communications, 1988)

10 Bradshaw, JE: *Healing the Shame that Binds You* (Deerfield Beach, FL: Health Communications, 1988), 13-14.

CHAPTER 11

1 Personal correspondence, 1995

2 "What Was It We Were Fighting For?" © Jallen Rix, rixartz.com, 1999

3 "I Would Choose You," for Jay and Ron on their wedding day, © Jallen Rix, 1997

4 "How a Mother Loves Her Son," © Jallen Rix, 1993

CONCLUSION

1 http://gayChristian.net/

2 "In My Shoes," © Jallen Rix, 1994

3 Manuaci T, Reznick F: *One Nation under God*, documentary, firstrunfilms. com, 1993

4 "Steadfast Outcast," © Jallen Rix, 1994

5 Rita Mae Brown: *Sudden Death* (New York: Bantam Books, 1983), 68 (I was surprised to find that it was neither B. Franklin nor A. Einstein who first coined this phrase)

6 "Where My Life Grows," © Jallen Rix, September 2009

Jallen Rix can be reached at:
DoctorRix.com

Nearly every set of lyrics in this book was recorded by Jallen
on CD or downloadable MP3s. Hear how they are sung
and performed by the author, at DoctorRix.com

FINDHORN PRESS

Life Changing Books

For a complete catalogue,
please contact:

Findhorn Press Ltd
117-121 High Street,
Forres IV36 1AB,
Scotland, UK

t +44 (0)1309 690582
f +44 (0)131 777 2711
e info@findhornpress.com

or consult our catalogue online
(with secure order facility) on
www.findhornpress.com

For information on the Findhorn Foundation:
www.findhorn.org